THE VITAL COG IN HITLER'S WAR MACHINE...

Without I.G.'s immense productive facilities, its far-reaching research, varied technical experience and overall concentration of economic power, Germany would not have been in a position to start its aggressive war in September, 1939.

From its laboratories and factories flowed vaccines, sera and drugs such as Salvarsan, aspirin, Atabrine and novocaine, as well as sulfa drugs, poison gases and rocket fuels. Few universities could match the profusion of Nobel Prizes earned by its scientists.

I.G. reduced slave labor to a consumable raw material, a human ore from which the mineral of life was systematically extracted. When no usable energy remained, the living dross was shipped to the gassing chambers and cremation furnaces where the SS recycled it into the German war economy—gold teeth for the Reichsbank, hair for mattresses and fat for soap.

The Crime and Punishment of I.G. Farben

Joseph Borkin

A KANGAROO BOOK
PUBLISHED BY POCKET BOOKS NEW YORK

Distributed in Canada by PaperJacks Ltd., a Licensee
of the trademarks of Simon & Schuster, a division of
Gulf+Western Corporation.

POCKET BOOKS, a Simon & Schuster division of
GULF & WESTERN CORPORATION
1230 Avenue of the Americas, New York, N.Y. 10020
In Canada distributed by PaperJacks Ltd.,
330 Steelcase Road, Markham, Ontario.

In the councils of Government, we must guard against the acquisition of unwarranted influence, whether sought or unsought, by the military-industrial complex. The potential for the disastrous rise of misplaced power exists and will persist. We must never let the weight of this combination endanger our liberties or democratic processes.

PRESIDENT DWIGHT D. EISENHOWER
FAREWELL ADDRESS TO THE NATION
JANUARY 17, 1961
WASHINGTON, D.C.

Contents

Preface

My first encounter with I.G. Farbenindustrie Aktiengesellschaft took place in the early summer of 1934. I had just been hired by the United States Senate Special Committee to Investigate the Munitions Industry as an investigator–researcher. By luck, my immediate supervisor was H. C. Engelbrecht, whose book *Merchants of Death* had been an important factor influencing Senator Gerald P. Nye to press for the investigation.

To ease me into the job, Engelbrecht handed me an agreement between the Standard Oil Company (N.J.) and I.G. Farben. My assignment was to summarize this involved contract so that it would be intelligible to the senators on the Committee. I had never heard of I.G. Farben before. But for the next forty-four years, it was my Moby Dick.

After the Senate Committee, I took I.G. Farben along with me to the Committee on Patents of the House of Representatives, where I served as a technical counsel on patent pooling and cross-licensing agreements. In 1938, I carted my industrial white whale to the Antitrust Division of the Department of Justice. There as head of the Patent and Cartel Section, under the great Thurman Arnold, I instituted the cartel program in which the attack against I.G. Farben continued throughout the course of World War II. In 1943, I co-authored *Germany's Master Plan,* a book outlining the details of this program. After the war, when I read the transcript of the trial of the I.G. war criminals at Nuremberg, I knew that someday I would write the present book.

Acknowledgments

Many persons provided valuable help in the making of this work. I should like to acknowledge my gratitude to Meg Leary and to Anne Greigg, whom I owe more than I can ever repay; to Terri Allen, Morris Amchan, Karen Daggle, Ellen Finkelstein, Newton Frohlich, Paul Gannt, Irene Gordon, Paul Green, Iris Linson, John Mendelsohn, Alice Mostoff, Anita Navon, John Pehle, Hyman B. Ritchin, John E. Taylor, Robert Wolfe, and the late Richard Bauer for their special contributions; to Charles E. Smith, Editor-in-Chief at The Free Press; to Madeleine Sann, who edited the manuscript; to Elly Dickason, who supervised production; to Mike McIver, the jacket designer; and to my wife Pauline, whose faith and encouragement go all the way back to the Nye Committee, where we both came across I.G. for the first time.

The Crime and Punishment of I.G. Farben

Introduction

"Without I.G.'s immense productive facilities, its far-reaching research, varied technical experience and overall concentration of economic power, Germany would not have been in a position to start its aggressive war in September 1939."[1] Such was the judgment rendered by a team of civilian and military experts assigned by General Eisenhower at the close of World War II to make an exhaustive investigation of I.G.'s contribution to the Nazi war effort. Extravagant as this conclusion may have sounded, the record sustains its accuracy.

I.G. truly was a mighty industrial colossus. So huge were its assets admitted and concealed, so superior its technological know-how, and so formidable its array of patents that it dominated the chemical business of the world. I.G. fortified this commercial leadership by constructing a maze of cartels whose members included such industrial giants as Kuhlmann of France, Imperial Chemical Industries of Great Britain, Montecatini of Italy, Aussiger Verein of Czechoslovakia, Boruta of Poland, Mitsui of Japan, and Standard Oil (New Jersey), Du Pont, and Dow Chemical of the United States.

But I.G. was more than a corporate empire. Through the uncanny talents of its scientists and engineers, it secured the vital self-sufficiency that enabled Germany to maneuver in the world of power politics. From its laboratories and factories flowed the strategic raw materials that Germany's own territory could not supply, the synthetics of oil, rubber, nitrates, and fibers. So, too, I.G. produced vaccines, sera, and drugs such as Salvarsan, aspirin, Atabrine, and Novocain, along with sulfa drugs, as well as poison gases and rocket fuels. Few universities could match the profusion of Nobel Prizes earned by its scientists: Paul Ehrlich for Salvarsan, Fritz Haber for the fixation of nitrogen, Carl Bosch for synthesizing saltpeter and gasoline, and Gerhard Domagk for the sulfa drugs.

Gustav Stresemann, chancellor and foreign minister during the Weimar Republic, once said, "Without I.G. and coal, I can have no foreign policy." But it was for the Nazis that I.G. performed the greatest service. With I.G. and coal Adolf Hitler almost conquered the world.

Hitler was an apt student of the weaknesses that brought Germany to its knees during World War I. Defeat had drilled into him the doleful fact that Germany's impoverished land, devoid of the strategic raw materials with which modern wars are fought, had made the British blockade a decisive weapon. In planning for World War II he vowed to correct nature's imbalance with science and technology.

The result was a strange alliance between Hitler and I.G. Hitler despised I.G. for its international complexion and for its unusually large number of Jewish directors and scientists. Carl Bosch, the head of I.G. when Hitler came to power, was the most vocal anti-Nazi in the industrial community. In the light of succeeding events, it is ironic that the Nazis legally stigmatized I.G. as non-Aryan in the early years of the Third Reich. But Hitler needed I.G.'s genius and I.G. needed Hitler's support. I.G.'s first and major task for Hitler was to free German diplomacy from the bonds that shackled it to the oil wells and rubber groves of its enemies. How well it succeeded is written in the history of the world's most violent and mechanized war. For five and a half years, Hitler's tanks, trucks, and planes were propelled by I.G's gasoline, their wheels made of I.G.'s rubber. Success had rendered I.G. indispensable.

Mere indispensability, however, was not enough. As

the war progressed, I.G.'s embrace of Hitler became more passionate. With the help of the Wehrmacht and the Nazi bureaucracy, I.G. looted the chemical properties of the defeated nations (Austria, Czechoslovakia, Poland, Norway, and France). Moreover, it had similar plans to bring England, the United States, and the Soviet Union into its orbit.

I.G.'s moral descent did not end there. Before long it joined the Nazis in a vast forced labor program in which millions of victims from the conquered countries were enslaved in the service of German war production. But slavery was only a step in the dehumanization of victor and vanquished. I.G. found itself in the role of an industrial Faust, unable and unwilling to extricate itself from the compact it had made with Hitler to help prepare the Nazis for war. The depth of the partnership was reached at Auschwitz, the extermination center, where four million human beings were destroyed in accordance with the "Final Solution of the Jewish Question," Hitler's plan to destroy an entire people. Drawn by the almost limitless reservoir of death camp labor, I.G. chose to build a great industrial complex at Auschwitz for the production of synthetic rubber and oil. So enormous was this installation that it used as much electricity as did the entire city of Berlin. More than 25,000 camp inmates paid with their lives to construct it.

After the defeat of Germany, the horror of I.G. Auschwitz made it certain that those involved would have to face the consequences of their acts. An indictment charging twenty-four of I.G.'s highest official with war crimes was filed with the United States Military Tribunal at Nuremberg. In the opening paragraph of his statement to the court, General Telford Taylor, the chief prosecutor at Nuremberg, summarized the spirit of the prosecution's case.

The grave charges in this case have not been laid before the Tribunal casually or unreflectingly. The indictment accuses these men of major responsibility for visiting upon mankind the most searing

3

and catastrophic war in human history. It accuses them of wholesale enslavement, plunder, and murder. These are terrible charges; no man should underwrite them frivolously or vengefully, or without deep and humble awareness of the responsibility which he thereby shoulders. There is no laughter in this case; neither is there any hate.

Yet, despite the terrible gravity of the charges, the setting was more like that for an antitrust suit than that for a trial for slavery and mass murder as the defendants took their places in the dock at the Palace of Justice at Nuremberg. The twenty-three defendants (the twenty-fourth defendant, Max Brueggemann, was excused for illness) were among the industrial elite of Germany, not Hitler's black- and brown-shirted hooligans. They represented a combination of scientific genius and commercial acumen unique in a private industrial enterprise. They were the executives who made I.G. preeminent in the world of technology and commerce. They served on the boards of directors of the most prestigious corporations in their own country and abroad, where they were treated with awe and admiration. When their government called, they accepted official posts in the spirit of public service. Like their counterparts everywhere, they were among the leading supporters of culture, charity, and religion, donating their names, time, and money.

How this group finally arrived at the courtroom at Nuremberg, branded as the "Devil's Chemists," charged with unparalleled atrocities, is a profound lesson for the world.

Until 1856 all the dyes by which man colored clothing, homes, and art came from natural sources such as insects, barks, flowers, berries, animal organs, and eggs. In 1856 an eighteen-year-old chemistry student at the Royal College in London, William Henry Perkin, while experimenting with coal tar in the search for synthetic quinine, found something a great deal more valuable. Instead of quinine, a bright purple solution filled Perkin's

4

test tube. And with the first of the aniline dyes, a new industry was born.

Although Perkin's remarkable discovery may have been an accident, he had the genius to perceive its immense potential. After he applied for a patent, he opened a factory for commercial exploitation. But Perkin was destined to suffer the fate of prophets. His own countrymen did not fully appreciate either the seminal nature or the industrial potential of the discovery. The Germans, however, did recognize the great future of synthetic dyes. Scientist-businessmen from Germany settled in England long enough to learn the new technology and then carted it off bodily to their homeland.

What they did with their booty was nothing less than an industrial miracle. With the German knack for turning garbage into wealth, these talented borrowers transformed the mountains of coal tar, the costly waste of the steel production of the Ruhr, into an immensely valuable product, the raw material for a new and exciting dyestuff industry.

By the turn of the twentieth century, six German companies had emerged to dominate the world's production and distribution of synthetic dyestuffs. Both in Germany and abroad, these firms were recognized as the "Big Six." There were three very large enterprises:

BASF   (Badische Anilin und Soda-Fabrik of Ludwigshafen)

Bayer   (Farbenfabriken vorm. Friedrich Bayer & Co. of Leverkusen)

Hoechst   (Farbwerke vorm. Meister Lucius und Bruening of Hoechst am Main).

Not far behind were three lesser concerns:

Agfa   (Aktiengesellschaft fuer Anilinfabriken of Berlin)

5

Cassella   (Leopold Cassella & Co. of Frankfurt)

Kalle   (Kalle & Co. of Biebrick).

But the very success in gaining a worldwide monopoly led the German producers into a bitter and costly competition for a larger share of the lucrative foreign and domestic markets. Price cutting, protracted patent litigation, kickbacks to customers, and bribery to gain technical secrets—in fact, every known form of cutthroat competition—afflicted the industry. With the consequent loss of profits and reduction of growth, the leaders of the industry began casting about for a solution. It remained for Carl Duisberg, the general manager of Bayer and a dominant figure in the industry, to take the first step in bringing order out of chaos.

Duisberg, by training and ability, was well suited to this role. He was a respected, even brilliant, dyestuff scientist—a fact attested to by an array of valuable patents. His business acumen was reflected in the financial success of his company and the worldwide network of agencies he organized for distributing Bayer's products. Duisberg's personality was both domineering and flexible. He was an imperious Prussian who would not tolerate dissent in either his personal or his business life. Politically, Duisberg was an ardent Pan-German who believed passionately in Germany's mission in world affairs. Devoted to the "Fuehrer principle" in the organization of political and industrial life, he specifically used the term long before Hitler was ever heard of. At the same time, Duisberg was a superb opportunist, never permitting devotion to principle to interfere with expediency. Whether under the Kaiser, the Weimar Republic, or the Nazis, he always made the required adjustments, and he never failed to prosper.

In 1903, Duisberg made a trip to the United States to lay the cornerstone for a new Bayer factory at Rensselaer, New York, designed to produce a limited number of dyestuffs and pharmaceuticals. He was not happy about the project, mainly because it ran counter to the industry's policy of protecting its monopoly by not building plants outside Germany. This policy protected German technical secrets and trained personnel from being pirated by foreign interests. Unfortunately, the only way to get around the provisions of a new American tariff law that Duisberg believed was directed at Bayer was to construct the Rensselaer plant. Even so, its production was limited to a few dyestuffs and aspirin.

The trip, however, had an unexpected benefit. Duisberg was snapped out of his dismal mood by a sudden awareness of the trust movement in the United States, which despite passage of the Sherman Antitrust Act some thirteen years earlier was booming. John D. Rockefeller's Standard Oil trust particularly caught Duisberg's attention. He went back to Germany to persuade his colleagues and competitors that the Standard Oil formula represented their salvation.

The other members of the Big Six were all receptive to Duisberg's major goal of ending costly competition. They had reservations, however, about surrendering as much control over their own corporate affairs as contemplated in the Standard Oil trust type of organization. But the thrust of Duisberg's proposal was not wasted. Bayer, BASF, and Agfa adopted a loose-knit joint organization of the type used by a number of industries in Germany, that is, an *Interessen Gemeinschaft* (roughly a "community of interest"). Not long after, Hoechst, Cassella, and Kalle organized a similar *Interessen Gemeinschaft*. In both cases the function of the community of interest was to reduce competition among the parties, mainly by setting up a formula for sharing profits. Each enterprise kept its identity intact and retained control over its own policies and activities. And of vital importance, dyestuffs alone were subject to the community of interest's regulations. The parties were free to exploit and develop other products without reference to the cartel's rules or restrictions.

Historically and industrially, the omission was a matter of some moment. Although dyestuffs remained the "cash crop" of the industry, the more dominant companies developed other significant and highly profitable lines of business activity. These outside activities eventually rivaled dyestuff production. Agfa became the largest European manufacturer and supplier of photographic materials. Its trademark, the Agfa signature, was a feature in photographic shops the world over. Bayer and Hoechst developed highly profitable pharmaceutical divisions that were giants in the field, with worldwide systems of distribution. Hoechst, for example, supported the research of Paul Ehrlich that led to his discovery of Salvarsan, the cure for syphilis. The result was everlasting fame and a Nobel Prize for Ehrlich and a patent monopoly of an enormously profitable pharmaceutical product for Hoechst. Hoechst also developed Novocain, a painkiller that physicians and dentists came to rely on universally. These products gave the Hoechst trademark acceptance everywhere.

Bayer's pharmaceutical venture was even larger. Out of its laboratories emerged aspirin, the world's most famous home remedy for pain and fever. Bayer was also responsible for the introduction of heroin, which it sold as a cure for morphine addiction and as a cough suppressant, especially effective in children. Later the Bayer laboratories developed methadone, in preparation for World War II, as a synthetic substitute for morphine. It was originally named Dolophine, in honor of Adolf Hitler. Today methadone is used principally in the treatment of heroin addiction. The sulfa drugs also had their inspiration in the test tubes of Bayer's laboratories, as did Atabrine, the most effective malarial suppressant. Indeed, no hospital and no pharmacy can be found without some Bayer product.

To BASF, however, must go the credit as the most venturesome of all the I.G. companies. Unlike Bayer, Hoechst, and Agfa, however, BASF did not gear its non-dyestuff products for the consuming public; hence, for a long time BASF was not a household name. But in corporate board rooms and in scientific organizations worldwide, its name and power evoked respect and admiration.

BASF's corporate personality began taking shape during the developing stages of the new dyestuff technology. The first colors to come out of this industry

8

were reds and yellows, which were mastered quite early. But unlocking the secret of synthetic blues proved more troublesome. As a result, the world for a time was forced to rely on China, the age-old source for natural indigo dyes. Great rewards awaited the discoverer of an acceptable synthetic. And BASF's part in this race has become a legend in the industry.

Heinrich von Brunck, the chairman of the managing board of BASF and a dyestuff chemist of extraordinary talent and imagination, convinced the BASF board of directors to make the search for synthetic indigo a major effort. Long before the project had run its course, Brunck had committed the greater part of BASF's capital to this undertaking. Some of the directors demanded the abandonment of the search, charging that the enormous investment was threatening the corporate structure of the company itself. Fortunately, before this internal dispute came to a head, the technicians and scientists at BASF reached their goal. The vats of BASF began pouring out gorgeous synthetic indigos. Brunck was vindicated as the company's profits began to soar. The project rang the death knell for the natural dyestuff industry, and BASF's discovery and consequent success catapulted this company into leadership of the industry. Commercial boldness and technological excellence became the decisive elements in its corporate character.

BASF's willingness to make big corporate gambles further crystallized in another audacious project that followed the indigo success. This time it was the search for a synthetic nitrate to free Germany from dependence on Chile, which monopolized the natural nitrate supply. For BASF this undertaking involved a scientific and business risk far exceeding that in the indigo gamble. Brunck, his confidence bolstered by the indigo breakthrough, made the decision to go all out.

During the latter part of the nineteenth century, a number of prominent scientists expressed the belief, supported by facts and figures, that an exploding world population clearly threatened to outrun the food supply. The ghost of Malthus had returned to haunt the world. The most promising solution was the increased use of fertilizers. But, as some of those who sounded the tocsin warned, this approach was complicated by the uneven distribution of the earth's resources. Chile had a monopoly of the world's supply of natural nitrates, the most effective of all fertilizers, and as is the custom of monopolists Chile charged what the traffic would bear. But many concerned scientists, such as the renowned Sir William Crookes, expressed the fear that Chile's natural reserves of nitrates would soon be depleted. The grimness of the prospect of a starving world underscored the opportunity for realizing great financial profits should a synthetic nitrate be produced.

There was another opportunity that also should have spurred the effort to break Chile's monopoly. Nitrates were an essential ingredient of all explosives, including gunpowder. But for reasons not altogether clear—unless one is willing to accept the conventional wisdom that the military mind is incapable of seeing beyond the last war—the German General Staff did not appear to be concerned that Chile controlled the supply of a raw material so essential for waging war. And the military implications of Chile's monopoly did not excite the interest of the private manufacturers of explosives in finding alternatives. From a commercial point of view, it was cheaper for explosive manufacturers to import nitrates from Chile than to undertake the uncertain and expensive venture of inventing a synthetic substitute. In times of peace, gunpowder was no great source of profits.

The impending food crisis was another matter. The farmers of the world represented an enormous market for fertilizers. Attracted by prospects of fame and profit, a number of scientific institutions and private concerns entered the race to synthesize nitrates Not the least active of these was BASF. Not only did its talented scientists and engineers conduct experiments on a variety of systems to make synthetic nitrates but also the concern made available sizable subsidies to independent university researchers.

In 1909 BASF's "Project Nitrogen" struck the jackpot. Fritz Haber, a technical school instructor supported by a BASF grant, scored a major scientific breakthrough. Using enormous pressure and extremely high temperature he succeeded in combining the nitrogen of the atmosphere with the hydrogen of water to form ammonia. The fixation of nitrogen became a landmark in creative chemistry, earning for Haber the acclaim of the international scientific community.

Before Haber's great discovery could be made profitable, one more step had to be completed: BASF had to turn Haber's laboratory feat into a large-scale industrial operation. Brunck, nearing the end of his active life, delegated the task to his protégé, Carl Bosch, a promising, thirty-four-year-old metallurgical engineer who was among the first to grasp the colossal implications of Haber's work. Technically Brunck had little doubt that Bosch was equal to the task. But the BASF board of directors questioned the proposed financial investment in a technologically unknown terrain. To place this responsibility in the hands of an untested thirty-four-year-old was not exactly a prudent business decision. But Brunck was not to be denied. He compared the venture with the earlier indigo gamble. The directors capitulated and the decision was made to go ahead.

The challenge Bosch faced was to design and to build an industrial-size installation that could contain the great pressures and high temperatures required in Haber's process. Taming these wild forces called for the discovery of catalysts to speed up the reactions and for the invention of alloys to keep the outsize equipment intact.

· Bosch chose Oppau near BASF's headquarters at Ludwigshafen as the site for the new plant. Recognizing that Brunck's health was failing and that support among board members was paper-thin, Bosch worked like a man with a mission. As the technological difficulties and the costs mounted, the board became more restive. Brunck's death at the end of 1912 complicated Bosch's problems. But in the fall of 1913 he reached his goal ahead of schedule. The Oppau plant, completed and operating, began mass-producing synthetic ammonia. Bosch's feat of technical macrodynamics was recognized throughout the world as an engineering achievement of the first rank. Before long the scientific community elevated him to near equality with Haber by referring to the "Haber-Bosch process." For an engineer this was an extraordinary accolade from the world of pure science. And twenty years later this achievement earned for Bosch a Nobel Prize, the first engineer so honored.

For BASF, immense financial returns seemed assured and Bosch emerged as one of the stars in the company's hierarchy. He was elected to the board of directors, clearly destined for future leadership of the company.

1

World War I

By July 1914, with war barely a month away, the Oppau plant was producing forty tons of synthetic ammonia a day, mainly as the raw material for nitrate fertilizer. The military possibilities of the plant's operation, however, had not escaped Bosch. For some time in his laboratory he had been producing experimentally a limited amount of saltpeter ($NaNO_3$), the essential raw material for gunpowder, by oxidizing Oppau's ammonia. Lacking any expression of interest from governmental authorities, Bosch saw no reason to expend the money or the time to go beyond his laboratory effort. He stored the experience for future reference.

So little did the saltpeter problem concern the German General Staff or the Ministry of War that when war erupted on August 1, 1914, so many of Oppau's key technicians and workers were drafted for military service that the plant was forced to shut down. The day of reckoning was barely six weeks away. The closing of the Oppau plant, however, was by no means the result of blunder or the mindlessness of the German military establishment. Rather, it was the logical outcome of the basic war philosophy successfully followed by the General Staff in the 1871 victory over France and, ever since then, reworked and refined for the war that was now being waged with France, Britain, and Russia. Perfected by the late General Count Alfried von Schlieffen, chief of the General Staff from 1895 to 1906, this policy had become the bible of the German General Staff.

The goal of the Schlieffen plan was not mere victory but swift victory. This was to be achieved by an overwhelming assault on France with the bulk of the German army, while a minimal force held Russia in check. Once France was defeated, Russia would be easily crushed by the full fury of German arms. An isolated England would have no recourse but to sue for peace.

According to the Schlieffen plan, a long war for Germany could not even be considered in the formulation of military plans. He held that the political-industrial structure of modern states was so delicately balanced that they could not survive for long the disruptive power and violence of twentieth-century military technology. The consequent social unrest in the rear would disastrously affect the fighting at the front. Schlieffen had no interest in the manufacturing capacity of the industrial community. All he wanted from the civilian population was civil order and no interference with military operations. The problem of raw materials was a long-term industrial concern and hence an irrelevant distraction from achieving a quick victory. In a short war, industry could play no vital part; in a long war, it would be an impediment. Such was the inflexible blueprint Schlieffen bequeathed to the General Staff. What both he and they failed to understand was that industrial mobilization was the very element that made wars of exhaustion possible and that industrial supremacy was the key to victory. This oversight had fatal consequences.

It remained for an industrialist to challenge the General Staff's war plan. When the war was barely a week old, Walther von Rathenau, head of the A.E.G. (Allgemeine Elektrizitaetsgesellschaft), the German electric power and equipment combine, called on General Erich von Falkenhayn, the minister of war, with a grim message. The military establishment, Rathenau charged, had made a blunder of such dimensions that unless corrected promptly could lead Germany to defeat.[1] Rathenau was no ordinary industrialist. He was the director of more than 100 large corporations in Germany and elsewhere in Europe and a recognized intellectual whose books were seriously received in university and diplomatic circles. No less important, Rathenau was also a political figure: seven years later he became Germany's foreign minister. It is probable that the war minister was already suspicious of the euphoria exhibited by his military colleagues in charge of Germany's war effort for despite the enormous press of other duties he took time to hear Rathenau out.

According to Rathenau, the German General Staff was so deeply committed to a short war that it had formulated no contingency plan for a long one and it had ignored the role of industry in all of its meticulous preparations for waging war. Rathenau cited the lack of preparations for insuring a continuous supply of raw materials for industrial production, even for those factories engaged in the manufacture of gunpowder and other military goods. Aggravating the plight of a Germany at war was the dismal fact that nature had made it poor in raw materials. A broad range of stragetic raw materials such as nitrates, oil, rubber, and many metals were available only from overseas sources. Without these basic imports, Germany's war production would be precarious. Denied these raw materials for a prolonged period, a number of vital industries would grind to a halt.

To Rathenau it was incredible that the General Staff should have ignored this obvious German weakness. The enemy was certainly aware of it. The Allies' main strategy focused on this visible Achilles' heel. The mission of the British fleet was to strangle Germany into ultimate submission. If the German General Staff did not appreciate the full meaning of the blockade, German industry did. Already it could feel the effects of the tourniquet of enemy warships as they progressively shut off the arteries of supply. Shortages of raw materials would soon occur. By keeping industrialists out of war planning and ignoring the problem of raw materials, the

15

General Staff had played into the hands of the enemy, Rathenau argued.

But it was not Rathenau's purpose to be a harbinger of doom. Instead, he came prepared with specific proposals to correct the military myopia at which he had directed his barbs. He recommended the establishment of a system of controls, including rationing, and a system of priorities to husband the limited stockpiles of strategic raw materials, the import of which was now prevented by the British fleet. Of no less urgency was Rathenau's proposed program to develop, wherever possible, synthetics and other substitutes to replace scarce raw materials.

General Falkenhayn, an officer of superior intelligence, was convinced by Rathenau's dissertation. He also had sufficient rank to act on Rathenau's advice. In a frontal attack on the problems raised by Rathenau, General Falkenhayn ordered the creation of a War Raw Materials Office within the Ministry of War and he immediately appointed Rathenau to be its head. Rathenau lost no time in staffing the agency with a selected group of scientists and industrialists. The first task of the new agency was to evaluate accurately the raw materials supply. Pressed by Rathenau the agency promptly undertook a survey of 900 concerns engaged in war production. The survey confirmed Rathenau's worst fears. It disclosed that German industry had no more than a six months' supply of imported raw materials.[2] The limited stockpile of nitrates made gunpowder production particularly vulnerable. As long as the British fleet controlled the seas, the prospect of replenishing the nitrate supply by shipments from Chile was slim. A munitions crisis of major dimensions loomed if the war continued for another half year. An army running out of gunpowder was a military disaster beyond contemplation. To come to grips with the problem Rathenau appointed Fritz Haber, then at the Kaiser Wilhelm Institute for Physical Chemistry and Electrochemistry, to head up the chemical division of the new agency. The creator of synthetic ammonia brought with him an assortment of Nobel Prize winners and other scientific luminaries, and soon this division became known as the "Bureau Haber."

The rapid expansion of the Bureau Haber indicated the priority that Rathenau assigned to the nitrate problem. He warned the military officers in the War Ministry that the British blockade had completely shut off shipments from Chile. The stockpile of nitrates was dangerously low and any major military offensive by either side would make the gunpowder situation critical. The War Ministry bureaucracy—still under the influence of Schlieffen's philosophy and confident of the success of his so-called plan—remained indifferent to Rathenau's plea for affirmative action. Despite the fact that Rathenau was an eminent industrialist appointed by Falkenhayn himself, the traditional Prussian officers in the War Ministry resented him as a Jew and a civilian. In a direct answer to his warning that the nitrate shortage would soon adversely affect the German war strategy, they responded with a curt note instructing Rathenau not to interfere in purely military affairs.[3]

But arrogance precedes disaster and the day of reckoning was not far off. In the historic Battle of the Marne during the second week of September 1914, with Paris almost in sight, the German army's headlong rush to victory was stopped cold by an unexpected French counter-attack, shattering the Wehrmacht's design for a quick victory. The Schlieffen plan lay in ruins, buried in the trenches the opposing sides were forced to dig. Confronted by the dreaded long war of exhaustion, the military bureaucracy could no longer ignore Rathenau. The violence of the battle had used up more of the gunpowder than anticipated. Suddenly the dullest officers in the War Ministry understood the terrible meaning of the British blockade.

The munitions crisis expanded Rathenau's influence dramatically. Nitrates became the War Ministry's number one priority. The "Chemists' War" was about to begin. Rathenau, supported by Haber, persuaded the War Ministry to summon Bosch to Berlin as quickly as possible.[4] Time was now Germany's immediate and most pressing enemy. The moment Bosch arrived he was hustled into a meeting with the military officials concerned with the gunpowder shortage. Bosch was appalled by their ignorance. Some were not even aware of Germany's utter dependence on Chile for saltpeter. Bosch explained that the production of synthetic ammonia by the Haber-Bosch process solved only part of the problem. Before ammonia could be used in the manufacture of gunpowder, it first had to be converted into nitric acid. Though conversion in the laboratory was a well-known process, adapting it to large-scale factory production called for a monumental effort. Among other things, such an undertaking meant the immediate return of the skilled Oppau personnel who had been drafted and a guarantee that building materials, technical equipment, and heavy machinery already in short supply would be readily available. Not unmindful of the interests of BASF's stockholders, Bosch demanded a substantial subsidy. Prodded by Rathenau and Haber, the War Ministry agreed to all of Bosch's demands.

A determined Bosch returned to Oppau and a massive effort to get the project under way began. This represented a prototype of the Manhattan Project—an all-out effort by government, industry, and science sparing neither money, matériel, nor manpower to solve a specific military-industrial problem upon which the outcome of a war may depend.

Although adequate gunpowder reserves could not insure victory, everyone involved recognized that defeat could very well hinge upon Bosch's success or failure. Rarely has the military future of a great power rested so heavily on the shoulders of a single civilian. Should Bosch fail, it was generally agreed that Germany would have to abandon the war in six months.

As Bosch set about to convert ammonia into nitric acid, the munitions crisis intensified. Confronted with the specter of an army without gunpowder, the War Ministry frantically scoured Germany and the conquered territories for nitrates. Even tiny amounts of fertilizer were commandeered from peasants.[5] The shortage was temporarily eased in early October when a cache of 100,000 tons of Chilean saltpeter was discovered in cargo ships in the harbor of occupied Antwerp.[6] However, as Fritz Haber later reminisced, "The Belgian saltpeter supply had so little effect on the matter that in the fall of 1914 every expert recognized the necessity of ending the war in the spring of 1915."[7]

The nitrate shortage began to affect seriously the strategy of fighting the war itself. Unfortunately, having relied so completely on Schlieffen, Germany's military leaders were now in no mood to gamble everything on Bosch's success. Prudence dictated that alternatives be explored without delay. Being miltary men, Germany's military leaders sought a military solution. Accordingly, they called for a plan to blast a hole in the British blockade and reopen the supply line from Chile to the German gunpowder plants.

Charged with this mission, the German Admiralty devised a bold and imaginative plan worthy of the stakes involved. Its goal was the capture of the British-owned Falkland Islands, an unfortified coaling and supply base for British naval vessels at the tip of South America. These bleak and windswept islands were the southernmost hinge of the British blockade, standing guard over the trade routes from the west coast of South America to Europe.

The mission to capture the Falklands was assigned to Admiral Graf von Spee, who was in command of a powerful naval squadron on duty in the Indian Ocean. At about the time that Bosch returned to Oppau to embark on his own "Battle of Nitrogen," Spee's squadron was ordered to the South American theater.

The German General Staff had no monopoly on shortsightedness. When the British Admiralty learned of Spee's presence off the coast of Chile, it concluded that the German commander's main objective was to disrupt the trade between East Asia and Europe. The Admiralty even suspected that Spee's target was the Panama Canal. The British did not have the slightest idea that Spee's mission was related to the German nitrate crisis—or at least this possibility escaped the British entirely. In any event, a woefully inadequate naval force stationed at the

Falkland Islands was dispatched to intercept Spee. So little did the Admiralty appreciate the critical nature of Spee's mission that it refused the British commander's urgent appeal for reinforcements. This failure was soon to be regretted. On November 1, the enemy squadrons met at Coronel, off the coast of Chile. Outgunned and outmaneuvered, the British were swiftly defeated. Those ships not sunk fled through the Straits of Magellan to their base in the Falkland Islands.

Now aware of Spee's goal of capturing the Falklands although still unable to divine the reason, the British Admiralty set out to repel the anticipated invasion. It ordered the sinking of an old battleship in the mud flats of Port Stanley, the main Falkland harbor, to act as an artillery platform. The British then dispatched a powerfully reinforced squadron to intercept Spee's ships. As the German flotilla approached, observers on the cliffs of the Falklands observed heavily armed landing parties preparing to invade. Before the invasion could begin, however, the reinforced British flotilla reached the battle scene. This time the superiority of the British naval forces was overwhelming. With one exception every German warship, as well as Spee himself, was sent to the bottom. Not a single British ship was lost.

After the defeat at the Falkland Islands, Germany's nitrate position became more desperate. Surprisingly, however, the British never fully understood the strategy behind Spee's action. No less a figure than Winston Churchill, who had been first lord of the Admiralty during the Battle of the Falkland Islands, was still in the dark ten years later when he wrote *The World Crisis*, his monumental history of the first world war. Apparently unaware of Germany's crucial nitrate shortage, Churchill was able to say of Spee's mission only that "We do not know what were the reasons which led him to raid the Falkland Islands, nor what his further plans would have been in the event of success. Presumably he hoped to destroy this unfortified British coaling base and so make his own position in South American waters less precarious."[8]

In any event, for Germany the life and death Battle

of Nitrogen extended beyond the naval engagement off the southern tip of South America. The next phase was centered in the Oppau laboratories, where work continued around the clock. Bosch was Germany's last hope.

Falkenhayn, who had succeeded Field Marshal von Moltke as chief of the Supreme Command after the disaster of the Marne, was acutely aware that time was running out for the Wehrmacht. Until a steady supply of gunpowder could be assured, no offensive could be mounted and the western front would be frozen in place. In the meantime, some other method would have to be found to break the stalemate. Falkenhayn assigned the search for a solution to Major Max Bauer, an aggressive and imaginative officer who was the Supreme Command's liaison to heavy industry.[9]

Bauer discussed his assignment with a number of the War Ministry's scientific consultants, members of the Bureau Haber. This impressive group included, in addition to Haber, Nobel Prize winners Walther Nernst, Emil Fischer, and Richard Willstaetter. Bauer learned from them that the German dyestuff industry was the source of poisonous chemicals such as bromine, chlorine, and phosgene, which could easily be converted into terrible instruments of mass asphyxiation.[10]

Though all poisonous weapons had been outlawed by the 1907 Hague convention, to which Germany was a signatory, the attractions of poison gas warfare were too great for the Germans to be constrained by the treaty. To the contrary, the very fact that poison gas was barred by the convention assured Germany of the advantage of surprise.

Bauer and Nernst paid a visit to the acknowledged spokesman of the German dyestuff industry, Carl Duisberg, who saw immediately that poison gas warfare could revive the moribund dyestuff industry, which was almost at a standstill since the beginning of the war. As a German patriot Duisberg also recognized the possible decisiveness of the new weapon. Accordingly, he not only committed Bayer to the poison gas project but also involved himself personally in the experiments. In a letter to Bauer in early 1915, Duisberg wrote of his firsthand knowledge of the effects of phosgene: "How uncomfortably it works you may best gather from the fact that for eight days I have been confined to bed, although I inhaled this horrible stuff only a few times . . . if one treats the enemy for hours at a time with this poisonous gas-forming product, then, according to my view, he will not immediately leave the country."[11]

The first gas to be used by the German army, a bromide, came out of the Bayer laboratory. Its secret code name was "T-Stoff." The army decided to use it against Russian troops at the end of January. But the new weapon was a dismal failure. The Russian winter was so cold that the gas froze and sank into the snow.[12]

Fritz Haber, whose bureau in the War Raw Materials Office was deeply involved in the poison gas project, regarded chlorine as a more effective weapon and the spring as a more advantageous time for its introduction. Chlorine was in plentiful supply in the dyestuff plants. Moreover, Haber knew of BASF's successful attempt to store chlorine in metal cylinders rather than the traditional glass containers, an obvious advantage on the battlefield. Haber's staff at the Kaiser Wilhelm Institute, in cooperation with the I.G. companies, began preparing chlorine for the coming test on the field of battle. This project was one of the most closely held military secrets in all Germany. An explosion in the laboratories of the Institute, which killed Haber's assistant, who was experimenting with phosgene, almost gave the secret venture away. Quick and successful suppression of news of the event prevented any serious leakage.

Chlorine gas was scheduled to be tested on the western front in April 1915. Haber, who was certain that the attack would devastate the enemy, advised his superiors to assign large reserves of troops to exploit the opportunity. However, the military refused to regard the projected attack as anything more than a test and allocated only one company of soldiers to support it.

In the third week of April 1915, Haber and his small team of soldiers and technicians from the dyestuff companies, the Bureau Haber, and the Kaiser Wilhelm Institute arrived at a sector of the western front near Ypres in Belgium. Five thousand metal cylinders of liquid chlorine were placed in position along the front-line trenches. After several delays caused by unfavorable wind conditions, Haber finally ordered the cylinders to be opened late in the afternoon of April 22.[13]

The report of British Field Marshall Sir J. D. P. French tells what happened.

> Following a heavy bombardment, the enemy attacked the French Division at about 5 p.m., using asphyxiating gases for the first time. Aircraft reported that at about 5 p.m., thick yellow smoke had been seen issuing from the German trenches between Langemarck and Bixschoote. What follows almost defies description. The effect of these poisonous gases was so virulent as to render the whole of the line held by the French Division mentioned above practically incapable of any action at all. It was at first impossible for anyone to realize what had actually happened. The smoke and fumes hid everything from sight, and hundreds of men were thrown into a comatose or dying condition, and within an hour the whole position had to be abandoned, together with about fifty guns.[14]

The effect of the chlorine gas at Ypres was truly devastating. Before the day was over, 15,000 soldiers lay on the battlefield, one-third of them dead.[15] An enormous gap, over four miles wide, had been torn in the Allied lines. Nothing stood between the Germans and the vulnerable French ports, just across the channel from England.

But the failure of the German army to anticipate the overwhelming effect of its new weapon saved the Allies from annihilation. Haber was extremely bitter about this. As he wrote later, the military officials involved "admitted afterward that if they had followed my advice and made a large-scale attack, instead of the experiment at Ypres, the Germans would have won."[16]

After the attack at Ypres, Haber began to prepare for a gas attack on the eastern front. Haber's wife, Clara, pleaded with him to abandon the project and stay at home. He refused, insisting that it was his duty as a patriot to do what he could to help Germany. The night that Haber left for the eastern front, Clara Haber committed suicide.[17]

With Haber's gas attack at Ypres, chemical warfare became an essential element of the German military machine, and the dyestuff companies, together with the Kaiser Wilhelm Institute, became, in effect, the German chemical warefare service. As an English chemical warfare expert noted,

> Germany required no cumbersome government mechanism for the preparation of new war chemicals, for the semi-industrial work in developing processes for approved substances, nor for their production. By relying on . . . the German dyestuff companies and the Kaiser Wilhelm Institute . . . Germany escaped the necessity for comprehensive government organization, the development of which was such a handicap to Allied countries. . . .[18] There was no need to create a clumsy and complicated organization with an efficient one existing in [the German dyestuff companies] ready to meet Government demands.[19]

The dyestuff companies cooperated closely in their work in order to fulfill the army's requirements. When the German authorities wanted a new poison gas, according to an Allied report, "a conference with the various firms was held in Berlin to determine how manufacture should be subdivided in order to use the existing plants to best advantage."[20] Since producing a poison gas involves several stages of production, each stage was assigned to the company most suited to carry it out. The direct involvement of the military was very apparent. Masses of uniformed soldiers were constantly arriving at the various plants, where schools were established to train them in gas warfare. The total result was the emergence of a highly successful industrial, scientific, and military cooperative.

Unfortunately for Germany, poison gas was not the decisive weapon it was seeking. The attack at Ypres had dissipated the crucial element of surprise; the development of new and deadlier gases could not take the enemy completely off guard. With the war of exhaustion approaching reality, Bosch's success became more urgent. As the reserves of gunpowder dwindled, the General Staff waited anxiously for word from him.

In May, Bosch made his momentous announcement. He had succeeded. Oppau was ready to mass produce synthetic nitrate. Never again would the Wehrmacht's cannon be hostage to the nitrate beds of Chile. Throughout Germany Bosch was hailed as a hero.

For Germany Bosch's success meant salvation; for BASF it was a technological and financial bonanza. Bosch immediately began to press the Government to support an enormous expansion of BASF's synthetic nitrate capacity. He had the unexpected but welcome assistance of a young lieutenant in the War Raw Materials Office with the imposing title of Plenipotentiary for Chemical Production, Hermann Schmitz. With Schmitz's help, Bosch persuaded the German government to build a huge Haber-Bosch high-pressure plant in Leuna, in Central Germany.

Schmitz's performance in marshaling the facts and figures to overcome all bureaucratic opposition made a profound impression on Bosch. It marked the first step in a relationship that would lead Schmitz to succeed Bosch as the head of I.G. Farben some twenty years later. The new plant at Leuna, together with the one at Oppau, in time outstripped Chile in supplying nitrates. Never again was Germany to be troubled by a shortage of this raw material. The financial rewards for BASF were enough to justify a twenty-five percent return on invested capital to its stockholders during the rest of the war.

The other dyestuff companies also prospered in the Chemists' War. In the summer of 1915 Duisberg wrote Bauer about the surge of business that war production had brought his company. "You should see what things look like here in Leverkusen, how the whole factory is turned upside down and reorganized so that it produces almost nothing but military contracts. . . . As the father and creator of this work, you would derive great pleasure."[21]

Germany's introduction of poison gas shook the military foundations of the Allied powers. The German monoploy of dyestuff production had given it an incalculable military advantage. In the new technology of chemical warfare, any country without a dyestuff industry was vulnerable to its enemies. It was an intolerable situation and each of the Allied countries frantically undertook programs to close the gap.

Though the United States was still neutral, Army Ordnance strongly encouraged private companies to enter the production of dyestuffs. The most positive response came from the Du Pont Company, the largest supplier of gunpowder and explosives to the armed forces and the country's major chemical firm. Du Pont entered into a contract with a dyestuff manufacturer in Great Britain, to exchange technical information, know-how, and patent rights, as well as to cooperate commercially. It also enticed Morris Poucher, an executive of BASF's American agency, to leave his German principal and join Du Pont. Poucher's defection brought an angry response from Carl Bosch, enraged by what he regarded as a breach of business ethics by Du Pont and a treasonable act by Poucher—that Poucher was an American-born citizen made no difference to Bosch. As further encouragement to American producers like Du Pont to enter the new field, a protective tariff was enacted in the summer of 1916.

Carl Duisberg observed the growing competition from abroad brought on by military necessity with mounting concern for the commercial future. He suggested that the German dyestuff companies pool their resources into a single *Interessen Gemeinschaft* in order to strengthen their position in the postwar world against the new competition.[22] Such an arrangement would provide for the pooling of profits and patents. It would also lead to close cooperation among the various concerns without surrender of the independence or identity by individual members. In effect, such a community of interests would formalize the cooperation brought about by the gas warfare effort.

At first Duisberg's proposal met with a lack of interest by some of the companies. Very soon, however, the opposition evaporated in the wake of an unexpected event on the battlefield not unlike the surprise at the Marne.

At the Battle of the Somme in July 1916, the Germans were shocked by the strength, even superiority, of the British in men and matériel. They were amazed by the British capacity to sustain enormous losses and yet continue to fight. It now dawned on the members of the dyestuff industry that a German victory was no longer certain. The postwar implications of this unthinkable thought were obvious. In mid-August the major German dyestuff companies led by the so-called Big Three, BASF, Bayer, and Hoechst, and joined by five others, Kalle, Cassella, Agfa, ter Meer, and Greisham, accepted Duisberg's proposal and formed the Interessen Gemeinschaft der Deutschen Teerfarbenindustrie (the "Community of Interest of the German Dyestuff Industry"). This structure came to be known simply as I.G. and the individual members as the I.G. companies. (Years later the name I.G. was actually reserved in a court decision for the exclusive use of I.G. Farben.)

The Battle of the Somme was also a personal disaster for Falkenhayn. On August 28 he was removed as chief of the German Supreme Command, and Field Marshal Paul von Hindenburg was appointed in his place, with General Erich von Ludendorff second in command as first quartermaster general. This move was welcomed by the big German industrialists, who had become extremely dissatisfied with Falkenhayn's failure to push the stepping up of war production. Ludendorff, like Bauer, was an old and trusted friend of German big business.

Three days after Hindenburg took over the Supreme Command he announced a new munitions program that called for a big increase in war production—doubling the munitions supply and tripling the supply of machine guns and artillery by spring 1917.[23] Also included was a substantial increase in the production of poison gas and chemical products. All financial considerations were to be abandoned in this crash program. From the point of view of industrialists like Gustav Krupp and Duisberg the Hindenburg program could hardly have been more attractive if they had prepared it themselves.

On September 9 Bauer conferred a great honor on Duisberg and Krupp. He arranged for them to meet with Hindenburg and Ludendorff on the train of the Supreme Command to talk over the new munitions program. The two industrialists grasped the opportunity to complain about the critical shortage of labor. The goals of the Hindenburg program could not be fulfilled, they said, unless this problem were solved. Apparently, Duisberg was reassured by Hindenburg's response. The next day he wrote a rhapsodic note of thanks to Bauer.

> The ninth day of the ninth month 1916 was an eventful day in my life and one which I will not soon forget. It was similar to that time after the Battle of the Marne in late autumn of 1914. . . . At that time there was also a munitions shortage, and a much more threatening one than today's, which . . . permitted us to seize, in a practical sense, upon the spokes of the wheels of war.[24]

A week later, under pressure from the Supreme Command, the war minister held a secret meeting with thirty-nine of Germany's most important industrial leaders, including Carl Duisberg, so that they could air their grievances about labor. Max Bauer, who represented the Supreme Command at the meeting, made it clear in his opening address that the industrialists' demands would be heeded: "What industry must accomplish is just as important as what the army has to do. Only with your help can we march on to victory."[25]

Duisberg again complained about the labor shortage afflicting German industry. Wages were escalating and war production was dropping to dangerously low levels.

He proposed that the Supreme Command "open up the Belgian labor basin." He was aware that an earlier attempt to recruit Belgians to work in German factories had failed because the Belgians refused to help their conquerors. Bauer nevertheless assured Duisberg that his proposal would be put into effect.[26] And less than two months later, in November 1916, the German army began the forced deportation of Belgian workers to German factories. This decision and its consequent brutality was a shock to the Belgian nation.

Cardinal Mercier, the Catholic prelate in Belgium, in a moving protest, described to the world what the Germans were doing.

> Parties of soldiers begin to enter by force these peaceful homes, tearing youth from parent, husband from wife, father from children. They bar with the bayonet the door through which wives and mothers wish to pass to say farewell to those departing. They herd their captives in groups of tens and twenties and push them into cars. As soon as the train is filled, the officer in charge brusquely waves the signal for departure. Thus thousands of Belgians are being reduced to slavery.[27]

Neutral journalists dispatched similar reports—of men loaded into cattle cars at bayonet point, of hysterical women who threw themselves on the tracks to prevent the trains from leaving and who had to be removed by German soldiers.

The Belgians appealed to the United States government to stop the German action. After checking on the details of Germany's slave labor program, the United States dispatched a formal note to the German chancellor.

> The government of the United States has learned with the greatest concern and regret of the policy of the German government to deport from Belgium a portion of the civilian population for the purpose of forcing them to labor in Germany, and

is constrained to protest in a friendly spirit, but most solemnly, against this action, which is in contravention of all precedents, and of those humane principles of intenational practice which have long been accepted and followed by civilized nations in their treatment of non-combatants.[28]

The Germans dismissed the American complaint. The German governor general of Belgium argued that the evacuation of Belgian laborers was not a hardship but a blessing. The German press pursued this theme: the *Koelner Volkszeitung* insisted that the deportation of Belgian workers was prompted by "true humanitarianism, protecting thousands of able-bodied workmen from going to ruin by remaining unemployed."[29]

By the middle of November 1916, German authorities had "captured" 40,000 men and sent them to German factories and mines; 2000 more were being added each day. Raiding parties searched homes, theaters, and markets. Ultimately, over 66,000 Belgians were transported to Germany.

The slave labor program, however, proved counterproductive. The deported Belgians refused to work despite threats and promises. The vehemence of the worldwide protest barred sterner measures, ultimately forcing the abandonment of the project; the enslaved Belgians were returned to their homes.[30]

During the fall of 1916, Duisberg continued his activities on behalf of the I.G. companies on other "battlefronts" at home. Inflation, the economic disease that feasts on war, reached so high a level that it began to threaten war production. By early 1917 inflation was rapidly approaching crisis proportions. Labor unrest mounted, accompanied by "exorbitant" wage demands and followed by a series of strikes. To halt the inflation Duisberg, as spokesman for the industrialists, demanded a ceiling on wages and a prohibition on labor's right to strike. At the same time he took the lead in the industrialists' resistance to any attempt by the government to control profits or prices. The inflation rolled on.

A new agency, the War Office, decided to exert its influence toward halting the inflationary excesses. It had been set up several months earlier at the suggestion of Bauer and with the support of Ludendorff; its purpose was to divert all matters relating to the economy from the relatively independent War Ministry. Into this strategic position was placed General Wilhelm Groener, who had served with Bauer and Ludendorff before the war on the General Staff and whose personal devotion they were sure of. But they misjudged their man.

Groener initially chose to keep the War Office neutral with regard to the pressures of labor and industry. The approaching fiscal disaster changed his mind. He hinted at this new posture in his response to a request from the steel industry to restrain wage demands. Groener's reply was not the kind industrialists had come to expect from a German general. He observed that "industry has gone chasing after war profits in an unheard of manner." He then went on to cite some invidious examples of the conduct of some businessmen: "I wonder . . . whether you know that the War Office has had to stop a company from making a profit of thirty-five million; whether you know that a German employer permits four women who work for him to sleep in a barrack in one bed that is also full of lice."[31]

It was suspected that Groener had adopted this viewpoint because of the influence of one of his aides, Captain Richard Merton, a Jew and a political moderate. However, Merton was no reckless radical or academic reformer. In private life he headed the Metallgesellschaft empire, the leading enterprise in the nonferrous metals industry of Germany and the largest metals trader in the world with branches and subsidiaries in every major country.

Captain Merton's views on the wage—profit—price spiral made a deep impression on Groener and the general requested his aide to commit these thoughts to paper. The result was a document entitled "Memorandum on the Necessity of State Intervention to Regulate Profits and Wages."[32] In this memorandum Merton pointed out that the growing power of the workers and the shortsightedness of the industrialists engaged in war production interacted to inflate prices. Cost-plus contracts with the price determined after delivery encouraged producers to pile on expenses rather than resist higher prices for raw materials and higher wages. The state, which was the final purchaser, "can do nothing else under the present circumstances than agree to the price which is demanded of it." Certain to offend the industrial community was Merton's assertion that profits were already so great that wages could be raised without a corresponding increase in prices. Merton compounded his heresy by three recommendations. Prices should be fixed at the time war contracts were made, not after the goods were delivered. War profits should be taxed at a much higher rate. And finally, the chancellor should be empowered to take over the factories of recalcitrant owners or to intervene in the event that a labor dispute reached an impasse.

Groener approved the memorandum and dispatched it to the head of the government, Chancellor Georg Michaelis.[33] When Duisberg learned of the contents of the memorandum and that Merton's recommendations were being seriously considered in the highest levels of government, he was stirred to action. As spokesman for the I.G. companies he invited a small but influential group of industrialists to a meeting on August 19 at the Düsseldorf Industry Club. The opening lines of the invitation sounded the alarm: "Measures designed to assault the employers by limiting profits are . . . being considered. Speed is . . . necessary to counter this." Duisberg guaranteed the support and presence of the industrialists' ally Max Bauer, who would appear as a representative of the Supreme Command.[34]

In the meantime, pressures within industry and the Supreme Command were mounting for Groener's removal. By the end of July, Ludendorff had made up his mind to get rid of the controversial general. Within days of the decision, but two weeks before Groener himself learned of it, Duisberg assured his colleagues in the steel industry that Groener would soon be relieved of his position in the War Office and sent to a command division at the front. Groener later charged that Duisberg and Bauer had conspired to secure his removal. Duisberg insistently denied any part in it. However, historian Gerald Feldman, who studied the available documents, came to the conclusion that "In the light of the evidence . . . it is virtually impossible not to conclude that Duisberg was a liar."[35]

Groener formally requested that Merton continue on his staff, but Ludendorff vetoed the application with the remark, "This marriage must be ended."[36] Instead, Merton was scheduled for transfer to a dangerous battle area on the western front.

Unlike Groener, the young industrialist was wise to the ways of Duisberg and Bauer. He had established his own avenues of intelligence and influence. Major Kurt von Schleicher, a friend (who fifteen years later would precede Hitler as Chancellor of Germany) had earlier warned Merton of Groener's impending removal. Schleicher also arranged a safer post than the one planned for Merton. As a result of Schleicher's intervention, Merton was issued orders "to investigate industrial bribery in the occupied areas."

Inflation was not the only problem confronting Germany, and labor was not the only shortage afflicting the German war effort at this time. The mechanization of the war exceeded any of the projections by either side. The vast armadas of ships, trucks, and planes almost drank Germany dry of liquid fuel. In August 1916, the fuel problem was further complicated by the defection of Rumania, Germany's principal source of oil, to the Allied side. As a consequence Germany was forced to divert troops from the western front to mount an attack on Rumania in an attempt to gain control of the oil fields. Although the Germans quickly defeated the Rumanians, by the time they reached the oil, the Allied forces had succeeded in blowing up the wells and refineries. Without Rumanian oil, Germany's fuel supply fell to a dangerously low level.

A number of attempts were undertaken to find a substitute for natural oil. One of the most promising was synthetic gasoline, produced from coal and hydrogen under high pressure by a process known as hydrogenation, not unlike the Haber-Bosch process. In fact, it had been invented in 1909 by Friedrich Bergius, who had his first experience in high-pressure chemistry as Fritz Haber's assistant during the search for synthetic ammonia. In the laboratory the Bergius process showed great promise, and in 1916 Bergius set about to adapt his hydrogenation process to large-scale production. However, he had still not succeeded by the end of the war. What he lacked was an engineering genius, someone like Bosch to adapt his laboratory process to large-scale factory production.

A serious rubber shortage was also developing. The British navy had placed rubber at the top of its list of contraband products, and Germany was compelled to adopt extraordinary measures to elude the blockade. Twice in 1916 the famous submarine *Deutschland* was able to spirit a load of rubber and tin from United States ports in exchange for a delivery of I.G. dyestuffs and drugs like Salvarsan and Novocain.[37] Germany was scoured for every scrap of used rubber that could be reclaimed. The shortage became so acute that even wood and rope were tried as tires.

Bayer and BASF stepped up their laboratory efforts to find synthetic substitutes for rubber. They finally succeeded in developing a substance that, although too hard and inelastic for tires, could be adapted for use in submarine batteries, magnetos, and other electrical equipment. During the course of the war, Bayer alone turned out 2,500 tons of this hard synthetic rubber. But no way could be found to make synthetic rubber suitable for the desperately needed tires.

In April 1917 the United States entered the war against Germany. Walther Nernst, who had been in the United States at the time and was briefly interned until he could be repatriated, upon his return called on Bosch. He described the great raw material resources and enormous productive capacity the new enemy would be able to draw upon in the war. Of specific interest to an embattled Germany, the United States was the largest producer of oil and gasoline in the world. Bosch, who since the nitrate crisis had concerned himself with synthetic solutions to Germany's raw material weaknesses, was troubled by Nernst's visit. He was now convinced that the entrance of the United States into the war would end any major oil problem for the Allies. For Germany no solution appeared to be in sight. Bosch lapsed into a deep depression, an affliction that periodically returned to him in the wake of disappointments and crises.

The British blockade ultimately proved the decisive element in ending the war. A raw materials famine, complicated by actual hunger, finally cracked the German will to resist. By the middle of August 1918, the German commanders knew that continuation of the war was futile and defeat only weeks off. Ludendorff asked Carl Duisberg and other industrialists to carry this message to the Kaiser, but they all refused. Duisberg was in fact preparing to adjust to the coming shape of things.[38]

The German surrender was signaled by the signing of an armistice on November 11, 1918. With barely any delay, the German authorities began preparations for the conference that would ultimately lead to the conclusion of a formal treaty of peace. Johann von Bernstorff, who as ambassador to the United States had developed a friendship with President Wilson, was chosen to direct this project. Not long afterward, Duisberg was asked to join these preliminary efforts as the representative of the chemical industry. But Duisberg, unsure that his conversion to democracy would be accepted by the Allied conquerors or by the revolutionary German workers, decided that he would be unavailable and recommended the appointment of Bosch instead.[39]

Bosch accepted. His mission was to save the I.G. companies. Germany may have lost the war, but the I.G. companies did not intend to lose the peace.

Within a few weeks caution dictated that Duisberg leave the country. A *New York Times* dispatch of December 24, 1918, took note of his departure: "Dr. Carl Duisberg of Leverkusen, head of the German aniline dye industry, is reported to have fled to Switzerland. He was generally looked upon as the link between business and General Ludendorff and was one of the most active Pan Germans."[40]

At the same time, Fritz Haber, who took the brunt of the scientific world's condemnation of gas warfare, disguised himself with a beard and, like Duisberg, took off for Switzerland. The fears of men like Duisberg and Haber were not entirely groundless. Within weeks after the armistice, Allied troops poured into the Rhineland. No sooner had the occupying forces settled down than the infant chemical warfare services of the Allied armies began to press for the disclosure of the secret processes and production methods in use at the various I.G. plants turning out poison gases, explosives, dyestuffs, and nitrates. The I.G. companies resisted on the ground that such disclosure would adversely affect their commercial position in the postwar world. Unlike the French, the Americans and the British were careful not unduly to upset the I.G. officials. Assurances were given that the investigators would not "pry into secrets of commercial value in times of peace." No technology would have to be revealed nor questions answered unless they concerned weapons or military applications. "This reassurance," reported a U.S. Chemical Warfare Service officer, "established a more or less cordial relation between us."[41]

In keeping with this decision, the Allied peace commission directed the investigators to limit their inquiries to war products only. The Allied investigators promptly sent out an order to the I.G. companies requiring them to provide complete details on the manufacture of poison gases, gas masks, gunpowder, and other clearly military items. Failure to comply could result in the shutting down and even the dismantling of the noncompliant plants.

The investigators, bound by the Allied peace commission guidelines, did not press to examine the dyestuff technology. But the inquiry into poison gas proved to be a disappointment. The scientists on the U.S. team reported that they learned nothing about poison gases that was not known generally to the scientific commu-

36

nity. They noted that the Germans simply selected with great skill and imagination chemicals already available from commercial dyestuff processes. Whatever advantages the Germans had came from their domination of the peacetime dyestuff industry and not from the invention of new poisons.

The Haber-Bosch nitrate plant at Oppau was another matter. The investigators soon became aware that this facility represented a fundamental scientific breakthrough as well as a triumph of ingenuity and skill without which Germany could not have continued to fight as long as it did. They learned, for example, that in the last year of the war the Oppau plant had produced 90,000 tons of synthetic nitrates (equal to one-fifth of the natural, Chilean saltpeter consumed by the rest of the world).

However, when the French members of the investigating team demanded that the plant be started up so that it could be observed in operation, Bosch stubbornly refused. All attempts to move him, including threats of severe consequences, proved futile. The outraged French petitioned the Allied commission to force Bosch to operate the equipment and reveal the know-how and basic elements of the process of nitrate synthesis. To the disgust of the French, the commission ruled in support of Bosch, holding that the process was a commercial, not a military, affair.[42]

The leading British authority on chemical warfare, Major Victor Lefebure, vigorously opposed this decision as well as the earlier directive not to inquire into the know-how and technology of the "commercial" dyestuff plants. Later he amplified his views in a book entitled *The Riddle of the Rhine*: "Only the French," he concluded, "recognized the full war significance of these factories."[43]

In April 1919 the German delegation arrived at Versailles. Its members, including Bosch, were placed in protective custody behind barbed wire fencing surrounding the Hôtel des Réservoirs. Bosch, present as an expert in his field, was sent to the peace conference to protect the interests of the I.G. companies. The most stringent Allied demand as far as the I.G. companies were concerned was voiced by the French, who advocated the destruction of all of Germany's armament facilities, which, they insisted, included the dyestuff and nitrate plants. Marshal Foch had already made it clear that this issue was not negotiable. The only argument with any force that Bosch was able to muster against this demand was that the Allies needed a strong Germany as a bulwark against Russian communism.

The American delegation also was pushing a demand of its own. It was no secret that Du Pont, with the support of U.S. Army Ordnance and the congressionally chartered Chemical Foundation, wanted to keep the vested German properties and patents from being returned. The most valuable of these belonged to the I.G. companies. To counter the American demand, Bosch marshaled the arguments against it in a position paper for the use of the German delegation: "The German Chemical Industry and Its Desires during the Peace Negotiations."[44] Bosch argued that morality and international law required that all confiscated properties and patents be returned to their German owners. But Bosch was not content with mere repatriation. He insisted that the life of each patent seized should be extended to make up for the period of the confiscation.

In another position paper Bosch took issue with the possible Allied demand for separation of the east and west banks of the Rhine.[45] This would have played havoc with the I.G. companies, especially BASF, whose plants were situated on the west bank. The French were particularly active in pushing for a takeover of the left bank or at least the establishment of an "independent" Rhineland republic. The annexation of Alsace-Lorraine by the Germans in 1871 was a precedent that led the Germans to fear the worst.

As the representative of the defeated side, the German delegation had to await the proposed terms of the victorious Allies. It was an anxious time for Bosch. On May 7, the Allies delivered the proposed terms of the peace treaty to the German delegates. Carl Bosch promptly proclaimed, "The peace conditions are unacceptable in every respect."[46] He was speaking for himself, for the dyestuff industry, and for Germany.

The clauses dealing with the so-called points of honor were especially obnoxious. The German delegation was appalled by the demand for a public trial of the Kaiser before an international tribunal "for a supreme offence against international morality and the sanctity of treaties." Other "persons accused of having committed acts in violation of the laws and customs of war" would be brought to trial before military tribunals.[47] Those I.G. executives and scientists involved with poison gas could not have read these clauses without a sinking feeling. To the Allies, I.G. and poison gas were synonymous. Even so, a war crimes trial with such eminent scientists and industrialists in the dock seemed unthinkable.

Bosch was also bitterly disappointed by the Allied terms concerning the German patents and plants seized by Allied custodians. To BASF and the other I.G. companies their loss was a serious blow. These were not to be returned to their prewar German owners.[48] Whatever remedy remained, it was unlikely that it could be achieved at Versailles. Also a matter of some concern to the I.G. companies was the inclusion of dyestuff in the reparations payments to the Allies for war damages.[49] It was a requirement that could have unfortunate political consequences—and it did. The anxieties about the Rhineland were not realized. The essential clause involving this sensitive issue required only demilitarization not annexation.[50] The west bank would remain German.

But all of these concerns were minor in the face of the greater danger. The provisions that struck terror in the hearts and minds of the I.G. companies related to the disarmament of Germany. The Allies demanded that except for certain approved factories such as those required for internal security, "All other establishments for the manufacture, preparation, storage or design of arms, munitions or any war materials whatever shall be closed down."[51] The military leaders of France and England, including Field Marshal Foch and Field Marshal Sir Henry Wilson, left no doubt that this provision meant the smashing of the I.G. plants that made poison gas and nitrates. Unless modified these terms spelled doom for the German chemical industry.

On May 29, 1919, the German delegation submitted its formal memorandum of counterproposals to the president of the peace conference. In it the delegates complained that "the time limit given us for the drawing up of this memorandum was so short that it was impossible to exhaust all questions." They repeated their request for a personal confrontation and oral negotiations: "This peace is to be the greatest treaty of history. It is without precedent to carry on such vast negotiations by means of written notes only."[52]

The German plea for some kind of personal negotiation was ignored. On June 16 the final terms of the Allies were presented to the German delegation. So few alterations had been made in the proposed terms already submitted that the same document was used and the changes were added by hand in red ink.

Frantically the German government explored a variety of suggestions to soften the harsher provisions of the treaty. At one point the futility of their effort drove the Germans to consider resuming the war. The thought was short-lived. On June 28, 1919, the treaty of peace was signed.

Although the disarmament clauses that threatened the end of the I.G. companies remained intact, there was one more diplomatic round left to eliminate their lethal impact. Before I.G.'s fate was sealed, experts from both sides were to reconvene at Versailles to clarify and interpret those terms of the treaty that were considered ambiguous.

In the interim, Bosch left for Ludwigshafen to attend a meeting of the BASF hierarchy, where, as anticipated, he was elected chairman of the managing board. Together with Duisberg, Bosch was now one of the two most powerful figures in the German chemical industry. Immediately after his election, he returned to Versailles to resume his efforts at softening the French position. But the French refused to be reasonable. After one difficult session, Bosch told his friend Baron von Lersner, the new chief of the German delegation: "The dictate of Versailles demands the complete surrender of the German chemical industry." But with the confidence of a man in possession of a powerful secret, he added, "Trust me—the German chemical industry will never be destroyed." The unusual display of confidence, Bosch indicated, without being specific, stemmed from a "special trump card" that he had been planning to play at the right moment.[53] That time had now arrived.

The trump card turned out to be Joseph Frossard, a French official who had just been put in charge of all I.G.'s confiscated dyestuff plants in France, now consolidated in a French government-owned corporation (Compagnie Nationale des Matières Colorantes et des Produits Chémiques—the "National Dyestuffs and Chemical Products Company"). If such a strategically placed French official was truly Bosch's trump card, he was obviously in a position to help Bosch rescue the I.G. companies from their threatened annihilation.

Frossard was a shadowy figure about whom there is still not an abundance of solid information. For some years before the war he had worked for the Russian textile industry, then dominated by the German dyestuff cartel. During the war, as an official in the French chemical warfare service, he had helped in the acceleration of mustard gas production. After the war, the French had assigned Frossard to watch over the occupied BASF plants at Ludwigshafen. Now at Versailles he had turned up as an adviser on dyestuffs and chemicals to the French delegation.[54]

In some mysterious way never disclosed, Bosch made arrangements for a clandestine meeting with Frossard. At their secret rendezvous Bosch revealed his plan to temper the French demand for the demolition of the I.G. plants. In its essence, the plan provided for the French government and the I.G. companies to become partners in exploiting the French dyestuff market. The German companies would surrender their jealously guarded secret know-how, without which the French, as Frossard knew, were already having trouble operating the confiscated dyestuff plants. It was an offer only desperation could force Bosch to make. In return, the

41

I.G. companies would regain a half interest in their prewar dyestuff plants—and of overriding importance, the I.G. plants in Germany would be spared. As Bosch fully expected, Frossard agreed to his plan.

His next step was to convince the French military to to abandon their intransigent insistence on the destruction of the I.G. plants. Frossard promised to arrange a meeting with the appropriate French official, a General Patard. He therefore asked Frossard to arrange a meeting with the French general in charge of such matters, and Frossard promised to do so promptly. Their meeting concluded, Bosch sneaked back to the German compound, undetected, he hoped.

The next morning, however, Baron von Lersner received a formal note from the French commandant: "Last night in violation of law, Professor Bosch left the German quarters surrounded by barbed wire and scaled the wall of the Versailles Park. After two hours and five minutes he returned the same way."[55] Such was the extent of the French objection. They did not pursue the affair any further.

Bosch's faith in Frossard was not misplaced. In a few days he was invited to Paris by General Patard to discuss the future of the nitrogen plants at Oppau and Leuna. As a result, Bosch was one of the first Germans permitted to move freely in Paris after the war.[56] Although Patard had been briefed on the plants and on Bosch's scientific reputation and engineering accomplishments, the negotiations at first did not go well. The two men exchanged bitter words. Patard insisted that the Oppau and Leuna plants had to be destroyed because of their military value. Bosch countered that with famine facing many of the war devastated areas, these plants were desperately needed to produce fertilizer. Bosch finally began to impress Patard with the depth of his intellect. The general relaxed his hard position. If the synthetic nitrogen plants were so vital to agriculture, Patard said, France should have them as well as Germany. Therefore, if Bosch would support a French nitrogen project, Patard would permit Oppau and Leuna to continue to operate. Patard was specific in his terms. BASF should help the French government build the nitrate plants, deliver the necessary equipment, make available all secrets, know-how, and technology, send experienced personnel to train French technicians, and expend their best efforts to create a successful French nitrogen industry. In return, the French would drop their demand that the German dyestuff and nitrate plants be destroyed.[57] Bosch was aware of the criticism he would face in Germany for giving up the Haber-Bosch monopoly, but he readily agreed to Patard's terms. A more important consideration was involved: it was the only way to save his beloved Oppau and Leuna and possibly I.G. itself. At the conclusion of this meeting it was agreed to start negotiations in November on a formal agreement.

Before Bosch left Versailles, he had one more mission to accomplish. Hermann Schmitz, the bright young man in the War Raw Materials Office who had helped him secure the approval of the German Government for the building of the Leuna high-pressure chemical plant in the spring of 1915, was present at Versailles as a nitrate and fertilizer expert representing the Ministry of Economics.[58] Bosch arranged for Schmitz to join BASF as its chief of finance and foreign operations.

In the flush of the excitement of this important step upward in the industrial world, Schmitz could not possibly imagine what the future held.

In the fall of 1919, at just about the time Bosch was concluding his deal with General Patard, the issue of war criminals became front-page news for the first time since the Versailles treaty was signed. It was raised accidentally by the Nobel Prize committee in Stockholm, which announced that Fritz Haber had won the Nobel Prize for chemistry for his synthesis of ammonia.[59] The scientific community of the world reacted with outrage. The comment of the foremost British scientific journal, *Nature*, was typical: "It will not be forgotten that it was at the Kaiser Wilhelm Institute for the Promotion of Science that Geheimrat Haber made his experiments on poison gas, prior to the Battle of Ypres, which initiated a mode of warfare which is to the everlasting discredit of the Germans."[60] French scientists were especially resentful of the Nobel committee selection, and two French winners announced publicly that they would refuse to accept their prizes as long as Haber was to be honored with them.[61]

Supporting the French scientists, the *New York Times* editorialized on January 27, 1920:

> So, though Dr. Haber undoubtedly has many scientific achievements to his credit besides his work in poison gas, and though the Swedes who made the award had probably no invidious intention, general sympathy will be felt with the Frenchmen who did not care to be honored in such company. One may wonder, indeed, why the Nobel prize for idealistic and imaginative literature was not given to the man who wrote General Ludendorff's daily communiqués.[62]

The Swedish government, troubled by the extent of the protest, sought to correct the impression that Haber was being honored for contributions to the horrors of war. Upon orders from Sweden, Dag Hammarskjöld, first secretary of the Swedish legation in Washington, wrote a letter to the *New York Times* pointing out that

> the report on which the award was made stated that the Haber method of producing ammonia is cheaper than any other so far known, that the production of cheap nitric fertilizers is of a universal importance to the increase of food production, and that consequently the Haber invention was of the greatest value to the world at large. . . . Ammonia, the product of the Haber method, must be converted into nitric acid in order to give rise to explosives or corrosive gases. As a matter of fact, the Haber plants in Germany were erected with a view of producing agricultural fertilizers.[63]

A few days later Haber's role in Germany's poison gas warfare became an official matter. The Versailles treaty, in one of its most bitterly contested provisions, had called for a war crimes trial before a special tribunal of "persons accused of having committed acts in violation of the laws and customs of war."[64] On February 3, 1920, a list of over 900 alleged war criminals was submitted by the Allies to Baron von Lersner as head of the German peace delegation. On the list were military and political figures, including the Kaiser, Hindenburg, Ludendorff, Bernstorff, and princes of the Royal House of Hohenzollern. Fritz Haber was also on the list—the only person remotely within the I.G. orbit to be charged as a war criminal.

The collection of names presented by the Allied powers proved to be entirely unmanageable. Many individuals were unidentifiable and a large number could not be located. Misspellings added to the confusion. The Kaiser was in Holland, which refused to surrender him. Recognizing that a reduction in the number was required, the Allies on May 7, 1920, submitted a drastically smaller list, omitting practically all the well-known names. The number of those accused of war crimes had been reduced from 900 to 45; the list was now composed mostly of obscure figures like submarine commanders and prison guards. Haber's name was no longer on the list. The German government agreed to commence proceedings against the accused in a German court at Leipzig.

The trials took place late in May 1921. Of the six defendants accused by the British, five were convicted and given short sentences; of the six on the Belgian and French lists, only one, accused of shooting a prisoner of war, was convicted and sentenced to two years.

The pointlessness of these trials became apparent, and a commission of Allied legal experts found, without a dissent, that many of the accused who should have been condemned had been acquitted and that the punishments generally were inadequate. They recommended that those not yet tried should be delivered to the Allies for trial instead. Their report was received by the Allies, pigeonholed, and forgotten. Almost half a century later a war criminal convicted at Nuremberg, Albert Speer, lamented that the failure of the war crimes trials in World War I may have had an effect on the commission of war crimes in World War II.

There was at least one more strong reverberation in the Allied countries because of poison gas warfare. In September 1921 a tremendous explosion shattered the Haber-Bosch synthetic nitrate plant at Oppau in one of the world's worst industrial catastrophes. Over 600 workers were killed, more than 2000 were injured, and the plant was demolished. Rumors spread that BASF was experimenting with some terrible new kind of chemical weapon. A *New York Times* editorial speculated:

> Nearly three years after the armistice, the Oppau plant of odious memory is blown to pieces by some mysterious explosive and 3,000 persons are killed, injured, or missing, and the scientists, including Professor Haber, do not know how it happened, can't understand it at all. It may never be explained to the satisfaction of honest scientific men; but when the fact is well known that there is an unrepentant and revengeful military party in Germany that looks to another war to restore her baleful power, and when the world believes that these dangerous reactionaries would welcome the discovery by their chemists of annihilating gases of enormous power, it is not inconceivable that the disaster at Oppau may have been due to covert experimenting by those chemists.[65]

An American reporter asked Haber for a possible explanation of the explosion. He replied that the Oppau explosion could not possibly have been caused in the production of synthetic nitrates by the Haber-Bosch process; neither the nitrates nor the enormous pressures involved could lead to an explosion of such force. Haber added intriguingly that "an investigation may reveal new and terrible forces."[66]

Whatever the cause, it was certain that BASF faced an enormous financial loss if the Oppau plant were not reconstructed quickly. However, BASF engineers estimated that the rebuilding would require at least a year. Bosch put Carl Krauch, whom he regarded as his most gifted protégé, in charge of Oppau's reconstruction, with orders to spare no expense.[67]

The most urgent problem was the recruitment of a huge labor force. At least 10,000 construction workers, mainly skilled craftsmen, were needed, as well as supervisory personnel. It seemed an impossible requirement. However, Krauch attacked the problem with imagination and boldness. He contracted with corporations all over Germany to suspend their own production and send complete units of workers and their supervisors to work at Oppau. Though expensive, the method proved a spectacular success.[68] Krauch was able to assemble the required work force in an incredibly short time, and Oppau was restored in only three months. The day after Oppau resumed operation, Bosch rewarded Krauch by appointing him to the BASF managing board of directors.[69]

The triumvirate who were to guide I.G. during the crucial years to come—Bosch, Schmitz, and Krauch— were now at the top of BASF, ready to play out their roles.

2

Postwar Germany
and
Bosch's Dream

The Versailles treaty clause providing that the Allied countries did not have to return seized German industrial property was a blow, of course, to the I.G. companies. But at least they were confident that the confiscated plants and patents could not be used to build up serious competition in the postwar dyestuff market. The non-German personnel in their foreign plants had not been entrusted with any of the vital technical information and know-how. The foreign patents had been intentionally worded so that only those with the know-how could work them.

The French had solved their problem by going into partnership with the I.G. companies to make dyestuffs in France—an opportunity afforded by the Bosch-Frossard deal at Versailles. The Americans, on the other hand, tried at first to develop a domestic dyestuff industry on their own, without the Germans. U.S. Army Ordnance still believed that a strong, independent American dyestuff industry was critical to national self-defense. Du Pont, Army Ordnance's chief hope, expended great sums of money in a futile attempt to make dyestuffs according to the specifications of the confiscated German patents. However, as Irénée du Pont, the firm's president said, ". . . an ordinary chemist couldn't work them. They were drawn for Germans who spent their life in the dyestuff field."[1]

It was finally decided to feel out Carl Bosch, the most international-minded of the top I.G. men, about a possible joint Du Pont-I.G. dyestuff venture. A Du Pont executive met with Bosch in Paris in November 1919, but Bosch was totally uninterested. He brushed the proposal aside with the explanation that he was not free to act on a dyestuff arrangement without the unanimous approval of all the other I.G. companies.[2] Du Pont was apparently not in the same strong negotiating position as the French had been: the dyestuff plants in Germany were no longer threatened with demolition under the Versailles disarmament provision. Perhaps of equal importance, Du Pont had no Frossard to do the negotiating.

Since Du Pont could not obtain the critical German dyestuff know-how through a partnership agreement, it resorted to a more direct method. In late 1920, a Du Pont representative, Dr. E. C. Kunze, succeeded in recruiting four Bayer chemists. Each signed a contract for $25,000 a year for five years—a tremendous sum at the time compared to what a chemist received in Germany. Dr. Kunze spirited the four chemists and a trunk containing drawings, formulas, and other important industrial information out of Germany. But the trunk was seized by the Dutch authorities when they accidentally discovered its contents, and, at the request of the Cologne prosecutor, a warrant was issued for the arrest of the four chemists for industrial espionage.[3]

The German press treated the episode as a major scandal. Newspapers carried stories with such headlines as "FOUR TRAITORS," "AN AMERICAN PLOT AGAINST GERMAN DYESTUFF INDUSTRY," and "THE POWER OF THE DOLLAR."[4] Two of the men, Joseph Flachslaender and Otto Runge, managed to make their way to the United States. They were detained at Ellis Island on the strength of the arrest warrant, but Du Pont was able to effect their release.[5]

The other two chemists, Max Engelmann and Heinrich Jordan, had a more difficult time. Meade wrote Irénée du Pont,

The Bayer Company has pretty effectively succeeded in getting the German government to do its will, in view of the fact that it has held Dr. Jordan in Holland and I presume by this time, under the Extradition Treaty, has had him returned to Cologne. Dr. Engelmann ... cannot secure a passport to this country under what we believe is a general order issued by the German government forbidding the issuance of passports to any German chemists.[6]

Du Pont did not intend to be blocked in its efforts to import German dyestuff technology. It called on the United States Army for help. One day in May 1921, a Washington D.C., attorney named Clement Lincoln Bouvé, appeared at the headquarters of the U.S. Army of Occupation in Coblenz. Bouvé, who had been an officer of the U.S. Army of Occupation, now belonged to a prominent Washington, D.C., law firm that included Robert Lansing, secretary of state under Woodrow Wilson. Bouvé was on no ordinary mission. Major General Henry T. Allen, commanding general of the U.S. forces in Germany, called in Captain H. E. Osann, chief of the Military Secret Police of the U.S. Army of Occupation in Coblenz, and assigned him, along with a company of soldiers, to Bouvé's project. This, the general explained, was to bring Dr. Engelmann and Dr. and Mrs. Jordan from unoccupied Germany to the American sector. Although the chemists were under German police surveillance, the skillful maneuvering of Bouvé and Osann made the mission a success. On July 5 the party arrived at Hoboken, New Jersey, on the U.S. Army transport *Somme*.[7] Within days they were in Wilmington, Delaware, working in the Du Pont laboratories. Du Pont was now in a position to compete effectively with I.G. in the world's dyestuff market.

By the fall of 1922 the Germans were finding it difficult to meet the reparations quotas required by the Versailles treaty, most of which were in the form of raw materials and manufactured goods then currently being produced in Germany. The French were inflexible in their demand that these quotas be met. They could never forget Bismarck's brutal terms of the peace treaty ending the Franco-Prussian War. "We will leave them only their eyes to cry with," the Iron Chancelor had crowed. But the French had not cried. In a burst of national pride they had paid the five billion francs demanded by Bismarck as war reparations. It was a pain the French would long remember.

The French, therefore, were not disposed to treat lightly Germany's failure to meet its reparations obligations set forth in the Versailles treaty. In late September 1922, the French filed a complaint with the Allied reparation commission that the Germans were delinquent in deliveries of sawed wood and telegraph poles. The commission, after an investigation and a hearing, found the Germans delinquent and ordered that delivery of the materials indicated in the reparations schedules be resumed. The Germans, either unwilling or unable, refused.

For several months the French took no direct action. On January 10, 1923, however, President Harding, bowing to popular sentiment in the United States, withdrew the American occupation forces from the Rhineland. The French took advantage of this American action and promptly moved into the vacated area, as well as into the industrial Ruhr. This move signaled the opening of what has come to be called the Ruhr war. The German government responded by declaring a policy of passive resistance and the factories along the Rhine and in the Ruhr came to a complete halt.

By mid-May 1923, the BASF plants had been idle for four months. As a result, they also had fallen far behind in the delivery of dyestuffs and nitrate fertilizers required for reparations payments. On May 22, Bosch received an urgent message from an informant that the French army would occupy the BASF plants the next day and members of the managing board would be arrested, charged with deliberately preventing the shipment of the reparations goods.[8] Bosch immediately issued orders to dismantle the high-pressure Haber-Bosch

51

equipment with utmost speed and remove it to Leuna, in unoccupied Germany. Within hours the massive machinery was loaded on rafts and hauled across the Rhine. At the same time the members of the managing board fled to Heidelberg and hid out under assumed names.

Bosch's information had proved correct. For the second time since the end of the war, French troops moved into the BASF plants at Oppau and Ludwigshafen. The employees, acting under Bosch's orders, refused to cooperate with the invaders.

Bosch, when asked by the press about the French occupation of the Ludwigshafen dyestuff plant, responded with a bitterness spiced by arrogance. "The French may be able to make bricks, but never dyestuffs."[9]

A French military court was convened at Landau, Germany, and the officials of BASF were charged and tried, in absentia, for impeding the delivery of fertilizers and dyestuffs to France. All were found guilty, fined 150 million marks, and sentenced to long prison terms. August von Knieriem, BASF's chief legal counsel, received the heaviest penalty, ten years, because he had signed the orders to the BASF workers directing noncooperation. The other directors, including Carl Bosch and Hermann Schmitz, were sentenced to eight years each.[10] All the members of the BASF managing board of directors were now fugitives from the French Army of Occupation.

By the summer of 1923, Germany was in near chaos. The rate of inflation, which had been accelerating since the end of the war, had become truly terrifying. The German mark was now worth a five hundred billionth of its 1918 value, and the world became used to pictures of German workers carting their wages in wheelbarrows. In mid-August, a new chancellor, Gustav Stresemann, assumed office to try to cope with the financial crisis. He concluded that Germany would have to settle its differences with the Allies before it could achieve any kind of stability at home. In late September, he announced the end of the government policy of passive resistance to the French and the resumption of reparations payments. It was only a short time before the I.G. plants in the Rhineland started operation again. And by November, Hjalmar Schacht, the head of the Reichsbank, had managed to stabilize the mark, an accomplishment that brought him his first public acclaim.

The shutdown of most of the I.G. plants during the Ruhr war had given the foreign dyestuff industries a golden opportunity. Without German competition American producers were now supplying almost ninety-five percent of the U.S. market. Du Pont dyestuff production, of course, had received an extra boost from the technical aid of the I.G. chemists they had spirited out of Germany in 1921, as well as from the active cooperation of Army Ordnance. The French also took advantage of the shutdown. Since early 1921 the I.G. companies, in accordance with the Bosch-Frossard agreement, had been supplying the Compagnie Nationale with their industrial secrets and know-how in the production of dyestuffs, in exchange for which under their partnership agreement they would receive fifty percent of the profits for the next forty-five years.[11] But in 1923 the Compagnie Nationale was absorbed by Etablissement Kuhlmann, the large French chemical and metallurgical concern. Shortly thereafter, Kuhlmann nullified the contract entered into by Frossard and Bosch on the ground that the I.G. companies had failed, during the shutdown, to supply the French with the dyestuff chemicals called for in the contract.[12] In effect, the Germans once again were thrown out of the French dyestuff market. The I.G. officials were extremely bitter, contending that the unilateral abrogation of the contract was illegal. The French now had I.G. know-how, for which the I.G. companies had received almost nothing in return. However, because of the delicate political situation, Bosch took no immediate action.

By the fall of 1923 the growing strength of foreign competitors convinced Duisberg that a basic reorganization of the foreign business of the I.G. companies was demanded. He proposed that the foreign sales agencies of all the German companies be merged into a single organization.[13]

Independently Bosch also had been giving thought to consolidation of the I.G. companies. But his horizons were much broader and his schemes more imaginative. For him the new technology, especially the high pressure chemistry which his own genius helped create, opened up boundless opportunities. But Bosch was no stranger to reality. BASF's resources were inadequate to support the staggering financial requirements of his soaring imagination. A broader and more substantial corporate base was needed. Using Duisberg's modest suggestion of consolidating the foreign sales agencies as a springboard, Bosch took a quantum leap beyond. He proposed that all the I.G. companies merge into a single corporation bringing all their industrial activities and financial strength into a gigantic monolithic entity. Once having set his course, Bosch was impossible to derail. Despite the reluctance of the other concerns to surrender their individual identities and their independence, Bosch's will and logic prevailed. By 1924 a firm agreement was reached by all eight I.G. companies to merge into a single corporation.[14]

All through 1924 and 1925 Bosch and his financial adviser, Hermann Schmitz, prepared the ground for the new entity. For a time it appeared as though the incorporation would be delayed because of an impasse reached by the two immovable objects, Bosch and Duisberg, over the name of the new organization. Bosch wanted to abandon the designation of the 1916 cartel, I.G. Farben. He argued that to retain the name would be misleading since the enterprise would no longer be an *Interessen Gemeinschaft*. Instead, he recommended as more appropriate Verein Deutscher Teerfarbenfabriken (Union of German Coal Tar Dye Firms). Duisberg regarded this suggestion as commercially infantile. He refused to abandon the enormous value of the worldwide acceptance of the I.G. Farben name. This was a commercial decision and Bosch's genius had no currency in that area. The other I.G. executives unanimously supported Duisberg and Bosch capitulated. On

54

December 9, 1925, in a procedure by which the other seven companies were incorporated into BASF, the merger was finally concluded. The name of the new entity was I.G. Farbenindustrie Aktiengesellschaft. Carl Duisberg was elected chairman of the supervisory board, retiring from an active managerial role in the new company. Henceforth he would limit his activities to matters of major policy. Bosch was elected chairman of the managing board, which made him chief executive officer of the company. From then on, wherever Bosch sat was the head of the I.G. table.

Fritz ter Meer, a leading I.G. executive and scientist, later summed up the meaning of the company. "The opening up of hitherto unknown chemical fields was the motif of the new combine."[15] Its prospects quickly caught the fancy of the investing public and, despite the very low ebb of the German economy, the value of the I.G. shares more than tripled during 1926. By any standard I.G. Farben was the largest corporation in Europe and the largest chemical company in the world.

Armed with vast financial resources the new company also took aggressive action in already established fields. One of its first moves was to gain control of Germany's munitions industry, including such dominant firms as Dynamit A.G., Rheinische-Westfaelische Sprengstoff A.G., and Koeln-Roettweil A.G. In this way I.G.'s nitrate plants were vertically integrated with the leading explosives concerns that had been their chief customers. I.G. also moved to strengthen its position in the foreign dyestuff markets. In the United States, for example, it formed the General Dyestuff Corporation and a little later the American I.G. Chemical Company. Through these vehicles it regained almost all of the properties seized from the I.G. companies by the U.S. alien property custodian during World War I.

In France, however, I.G.'s efforts met with a certain amount of failure. During the summer of 1926 it undertook to purchase secretly the shares of the Kuhlmann company, by now the largest dyestuff manufacturer in

France. I.G. concealed its identity by buying through Dutch and Swiss cloaks organized by Schmitz.

In seven weeks of feverish activity on the Bourse, Kuhlmann stock rose from 450 to 1000 francs. An investigation revealed that I.G. Farbenindustrie was behind the "raid" and in fact had already succeeded in its goal of buying control.

The I.G. assault on Kuhlmann caused a furor in France. As the *New York Times* noted: "To have such a vital part of the nation's defense in the hands of its late enemy would be intolerable for the French War Ministry, and there is every reason to believe that now the French dye companies are aware of the danger, everything will be done to prevent the complete success of the German plans."[16]

Something was done. Kuhlmann, with the support of the French War Ministry and a law quickly enacted by the Chamber of Deputies, issued a block of 100,000 new shares of capital stock that carried the controlling voting rights and was reserved for registered shareholders, who were required to be French citizens. The secret German owners were in this way rendered relatively powerless since their shares carried no voting rights. The result was the regaining of French control of Kuhlmann. With this action, I.G.'s takeover of Kuhlmann collapsed. Instead of retreating entirely, however, I.G. suggested to Kuhlmann a reestablishment of the original Bosch-Frossard cartel. The result was an agreement, signed in 1927, that provided for price fixing, common sales agencies, exchange of technical information, and division of markets. I.G. agreed to stay out of the French market and the French agreed to stay out of the rest of the European market.[17] In effect, if I.G. could not own the French dyestuff plants, it would at least exercise dominion over the French by cartel agreement.

By far the most ambitious undertaking of the new I.G. was a project which had become Bosch's dominant interest and, in fact, had been the real impetus for his insistence on the merger of the I.G. companies into a single financially powerful giant. It was Bosch's dream to liberate Germany from dependence on foreign oil wells. Without a single domestic oil well worthy of the name, Germany had been strangled by the British fleet during the war. Bosch would do for oil what he had done for nitrates. Through the magic of high pressure chemistry and his own genius he would convert Germany's plentiful coal into a torrent of gasoline. He would recreate a past triumph in a new setting.

Events were already taking shape in Germany that provided a pressing demand for oil. Clandestine rearmament through systematic violations of the Versailles treaty was under way. In 1924 mobilization plans projected a sixty-three-division army. The Black Reichswehr required a "safe" source of gasoline. In the mechanized war of the future the need for liquid fuel would be astronomical.

The lure of great profits in peacetime also entered into Bosch's calculations. The automobile boom was on its way, consuming great portions of the available gasoline, and promising to consume continually greater amounts. The immediate energy question confronting the industrial countries of the world was whether oil discoveries could keep up with the accelerating demand. The reply of oil authorities was generally negative, some even predicting the imminent exhaustion of the world's oil reserves. In the United States President Calvin Coolidge gave official recognition to this dismal prophecy by creating the Federal Oil Conservation Board, composed of the secretaries of war, navy, interior, and commerce. The board's mission was to investigate and report on the state of the world's reserves of petroleum.[18] The fact that it was considered necessary to involve such a commission was itself regarded as a grim portent. To the prescient the signs were already discernible that oil would be the vortex of international diplomacy and power politics. Such developments foreshadowed the time when the wealth of nations would be measured by the dipsticks of oil.

Finally, there was a more immediate concern nudging Bosch. His company's domination of the world's synthetic nitrate industry was coming to an end. He

57

had given France a plant as well as the secret of the Haber-Bosch process, and the other major industrial countries were developing their own nitrate capabilities. The time was fast approaching when these foreign plants would lead to a glut of the world's supply. Soon, Bosch recognized, he would have to shut down a large part of the costly, high pressure installations at Leuna and Oppau. Finding a new and profitable use for their expensive equipment became a pressing mattter.

To push the project forward, Bosh decided to acquire the Bergius process for converting coal into oil under high pressure. Bosch was aware that Bergius, like Haber, could carry out his process successfully only in the laboratory. All attempts during the war at large-scale industrial production had failed. It was a problem made to order for Bosch. He had the supreme confidence that what he had done for Haber he could do for Bergius. Only one impediment confronted him, but that was monumental: cost. Acquisition of the Bergius patents would be expensive enough; however, the outlays required to adapt the process to large-scale industrial production were beyond even the resources of BASF, already hobbled by the loss of the war. Only the combined financial resources of the merged I.G. companies could support such a project. It was also probably to this end that Bosch was so insistent that his private financial wizard, Hermann Schmitz, assume the post of chief financial officer of the new company. In fact, in 1925, when it was certain that the merger would soon take place, Schmitz, at Bosch's direction, had purchased the Bergius patents on behalf of the yet to be formed I.G. Farbenindustrie. It took all of Schmitz's skill at financial legerdemain, using Swiss banks and other cloaks, to swing the deal. Before long, work was under way to adapt the Oppau plant from nitrate synthesis to the conversion of coal into oil.

Although Bosch's plan was to rely on the financial resources of I.G. to develop domestic production, he planned to bring in an American company like Standard Oil (New Jersey) as a partner in the worldwide exploitation of the process. Moreover, Standard had more than enormous financial resources: it had a huge and well-staffed research and development organization that had achieved important breakthroughs in petroleum technology.

Standard, the dominant force in the American oil industry, was also one of its more imaginative members. Since the early 1920s, when depletion of the world's natural oil reserves first became a matter of concern, Standard had searched for alternatives to crude oil. It pioneered in testing shale as a commercial source, and in 1921 it even purchased 22,000 acres in Colorado in the hope that a commercially adaptable method of extracting oil from shale could be found.[19]* Standard was also exploring the feasibility of the Bergius process since the United States, like Germany, had tremendous coal deposits. In 1922, Frank A. Howard, head of the Standard Oil Development Company, had sent a young assistant to Germany to study the Bergius process but had been advised that it was still far from ready for commercial exploitation.[20]

In the spring of 1925 Bosch dispatched several senior BASF executives to the United States to explore the interest of the Standard Oil Company. When they arrived in the United States, the BASF representatives were given a tour of the refineries in the New York area and then invited to lunch with the Standard directors. Wilhelm Gaus, spokesman for the BASF group, made a speech of thanks in halting English. He said that he had been very impressed by the size and efficiency of the refineries and by Standard's new research and development organization. He then mentioned, almost as an afterthought, the progress that Bosch and his staff had been making in the development of the Bergius process—information that Bosch had specifically instructed Gaus to mention.[21] Gaus suggested that Howard visit Ludwigshafen when he was in Europe the

---

* In late 1916 the United States Geological Survey announced that, after a three-year survey, the agency's experts had concluded that the Colorado hydrocarbon shale beds would yield more than twenty billion barrels of crude oil, from which more than two billion barrels of gasoline could be extracted by ordinary methods.

next spring to see for himself, and Howard accepted the invitation.

In March 1926 Howard arrived at Ludwigshafen, as he had promised, and was given a tour of the BASF laboratories, by now officially a part of I.G. Farbenindustrie. He was stunned. Although Howard was the head of research and development of one of the world's largest and most scientifically advanced corporations, he reported that he was "plunged into a world of research and development on a gigantic scale such as I had never seen."[22] He was especially overwhelmed by BASF's experiments in synthetic oil. Howard fired off a message immediately to Walter C. Teagle, president of Standard Oil, then on a visit to Paris, to come to Ludwigshafen without delay:

> Based upon my observations and discussions today, I think that this matter is the most important which has ever faced the company since the dissolution [the breakup of the Standard Oil Trust by a Supreme Court decision in 1911]. The Badische [BASF] can make high grade motor fuel from lignite and other low quality coals in amounts up to half the weight of the coal. This means absolutely the independence of Europe in the matter of gasoline supply. Straight price competition is all that is left.[23]

The urgency of Howard's message brought Teagle to Ludwigshafen within a few days. An examination of BASF's high pressure installation left him just as impressed as Howard: "I had not known what research meant until I saw it. We were babies compared to what they were doing."[24] When Teagle and Howard retired to their quarters, they talked over "the effect the startling scientific developments . . . would have on the world's oil industry."[25] For Standard's own protection, it was obviously imperative to find a way for closer cooperation with I.G. The vision of thousands of obsolete oil wells was enough of a spur.

At first Howard and Teagle considered the possibility

of purchasing the world rights to the Bergius synthetic oil patents from I.G. However, millions had already been spent on the process, and it was obvious that only a tremendous price would be acceptable to I.G. At the moment Standard was not prepared to make a large expenditure on a process that was still in the early stages of development and not yet ready for commercial exploitation. Teagle and Howard decided to proceed cautiously. They concluded that at least for the present the most sensible arrangement was a simple partnership to develop and perfect the process without any large financial commitment. Bosch agreed in principle to the proposal. Although he would have preferred a broader agreement, it nevertheless was a concrete demonstration of Standard's interest.

Until this meeting Bosch had limited the hydrogenation project to a few experimental high pressure furnaces. After the reaction of the Standard executives, he threw caution to the winds. On June 18, he ordered a huge Bergius plant to be built next to the Haber-Bosch plant at Leuna. He had decided that the process was sufficiently advanced for I.G. to start mass-producing synthetic oil—100,000 tons a year. It was a step that many I.G. officials considered financially imprudent in view of the fact that the process still had some way to go before it was perfected. But Bosch was too powerful to be thwarted.

On September 1, 1926, at the first stockholders meeting of the incorporated I.G., plans were announced for construction of the big new synthetic oil plant at Leuna.[26] The wisdom of pushing the project seemed to be corroborated a few days later when President Coolidge's Federal Oil Conservation Board submitted its preliminary report on the question of "national petroleum conditions" in the United States. The board found that "the total present reserves in pumping and flowing wells . . . has been estimated at about 4½ billion barrels, which is theoretically but six years' supply . . . future maintenance of even current supplies implies the constant discovery of new fields and the drilling of new wells."[27] Even the worst pessimists were taken by surprise by the six-year estimate.

Shortly after the announcement of I.G.'s new synthetic oil plant, Bosch himself arrived in the United States to begin negotiations with Standard. He was interested mainly in financial support. By now Teagle and Howard realized that their enthusiasm and stunned appreciation of the hydrogenation process had reduced their bargaining power with Bosch. They decided to put on a counterdemonstration. Teagle invited Bosch to accompany him on his annual tour of Standard's vast properties. For three weeks they drove across the United States inspecting Standard facilities. On the trip it became clear to Bosch that the Standard Oil officials were not ready to make the large payment to I.G. he had expected. In mid-December he returned to Germany without a definite agreement or financial commitment. Again he slipped into the depression that periodically afflicted him.[28]

It took until August of the next year for Teagle and Bosch to reach a relatively limited understanding. Standard agreed to embark on a cooperative program of research and development of the hydrogenation process to refine crude oil. It also agreed to build a new plant for this purpose as soon as possible in Louisiana. In return Standard was given the right to exploit the process in the United States and to share half of the royalties with I.G. on licenses to other parties.[29] However, Standard was not entitled to exploit the process in any of its far-flung plants outside the United States.

Modest as the arrangement was, the *New York Times,* in its news story of the agreement dispatched by its German correspondent, was almost euphoric about the possibilities of I.G.'s synthetic oil process.

> What experts in chemical fields admit is that the world is on the threshold of a new fuel era, and that the often predicted failure of the gasoline supply is now shoved centuries in the future. . . . The discoveries in these fields are more marvelous than inventions which enable rapid strides in the

development of radio, other uses of electricity and in airplanes, a prominent industrialist told the correspondent of the *New York Times*.

It was estimated by "conservative authorities" that twenty percent of the gasoline used in 1928 would be synthetic and that within a very few years Germany would be completely self-sufficient. So great was the confidence in making synthetic oil, concluded the *New York Times* article, that the price for the synthetic fuel was expected to be less than that of natural oil imported from the United States and the Soviet Union.[30]

The story was a public relation man's dream. The true situation was quite different. The Bergius plant at Leuna, which had begun production in June, was beset by operational failures and extremely serious technological problems. Expenditures had soared so far beyond the original estimates that if continued they would threaten the very financial structure of I.G. Farben itself.

In the following months, pressure developed within the I.G. managing board to scrap the synthetic oil project entirely. Bosch paid no attention to the carping of his colleagues: "Nitrogen production took fifteen years to reach today's levels," he told them. "Obviously gasoline production has to be given more time before it becomes profitable."[31] As usual Bosch's power in I.G. was decisive. The managing board agreed to continue the costly synthetic oil project, at least for the time being. However, it was obvious that Bosch would have to find a way to relieve the severe financial strain on I.G. or face more trouble from the board.

In the meantime, Standard Oil officials, probably unaware of I.G.'s problems, had become increasingly bullish about the prospects for the Bergius-Bosch process. A research staff under the direction of Robert T. Haslam, a professor of chemical engineering on leave from M.I.T., had gone to work at the new experimental plant in Louisiana on the hydrogenation of crude oil, and Standard had already concluded that the process was the most important scientific development that had ever occurred in the oil industry. The application of the hydrogenation process to crude oil was nothing less than amazing. In the past, two barrels of crude oil had been required to produce a barrel of gasoline; with hydrogenation, only one barrel of crude would be required. However, under the terms of the 1927 agreement with I.G., Standard's affiliates all over the world were still not permitted to use the process. It could be exploited by Standard only in the United States and then only in conjunction with crude oil, not coal.

In August 1928, Teagle and other top Standard officials went to Germany hoping to convince Bosch and his I.G. advisers to expand the I.G.-Standard partnership to allow joint exploitation of the Bergius-Bosch process all over the world and to give Standard the right to apply the process to coal as well as crude oil. Bosch brushed the Standard request aside. Although he did not say so, he was having enough troubles with his I.G. colleagues about the cost of the hydrogenation project in Germany. This was obviously not the time for I.G. to embark on an expensive program of world exploitation even in partnership with Standard.

What Bosch really wanted was a large lump payment from Standard to extricate I.G. from its present financial difficulties and still enable him to continue the hydrogenation project in Germany. With the help of Hermann Schmitz Bosch devised a counterproposal that he did not believe Standard could afford to refuse. He offered to sell the world rights to the Bergius-Bosch hydrogenation process for the production of gasoline. The only territorial exception was that the rights in Germany were reserved to I.G.[32] Obviously, the German authorities would never permit I.G. to surrender to a foreign company the German rights to a process so crucial to military and economic self-sufficiency. Even so, I.G. did not reveal to its government that it was selling the hydrogenation rights to Standard. As Bosch anticipated, Standard jumped at the offer.

The parties negotiated their agreement in the manner of two great powers forging a treaty to divide the world into separate spheres of influence. They agreed to observe the sovereignty of each in their respective fields. In the words of a Standard official, "The I.G. are going to stay out of the oil business—and we are going to stay out of the chemical business."[83] To set up a mechanism to carry out the terms of the agreement the parties agreed to create the Standard-I.G. Company, incorporated in the United States, owned eighty percent by Standard Oil and twenty percent by I.G. This retained for I.G. a minority interest in any future success. I.G. then transferred the world patent rights (except for Germany) on the hydrogenation process to the new enterprise. In return, Bosch finally secured what he so desperately wanted. Standard turned over to I.G. two percent of its entire common stock: 546,000 shares valued on Standard's books at $35 million![84] As a slight bonus for I.G., Teagle agreed to serve on the board of I.G.'s newly formed holding company in the United States, the American I.G. Chemical Company.

After the agreement was concluded, Bosch undertook to interest Standard in a borderline technological development. It involved the manufacture of a synthetic rubber called Buna, which Bosch believed had the potential for rivaling, even supplanting, natural rubber as the raw material for tires. At the moment the I.G. laboratories were producing Buna experimentally from coal, but the cost was far too high to compete with natural rubber. Using oil instead of coal, however, promised to make the cost more competitive. With this purpose in mind, Bosch dispatched Carl Krauch to the United States to interest Standard in setting up a co-operative organization to develop a number of processes using oil as a raw material with particular emphasis on Buna.[85]

Krauch's mission was a success. In 1930 the Joint American Study Company (known as Jasco) was formed, owned equally by I.G. and Standard. Its stated purpose was to test and license new processes developed by either party in the "oil-chemical" field. Bosch had high hopes that Jasco's success in developing a Buna rubber from oil would lead to the offering of licenses to the American tire industry. With more automobiles in the United States than in the rest of the world combined, the potential market for the joint enterprise was full of promise.

Hardly had the I.G.-Standard marriage been completed than it received a series of staggering blows. The Great Depression, combined with the discovery of enormous oil reserves in Texas, dropped the price of oil so drastically that Standard abandoned any immediate hope for worldwide development of the conversion of coal into oil. The drop in the price of natural rubber was even more precipitous. Buna could not possibly compete. Standard's interest in Buna lay dormant until the clouds began to gather for World War II, and it took the Arab oil boycott in 1974 to rekindle Standard's interest in making gasoline from coal.

3

I.G. Prepares Hitler for War

The onset of the Great Depression and the sharp decline of the price of oil did not shake Bosch's commitment to his hydrogenation project. There was a strong element in the I.G. managing board, however, who thought differently. In July 1930 Bosch returned from a two-month vacation to find that opposition to the hydrogenation project had reached near-insurrection. He was told that Leuna must be shut down immediately.[1] Its opponents argued that it represented an unbearable burden on I.G.'s finances, which already were strained by the weakened economy. Although 300 million marks had been poured into the project, the process was still not ready for commercial exploitation.[2] The cost of the synthetic gas, they pointed out, was forty to fifty pfennigs a liter, whereas the world price of natural gasoline was only about seven pfennings.[3] The project was drowning in its own economics.

Although major disputes in the managing board of I.G. were extremely rare, the battle over synthetic oil was a bitter one. The contending parties finally agreed to assign the task of evaluating the project to two committees, one headed by Fritz ter Meer and the other by Friedrich Jaehne, the chief engineer.

Early in 1931 the committees reported to the managing board. The ter Meer committee recommended continuation of the project, and the Jaehne committee recommended its abandonment. The Jaehne committee reported that synthetic gasoline from coal could not be produced in the foreseeable future at a cost that would insure a profit. The only solution was a government subsidy, which Jaehne, a political conservative, opposed under any circumstances. He was "on principle against any kind of subventions by the State because this leads of necessity to influence by the State. It would be better to close down the plant."[4] But Bosch was too formidable a figure in the affairs of I.G. In the end, the managing board voted to accept the ter Meer recommendation. Bosch's hydrogenation project once again was saved.

Not long after this, Bergius and Bosch were awarded the Nobel Prize for chemistry "in recognition of their contributions to the invention and development of chemical high-pressure methods."[5] Bosch was the first engineer to be so honored. His image as a national hero grew even brighter.

At this time, an external problem menaced I.G. As Adolf Hitler grew in political strength, his attacks on industrial concerns in which Jewish officers and directors were readily identifiable became more ominous. I.G. Farben was a prime Nazi target as an "instrument of international finance capital" dominated by such well-known Jews as Max M. Warburg, Arthur von Weinberg, Alfred Merton, Ernst von Simson, Otto von Mendelssohn-Bartholdy, and Kurt Oppenheim. I.G. was cartooned as "Isidore G. Farber," a grotesque caricature of Shylock, and "I.G. Moloch," an ugly reference to the Canaanite god to whom children were sacrificed.

I.G. officials were deeply troubled by these attacks and made an effort to stop them through a promising young I.G. employee with good Nazi connections, Heinrich Gattineau, press secretary to Duisberg. Gattineau had been the student of one of Hitler's favorite intellectuals, Karl Haushofer, the Nazi geopolitician. In fact, Gattineau had written his doctoral dissertation, "The Significance of the Urbanization of Australia in the Future of the White Race," under Haushofer's direction.[6]

In June 1931, Gattineau wrote his old professor on

behalf of I.G.: "A short while ago you wrote to me that I could come to you with all issues that deal with the N.S.D.A.P. [Nazi party]."⁷ He hoped the professor could use his influence with the Nazis to stop the publication of articles characterizing Farben as an instrument of international Jewish finance. I.G., Gattineau pointed out, was already being attacked by the Social Democrats and by the Communists: "Therefore it is really not necessary for the National Socialists to follow the same line." The leadership of I.G. was composed of Christian, self-made men who had worked their way up from small-time merchants, engineers, and scientists. "It would be a good idea if you could talk sometime to Herr H. [probably Hitler] about our situation . . . I would be most grateful to you, Herr Professor, if you could help me in this instance." Gattineau met with some success in mitigating the attack on I.G. in the Nazi press. At the end of 1931 Bosch put him in charge of I.G.'s press center in Berlin, a more strategic place from which to deal with the Nazi hierarchy.

During the following year, Bosch and other I.G. executives took note of the electrifying growth of the Nazi party. In the election at the end of July 1932, the Nazis became Germany's largest political party, winning 230 of the 608 seats in the Reichstag. In August 1932 Hitler demanded the chancellorship in a coalition government. Hindenburg refused, and the Nazi Reichstag deputies then joined with the Communists to overthrow the Papen government. Hindenburg dissolved the Reichstag, and new elections were scheduled for November 6.

Bosch decided the time had come to establish lines of communication with Hitler and to feel him out about a commitment to I.G.'s synthetic oil project in case he was elected chancellor. However, Bosch was not yet willing for any of I.G.'s top executives to be seen associating with Hitler. He instructed Gattineau to arrange a meeting between Hitler and Heinrich Buetefisch, who although not yet forty was technical director of Leuna and an authority on synthetic oil production. Gattineau once again called on Haushofer and asked him to arrange such a meeting. Haushofer obliged, and Hitler's secretary, Rudolf Hess, set it for early November in Munich just before the election.[8]

When Hitler arrived for his meeting with Buetefisch and Gattineau, he was obviously very tired—too tired, the I.G. men feared, to understand so complex a matter as the hydrogenation of coal into oil. However, Hitler already knew all about the process and was eager to discuss it.

> Before you tell me your view, I would like you to hear my attitude on the whole problem. . . . Today an economy without oil is inconceivable in a Germany which wishes to remain politically independent. Therefore German motor fuel must become a reality, even if this entails sacrifices. Therefore it is urgently necessary that the hydrogenation of coal be continued.[9]

The meeting had been scheduled for only half an hour, but it went on for two and a half hours, with Hitler pressing for detailed information on the conversion of coal into oil. As Gattineau later recalled, "[He] surprised me again and again by his amazing understanding for technical matters."[10] Before the meeting ended, Hitler had outlined a program under which he planned to make Germany self-sufficient in oil with the help of I.G. Farbenindustrie. World War I had taught him that Germany's dearth of raw materials had rendered the British blockade a decisive weapon leading to Germany's defeat. By a program of self-sufficiency he was determined to change Germany from a country deficient in natural raw materials into a self-sufficient military power. Hitler assured the I.G. visitors that their company could depend on his support, both financial and political. Gattineau and Buetefisch, elated by Hitler's response, reported back to Bosch. After hearing the entire story of the extraordinary meeting, Bosch remarked, "The man is more sensible than I thought."[11]

In the November 6 election a few days later, the Nazis suffered a decisive setback. They lost 34 seats in the Reichstag, slipping to 196; the Communists, on the other hand, gained 11 seats and now had a total of 100. German industrialists and financiers, more terrified by the Communist advance than by the Nazi setback, came to Hitler's support at this critical moment. In fact, thirty-eight of them did so publicly[12]—including such powerful figures as Schacht and Baron von Schroeder from banking; Cuno from the North German Lloyd Lines; Krupp, Voegler, and Thyssen from steel; and Siemens and Robert Bosch (Carl Bosch's uncle) from electrical engineering and manufacturing; but no I.G. personnel. Carl Bosch was not yet ready to make a public commitment.

Hindenburg was unmoved by this coalition of financial and industrial strength. He chose General Kurt von Schleicher instead. But Schleicher was unable to establish a stable government. Finally, on January 30, Hindenburg capitulated and appointed Hitler chancellor. However, Hitler's hold on the office was tenuous. Another Reichstag election was scheduled for March 5.

On February 20, Hjalmar Schacht, now among the most active members of the financial community supporting Hitler, called Germany's leading industrialists and financiers to a secret meeting at the home of Hermann Goering. This time I.G. stood up to be counted. Among those present was Baron Georg von Schnitzler, one of the most important nontechnical members of the I.G. managing board and generally known as "I.G.'s salesman." His presence had a powerful effect on the business community of Germany. I.G., after all, was the country's largest corporation. Schacht announced that he expected to raise three million marks from the assembled businessmen for Hitler's election campaign.[13] At the direction of Bosch, Schnitzler pledged 400,000 marks, by far the largest single donation.[14] I.G.'s support of Hitler was now official.

In the March 5 election, the Nazis fared better than they had in the previous election. They gained 5.5 million votes—not enough to give them a majority of the seats in the Reichstag but enough to maintain Hitler as chancellor of a coalition government.

Shortly after the election, Hitler and Bosch met for the first time. The meeting seemed to go well at first. Hitler gave Bosch absolute assurance that his government would fully back the synthetic oil project, and Bosch agreed to expand the Leuna plant. Gasoline self-sufficiency for Germany was the common goal for both men. Bosch then moved to a subject that his associates at I.G. had urged him to avoid. He warned Hitler that if Jewish scientists were forced to leave the country both physics and chemistry would be set back 100 years in Germany. Before Bosch could proceed further Hitler roared, "Then we'll work a hundred years without physics and chemistry!" When Bosch tried to pursue the subject, Hitler rang for his adjutant and announced, with calculated insult, "The Geheimrat wishes to leave."[15]

Although Hitler did not let the episode interfere with his support of I.G.'s synthetic oil project, he never again would appear in the same room with Bosch. On one occasion, Hitler arrived at a meeting, saw Bosch sitting on the platform, and abruptly left. Thereafter Bosch's associates were careful to keep the two men apart. Bosch was undeterred by Hitler's hostility. He continued his campaign in defense of Jewish scientists in Germany. In April he learned that Fritz Haber had been forced to resign his position as a professor at Berlin University despite the fact that Haber was a convert to Christianity and one of Germany's most revered scientists. Bosch tried to organize a movement among non-Jewish Nobel Prize winners to resist the Nazi persecution but with very little success. The great physicist Max Planck, who was no anti-Nazi and whose eminence was sufficient to gain him an audience with Hitler, pleaded in vain with the Fuehrer to reverse the expulsion of Haber. Hitler's response was so violent that it was some time before Planck recovered emotionally. Another of the Nobel laureates exclaimed in fear and despair, "We cannot draw our swords for the Jews!"[16]

Haber left Germany, but a few months later he decided to return. On his way back, he met Hermann Schmitz in Switzerland; Schmitz urged him to stay out of Germany, pointing out that the Nazi terror should not be underestimated. A miserable Haber never set foot in Germany again. A broken man, he died in Basel in January 1934. Germans were not permitted to mourn his passing.

On the first anniversary of Fritz Haber's death, however, Bosch organized a memorial ceremony under the auspices of the Kaiser Wilhelm Institute, in defiance of the Nazis.[17] He sent a personal invitation to leading scientists and educators, I.G. executives, and government officials who had had some relationship with Haber. When the Nazi minister of education learned that some of his subordinates had been invited, he forbade their participation: "The intention . . . to sponsor a memorial service on the occasion of the first anniversary of Haber's death must . . . be interpreted as a challenge to the National Socialist State. . . . This interpretation is confirmed by the fact that the sponsors have not shrunk from urging those invited to the ceremony to appear in uniform." Over 500 people packed the hall, many from I.G., as well as Haber's military friends. His professional colleagues, however, were more cautious and a number did not come. Max Planck, despite his experience with Hitler, did attend and although he opened the meeting with a Nazi salute he paid tribute to the "German scholar and German soldier, Fritz Haber."[18]

I.G. itself continued to be harassed by some of the lesser figures in the Nazi hierarchy. For example, the pharmaceutical branches at Hoechst and Leverkusen were attacked because of their use of animals for testing drugs. Under the Nazis, vivisection had been declared a capital offense. Heinrich Hoerlein, I.G.'s most prominent medical scientist, tried to explain to a high ranking Storm Trooper the folly of such an edict. The reply was that the Nazis wanted nothing to do with I.G. since it was an "international Jewish organization."[19]

In the total picture, these problems were relatively minor irritations. I.G., in fact, was making great strides in cementing its position with the new regime. Hermann Schmitz was appointed an honorary Nazi deputy in the Reichstag, a position attesting to the firmness of his commitment to Hitler's goals. Schnitzler opened up a salon in Berlin where foreign industrial and political dignitaries were invited to mingle with high Nazi figures. Bosch's young favorite, Heinrich Buetefisch, became a colonel in Himmler's S.S. as did Christian Schneider, who was among the most eminent of the older "high pressure" scientists in I.G.

Relations with the military establishment were carefully nurtured. Max Ilgner, the nephew of Hermann Schmitz, had for some time acted as I.G. liaison to Army Ordnance. Over the years he had developed a good relationship with a young officer on the economic staff, Georg Thomas, keeping him informed of developments in the manufacture of synthetic oil at Leuna. By no means incidental to the friendship was Thomas's active role as an army officer pushing raw material self-sufficiency, especially in oil and rubber. In fact, back in 1928, he had written a secret memorandum on behalf of the Army Ordnance economic staff recommending the development of synthetics "through new discoveries and inventions" to replace the strategic raw materials that Germany had to import from abroad.[20] He specifically referred to I.G.'s synthetic oil development at Leuna, noting that when "substitutes for foreign raw materials can be developed only through very expensive processes, these must be supported by Army Ordnance." Technologically and financially, Thomas's thinking was the unconventional kind that I.G. appreciated. Thomas was still on the economic staff of Army Ordnance with the rank of lieutenant colonel when the Nazis came to power.

There could be little doubt that Ilgner was an effective emissary for I.G. For example, by June 1933 I.G. had become involved with the Third Reich in one of the most secret enterprises in Germany—the building up of an illegal military air force, a direct violation of the Versailles treaty. A special independent finance office was created by an extraordinary joint decree of the Finance, War, and Aviation ministries for the *secret purposes of military aviation* [emphasis in original]."

This finance office was placed under the sole control of Hermann Goering, minister of aviation, "who alone will authorize acceptance of deposits and payments." So secret was this decree that knowledge of its existence was limited to a small circle of the highest military and Nazi officials. Included in this select group was Max Ilgner, who was among the very few to receive an official copy of this highly classified document.[21]

It was not long after the secret decree to finance the Black Luftwaffe was promulgated that Carl Krauch received a visit from General Erhard Milch, state secretary of the Aviation Ministry and Goering's right-hand man. (Although Milch's father was Jewish, his mother, an Aryan, had signed an affidavit that she had borne her son out of wedlock to an Aryan. And Goering, who did not take anti-Semitism seriously when his own interests were concerned, had given Milch his protection, declaring, "I myself decide who is a Jew and who is not, and that's all there is to it.") Milch had been referred to Krauch as the expert in I.G. who could be relied on to give the most accurate report on Germany's liquid fuel capability. Primarily, Milch was interested in learning whether I.G.'s synthetic oil was suitable for aviation gasoline. Krauch assured him that it was. Milch then asked what level of production could be attained in the next few years. Krauch promised to investigate and send Milch a report.

On September 15, 1933, Krauch submitted his findings in the form of a treatise on the German motor fuel economy.[22] He proposed a four-year plan for the expansion of Germany's production of "domestic" motor fuel in which he recommended that the production of fuel from domestic raw materials such as coal be increased more than three and a half times in the next four years. I.G.'s hydrogenation process was central to Krauch's plan. He emphasized that "it would easily be possible to produce aviation gasoline as well as lubricants suitable for airplanes through domestic production." As a matter of fact, he said the Lufthansa was already engaged in exhaustive tests.

The next day Milch showed Krauch's memorandum

to the Army Ordnance Chief, Major General von Bockelberg, and his aid, Lieutenant Colonel Georg Thomas.[23] He told them that the Air Ministry backed Krauch's four-year plan and suggested "a joint energetic approach." The army officers concurred.

During this same period Carl Bosch was spending most of his time conferring with government officials in Berlin about the expansion of I.G.'s production of synthetic oil as contemplated in the understanding with Hitler. In July Bosch felt so confident about the progress of these negotiations that he told two visiting executives from Du Pont that plans were under way to increase production fourfold, from 100,000 to 400,000 tons a year.[24] He may have hated what Hitler stood for but he had little doubt that the commitment of the Fuehrer to I.G.'s synthetic oil project was genuine. Only I.G. could provide Hitler with oil self-sufficiency.

There were some officials in I.G. at that time who were expressing unequivocal support of the Nazi government. One was Carl von Weinberg, who had just become Deputy Chairman of I.G.'s Supervisory Board, a position on the board second only to Duisberg. Although Weinberg was a Jew, he told the Du Pont visitors that he gave the Nazi movement his full stamp of approval, adding that all of his money was invested in Germany, that he did not have one pfennig outside the country.[25]

On December 14, 1933, Bosch and Schmitz on behalf of I.G., as well as representatives of the Third Reich, with the personal approval of Hitler signed the formal agreement. By the terms of the contract I.G. was to expand the synthetic oil installation at Leuna so that in four years, by the end of 1937, it could produce 300,000 to 350,000 tons annually. The Reich, in return, pledged to guarantee a price corresponding to the cost of production, including a five percent interest on invested capital and generous depreciation, and to take measures to assure the sale of all synthetic oil not sold by I.G. through its own outlets.[26]

The agreement was a monumental technological achievement in modern power politics. It was now only a matter of time before I.G. would provide Hitler's Germany with total independence from foreign oil, a matter of profound diplomatic and military significance. Never again would Bosch have to worry about funds for his beloved project. And only after the U.S. Eighth Air Force bombed I.G.'s synthetic oil plants into rubble in April and May 1944 did Hitler have to worry about oil.

With Germany's plan for oil self-sufficiency set, Hitler turned his attention to the next most important strategic raw material import, rubber. Since the source of natural rubber was literally on the other side of the world, Germany needed to develop a synthetic substitute for this substance to protect itself against an embargo or naval blockade. Unfortunately, Hitler's concern with rubber autarky was not shared by some key members of the civilian and military bureaucracies. A number of civilian economists regarded it as sinful to allocate vast resources and funds to such a project when natural rubber for stockpiling was available at depressed prices on the world market. The military added another objection; none of the available synthetic rubbers appeared satisfactory for military use, and depending on future breakthroughs was too risky. In fact, between 1931 and 1932 I.G. had virtually suspended its Buna program as the bottom dropped out of the natural rubber market. With it disappeared any prospect for making Buna competitive. When Hitler came to power I.G.'s Buna operation was minimal. But shortly Hitler's plans for the future of Germany began to breathe new life into the project. In late 1933, at about the time that the synthetic oil pact was concluded, representatives of Army Ordnance and the Ministry of Economics approched I.G. to resume its work on Buna. However, mere encouragement was not enough for Bosch. Without the guarantee of a sufficient subsidy he feared a repeat of the financial difficulties that had beset the synthetic oil project. To move forward, solid government support was essential. Specifically, Bosch wanted the government to insure that commercial tire companies would provide "effective cooperation" in manufacturing

77

test tires out of Buna. In addition, he demanded that at least 1000 to 2000 Buna tires be tested on military and other government owned vehicles. In a memorandum to the interested government agencies I.G. stated its attitude quite bluntly: "Before we resume our efforts on a large scale, it is necessary that the government decide whether it is sufficiently interested in the manufacture of synthetic rubber in Germany to be prepared to support the project in [this] manner."[27]

It was still early in the Third Reich and neither Army Ordnance nor the Ministry of Economics understood the depth of Hitler's devotion to military self-sufficiency. When they refused to accede to Bosch's demands, the Buna project continued in relative limbo. In the fall of 1934, troubled by the lagging synthetic rubber production, Hitler personally took an interest in the matter. He appointed his own economic adviser, Wilhelm Keppler, as the plenipotentiary for raw materials and synthetics with the specific responsibility for synthetics. This placed Keppler in conflict with Hjalmar Schacht, who as acting head of the Ministry of Economics had official responsibility for "mobilization for economic warfare."

Schacht viewed economic self-sufficiency in terms of conserving foreign exchange; hence, cost was a decisive factor in determining the choice of synthetics to finance and develop. Keppler, who more accurately reflected Hitler's own views, favored raw material self-sufficiency, governed primarily by military need. Cost and conserving foreign exchange were secondary considerations. The plenipotentiary and the minister were thus on a collision course. Under normal circumstances, Keppler, who in private life was a mechanical engineer and the owner of a small glue factory, would have been no match for the overbearing and powerful Schacht. But Keppler was a dedicated Nazi, who enjoyed Hitler's confidence. That fact more than equalized matters.

Keppler called a meeting of the representatives of I.G., the Ministry of Economics, Army Ordnance, and the tire industry. He pointed out to the group Hitler's dissatisfaction with the progress of the synthetic rubber program. The Fuehrer wanted the project pushed ahead "with elemental force."[28]

Ter Meer spoke up in behalf of I.G. Although delighted with Hitler's directive, he thought it necessary to point out a number of factors impeding the program. The commercial tire manufacturers were not enthusiastic about synthetic rubber, especially Buna, as a tire material. He also mentioned the doubts expressed by Army Ordnance. Confronted with such negative attitudes, I.G., ter Meer said, was reluctant to invest considerable funds and effort in the mass production of Buna. Before making such a commitment, ter Meer needed assurances that the tire manufacturers would produce Buna tires on a large enough scale.[29] The tire manufacturers declared that it was imprudent to mass-produce Buna tires because of the staggering cost; a Buna tire cost ninety-two marks to manufacture as compared with eighteen marks for a natural rubber tire. The Army Ordnance officials were no more willing to go ahead with Buna than the tire people. Buna, they maintained, was not up to the standards required by military use.

Keppler brushed aside all these objections. He reminded those in opposition that the promotion of synthetic rubber production was a pet idea of the Fuehrer and must not be delayed.[30] Army Ordnance had no choice but to engage in a series of extensive tests over the next six months. Hitler, who had a propagandistic as well as a military need for Buna, had no intention of waiting for the technical results. On September 11, 1935, at the seventh Nazi party congress at Nuremberg, he announced to the world that "the problem of producing synthetic rubber can now be regarded as definitely solved. The erection of the first factory in Germany for this purpose will be started at once."[31]

A few days later Keppler met with ter Meer and was adamant that Hitler's announcement meant that a sure of Hitler's public statement, assured ter Meer still cautious, agreed to commit I.G. to such a project provided the financial risk was minimized. For this reason he wanted a purchase guarantee for the plant's output from Army Ordnance. Keppler, under the pressure of Hitler's public statement, assured ter Meer that this posed no problem. In fact, he promised to negotiate the purchase contract with the military authorities himself.

But Keppler had not accurately assessed either the situation or his own influence with the army at that moment. Army Ordnance, after its six-month test of the Buna tires, concluded that they were not satisfactory for military use. It refused Keppler's demand to enter into a purchase agreement with I.G. or to support the building of a Buna plant. Instead, the army decided to meet military requirements by stockpiling natural rubber.[32]

Army Ordnance's decision not to go ahead with a Buna tire for military use was a serious blow to I.G. hopes. At the same time, Schacht had no intention of helping either I.G. or Keppler by supporting a program of civilian use for Buna. Buna tires would be far too expensive, he argued, to produce foreign exchange for Germany in the export market. The army's evaluation of its inferior quality only buttressed Schacht's opposition. Buna appeared to be in serious trouble.

Keppler did not intend to let Schacht block Buna development. He took the problem up with Hitler himself. After receiving the Fuehrer's unqualified support, he wrote to I.G.: *"As you know, the Fuehrer is greatly interested in speeding up the construction of the installation as much as possible. I therefore ask you to carry on with your planning work as before and to start building as soon as an agreement between us has been reached* [emphasis in original]."[33]

That was all the encouragement I.G. needed. As a result of Keppler's assurance of Hitler's support, Bosch made the decision to build a large-scale Buna plant without waiting for a formal agreement with the government. He selected a large site in Schkopau near the high pressure equipment of Leuna and before long construction got under way. It was a bold move in the Bosch tradition.

In early 1936, oil was pushed to the forefront of international diplomacy. The Italo-Ethiopian war had been going on since October 1935 and all attempts by the League of Nations to stop Mussolini's aggression proved ineffective. Finally, the League decided on a drastic step. It set up a committee to consider the imposition of an oil embargo on Italy. The rationale was simple. Italy, without a domestic source of oil, was totally dependent on imports. An effective embargo by League members could bring its military adventures to a complete halt.

While Mussolini and the League of Nations were sparring, Hitler was planning aggressive military moves of his own. In mid-February, he issued a statement designed to catch the attention of his potential enemies and the League. At the opening of the annual German automobile show, he spoke of the fact that Germany had mastered the problem of making synthetic oil and synthetic rubber from coal: "You may rest assured that we are determined to exploit both of these discoveries to their utmost practical limit," Hitler told the large, enthusiastic audience. With an obvious reference to contemplated League action against Italy, he added that the "miracle of synthetic fuel" possessed "political significance" for Germany. An oil embargo, Hitler implied, held no terror for Germany[34]—I.G. was performing its miracles on schedule.

In the meantime, the League continued to press for an embargo. On February 22 the League's sanction committee was convened to prepare for such an action. Mussolini declared in response that if oil sanctions were imposed Italy would leave the League of Nations and no longer consider itself bound to support Germany's observance of the Locarno treaty. This announcement was calculated to put pressure on France, whose borders Italy was pledged to protect as a treaty signatory.

Mussolini's threat worked. On March 2 the British foreign minister, Anthony Eden, under pressure from

France, agreed to delay the decision on the oil embargo until a fresh appeal had been made to Italy to end the Ethiopian war. Mussolini was given until March 10 to respond. Mussolini sent word to the League within days that he would accept "in principle" the League's appeal to negotiate a peace in Ethiopia.

However, on Saturday, March 7, Italy's aggression in Ethiopia was completely overshadowed by a far greater menace to world peace. Hitler marched his troops into the Rhineland, in violation of the Versailles and Locarno treaties. The world stood on the brink of war, waiting for England and France to respond in support of their treaty oligations. However, England and France were unwilling to accept Hitler's challenge, and Hitler's occupation of the Rhineland proceeded without interference.

Although the League of Nations found that the Germans had committed a breach of peace, it shrank from imposing the kind of sanctions with which it was threatening Italy. Two countries that provided much of Germany's oil, the Soviet Union and Rumania, nevertheless did pursue sanctions of their own for a time; the U.S.S.R. stopped all oil exports and Rumania raised the price of oil sold to Germany.[35]

The Soviet and Rumanian actions created a serious fuel shortage in Germany. To cope with the problem, Hitler appointed Hermann Goering fuel czar. However, before Goering had time to do much in this position, a greater opportunity presented itself to him—to become czar of the entire German economy. This enormous delegation of power came about as the result of the strained relations between Schacht and Keppler. To end the dispute, Hitler assigned Goering the task of mediating between the two men. But by mid-March, conditions had so deteriorated that Schacht sent out a circular order to all his staff forbidding any official dealing with Keppler.

Schacht took these extreme measures not simply because of his personal distaste for Keppler but principally because the outcome of the conflict would decide who was to dictate the financial and economic policies of the Third Reich and whether sound economics was to dominate Nazi policy or vice versa. Nazi radicals like Keppler and Goebbels favored expansion of government expenditures to maintain employment and to prepare for war. Schacht, on the other hand, had become increasingly disturbed by the drain on foreign exchange caused by the rapidly accelerating military rearmament program and by his inability to control government expenditures and restrain the extravagances of the Nazi bureaucracy. He concluded that authority over foreign exchange and raw materials must be centralized in one organization headed by a leading Nazi, whose policies he could dominate. In Schacht's calculations, the nominal head would be a figure with enough authority in the Nazi hierarchy to be able to impose the unpopular measures he had in mind. Goering seemed to him the perfect choice for such a front. Since Goering knew nothing about economics, Schacht would be able to formulate policy. Through Goering, Schacht planned to get rid of opponents like Keppler and to assume tight control over all government expenditures.

As Goering recalled it, Schacht called on him and suggested that he should head up a commission for raw materials and foreign exchange: "It was agreed that I should not function as an economic expert, which I was not; but . . . I should be the driving power and use my energy." Goering, however, was wise to what Schacht intended: "His idea was that I did not know very much about economics and he could easily hide behind my back."[36]

Schacht had made a major miscalculation. When Hitler, on April 27, appointed Goering economic czar with the title of commissar of raw materials and foreign exchange, the official government release made it bluntly clear that Schacht had in effect become Goering's subordinate. By the terms of the appointment, Goering assumed authority over all the ministries on economic matters. The *New York Times* reported that "Colonel-General Hermann Goering in effect superseded Dr. Hjalmar Schacht today as dictator of the economic and financial policies of the Third Reich."[37] The *Times* correctly divined the true meaning of the event.

When Schacht learned the specific details of Goering's appointment, he was irate. On April 29 he met with Hitler and Goering and tried to get Hitler to issue a follow-up, "explanatory" announcement that would make it clear that Schacht was *not* subordinate to Goering in any way. But no "clarifying" communiqué was issued; the original announcement was permitted to stand.[88]

Goering did make one concession to Schacht. He agreed to use only a small corps of experts on his new raw materials and foreign exchange staff. He put Lieutenant Colonel Fritz Loeb, of the Air Ministry, in charge of the organization. And he asked Bosch to recommend a man from I.G. to head up research and development. Bosch chose his closest friend and confidant, Carl Krauch.[89]

Krauch was the logical choice. Since the preceding September, Krauch had been chief of a new military liaison office in Berlin "to provide for systematic cooperation within the I.G. in view of the current development of military economy"—particularly in connection with such strategic raw materials in the high pressure chemical field as synthetic oil, synthetic rubber, and nitrates.[40] Second to Bosch, Krauch was Germany's leading expert on high pressure chemistry. In fact, in some ways, he had become Bosch's alter ego.

When Krauch joined Goering's raw materials and foreign exchange staff, he did not give up his key positions at I.G. He retained his membership on the I.G. managing board and his powerful role as head of the I.G. division covering the high pressure chemistry field. He also continued to act as head of I.G.'s miltary liaison office in Berlin. Two of the top men from this office—Gerhard Ritter and Johannes Eckell—were transferred to Krauch's research and development office.

During the summer of 1936, Goering's new organization worked on a plan to ease the demand for foreign exchange and to assure an indigenous raw materials basis. Goering and Schacht were soon at odds. The Schacht-Keppler conflict was now drowned out by a battle for power between Schacht and Goering. Schacht continued to insist on adherence to traditional economic principles. Goering, like Keppler and other Nazi radicals, insisted that Germany must greatly increase expenditures in preparation for war—and this included a vastly expanded synthetic raw materials program. "If war comes tomorrow," said Goering, "we will have to rely on substitutes. Then money won't play any role at all. If that is the case, then we must prepare in peacetime...."[41]

Soon synthetic rubber became the subject of a bitter disagreement between Schacht and Goering. Goering declared that "rubber is our weakest point"[42] and accused Schacht of being the principal reason for this vulnerability. On May 27, at one of the first meetings of the council of ministers to discuss substitute materials, Goering, looking squarely at Schacht, asked if anyone had any objections to the production of synthetic "war raw materials." Schacht immediately spoke up to say that he had no objections in principle except "in cases where prices for synthetics are far beyond world-market prices so that the products cannot compete." He then cited Buna as an example; it was so much more expensive than natural rubber that its production was thoroughly uneconomical and unwarranted. Goering interrupted to explain that it was necessary to consider the issue only "from the standpoint of waging war."[43] Economic principles in that case had no validity. Schacht, who had become increasingly disturbed about the inflationary effects of rearmament, was unmoved and persisted in his strong opposition to Buna.

Despite Schacht's inflexible stance Goering ignored him. His raw materials and foreign exchange staff began to plan for a vast expansion of the Buna program. On June 15, Krauch, in his government capacity, invited representatives of Army Ordnance, the War Ministry, and the Keppler office to consider a dramatic enlargement of the productive capacity of the Schkopau plant, from 200 to 1000 tons a month. A few weeks later, plans were being drawn up for a second I.G. Buna plant, also with a production capacity of 1000 tons a month.[44]

Schacht was also strongly opposed to another self-sufficiency program that Goering and his raw materials and foreign exchange staff were planning to institute—a proposal to switch from the rich Swedish iron ore to Germany's own low-grade iron ore in the production of steel. Schacht argued that such a changeover would necessitate an extremely expensive transformation of the German steel industry's blast furnaces. The consequent increase in the cost of German steel, he argued, would make it impossible to export.[45] According to Schacht, Germany could not afford such a loss in foreign exchange.

Schacht continued to press for a reduction of military expenditures and insisted on the right to decide how the military budget should be allocated among the various ministries. He called on Goering to take immediate steps to solve the deepening foreign exchange crisis. Goering replied that nothing would be done until at least the end of September. The clash between these two powerful personalities was rushing toward a climax.

The conflict came to a head in late August. By then it had become obvious that only Hitler had sufficient strength to resolve the dispute. On August 26 he took the unusual step of preparing a memorandum—one of the few times that he ever gave a written order—setting forth his decision to institute a four-year plan to prepare Germany for war.[46] The plan concerned itself primarily with what Hitler regarded as Germany's principal economic problem, the pressing need for raw materials. The definitive solution, Hitler wrote, lay in the extension of Germany's living space in order to expand its raw material base. This would be accomplished by conquest. In the meantime, however, Germany would have to find a temporary solution within its own borders. Since Germany could not reduce its imports of food, a balance would have to be found by other means. And those other means must not be at the expense of rearmament:

I must reject here with the utmost vehemence the conception according to which a limitation of natural armaments, that is, a limitation of the production of weapons and ammunition, can bring an "enrichment" in raw materials which eventually could be profitable to Germany in case of war. Such a conception is based upon a complete misunderstanding—to put it mildly—of the task and military requirements lying before us.

Neither was the stockpiling of raw materials the answer. No country could stockpile for more than a year of war. And the accumulation of foreign currencies did not necessarily insure the acquisition of supplies during war. Hitler pointed to the experience in World War I when Germany had large currency assets but was unable to purchase sufficient fuel, rubber, copper, and tin.

Hitler next drew up a program for "a final solution of our vital necessities" during war. German fuel production must be developed with the utmost speed and brought to a definitive completion within eighteen months, a task that had to be handled with the same determination as the waging of war. The mass production of synthetic rubber must be organized and achieved with the same speed.

At this point Hitler became unmistakably clear as to which side he was taking in the quarrel between Schacht and Goering. (Schacht later suggested why Hitler sided with Goering: "My incessant struggle to ensure saving and careful use of raw materials and foreign exchange and my steady insistence on a slowing down of armaments must have gradually got on Hitler's nerves."[47] There was, however, more to it than that.) Hitler's attack on Schacht was specific. There was to be no more argument that the synthetic rubber project was premature: "This matter does not concern the Ministry of Economics at all. Either we have a private economy today, in which case it is its task to rack its brains about production methods, or we believe that the determination of the production methods is the task of government, in which case we do not need the private economy any longer." Hitler pursued the attack on Schacht by ridiculing the argument of cost: "The question of production costs of these raw materials is also of no importance, since it is still more profitable for us to produce expensive tires in Germany and utilize them, than to sell theoretically cheap tires but for which the Minister of Economics cannot grant any foreign currency." As far as Hitler was concerned, the cost of synthetic raw materials had ceased to be a decisive consideration.

Using the same logic, Hitler also ruled that German iron production had to be increased despite the fact that German ore contained twenty-six percent iron whereas Swedish ores contained forty-five percent.

> The objection that in this case all German blast-furnaces will have to be transformed is also unimportant—and, above all, it does not concern the Ministry of Economics. The Ministry of Economics has only to set the tasks of the national economy; the private industry has to fulfill them. But if the private industry considers itself unable to do this, then the National Socialist State will know by itself how to resolve the problem.

Hitler was warning the recalcitrant steel producers that if they did not fall into line and begin using German iron ore the Nazi government would construct state owned steelworks that would do so. In fact, that was later done.

Hitler concluded his memorandum by pointing out that almost four precious years had been wasted during which Germany could have become completely independent of foreign countries in fuel and rubber and partly independent in iron ore supplies.

> Just as we produce 700,000 to 800,000 tons of gasoline at the present time, we could be producing 3 million tons. Just as we produce several thousand tons of rubber, we could already be producing 70,000 to 80,000 tons per year. Just as we increased our iron ore production from 2½ million tons to 7 million tons, we could process 20

to 25 million tons of German iron ore and if necessary 30 million.

These deficiencies had to be overcome. During the next four years, Hitler demanded that the German armed forces be made ready for combat and the German economy fully mobilized for the war that Hitler left no doubt was inevitable.

A few days after writing this memorandum, Hitler informed Schacht, who deliberately had not been given a copy, that he planned to announce his new economic program of German self-sufficiency at the Nazi party congress in Nuremberg the following week. Schacht, appalled by the potential consequences of such a program for the economy, appealed to Minister of War Werner von Blomberg to talk Hitler out of making the statement.[48] But Blomberg refused—for good reason. He had been one of the small select group to whom Hitler had given his memorandum and he had decided to throw his lot in with Goering. In fact, Blomberg had already written to Goering, who would be the determining factor in the allocation of funds for the armed forces, requesting a forty-two percent increase in military funds for 1937.[49] Schacht pressed his opposition but it was a futile exercise.

True to his warning to Schacht, Hitler announced the four-year plan at the Nazi party congress: "In four years Germany must be wholly independent of foreign countries in respect to all those materials which can in any way be produced through German capability through our chemistry, engineering, and mining industries."[50] Six weeks later, on October 18, Hitler designated Goering plenipotentiary for the four-year plan to "put the entire economy on a slate of readiness for war."[51] In the words of the leading Nazi newspaper, the *Voelkischer Beobachter*, "There will be only one ultimate authority in all economic questions—Party Comrade Goering."[52]

One of Goering's first decrees in his new position was to announce the organization for the execution of the four-year plan. Although provision was made for the participation of both Schacht and Keppler, Goering made it clear in this decree that "all persons and organizations of the Party and of the State participating in the Four-Year Plan have to obey *my instructions* [emphasis in original]."[53]

Goering's raw materials and foreign exchange staff was transferred to the office of the four-year plan and was given responsibility for developing a specific program of investments for the four-year plan, a matter of considerable interest to I.G. Carl Krauch continued as head of research and development with a staff made up almost entirely of I.G. men. One of these, Johannes Eckell, was put in charge of the rubber sector.[54] From now on I.G. would deal almost exclusively with Eckell in its synthetic rubber negotiations,[55] a not unpleasant prospect.

The preliminary four-year plan for German self-sufficiency, drafted by Loeb's staff in the summer of 1936, had been based mainly on coal, iron, and chemicals. Coal production, it was decided, was sufficient, requiring no expansion. In the case of iron, it had become evident by the fall of 1936 that the German steel industry was not willing to open up the low-grade iron ore fields in the cause of German self-sufficiency, and Goering had begun to consider building a state owned plant. That left the chemical industry, which in the next few months was to be allocated ninety percent of four-year plan investments. And of that share, I.G. was to receive 72.7 percent.[56] So large was I.G.'s share that the chief of the chemistry department of the Ministry of Economics remarked later, "The Four Year Plan was, in fact, an I.G. plan." Some companies objected to such dominance, and Schering and Merck, two pharmaceutical firms, refused to participate, fearing their operational secrets would become available to I.G. with no consequent benefit to themselves.[57]

Schacht joined the opposition to I.G. If there had to be a four-year plan, it should not be an I.G. plan. He made this point as strongly as he could with Goering. Goering was still willing to try to placate Schacht since Hitler wanted to keep him on the cabinet as a symbol of "conservatism." However, an official of the Ministry of Economics observed, Goering was unwilling to go so far as "to make any concessions which would be to I.G.'s disadvantage."[58]

Schacht's antagonism toward I.G. was nothing new. As early as 1933, he had tried to create a union of independent chemical companies in order to offset I.G.'s power. However, the independent companies had been afraid to challenge I.G., even with Schacht's support.[59] Finally, Schacht took his objections to I.G.'s domination of the four-year plan directly to Hitler.[60] But Hitler had settled on his course of action; Germany must become self-sufficient in oil and rubber in eighteen months and that required the genius and facilities of I.G. Preparation for war was Hitler's guiding light in shaping the economic policies of the Reich. To Hitler, Schacht's demand that sound and conventional economic policies be followed was irrelevant.

This became more obvious as the plans for synthetic rubber production moved ahead. The office of raw materials and synthetics was negotiating with I.G. for a *second* Buna plant while Schacht and Army Ordnance were strongly opposing even the *first* plant. Despite such formidable opposition, Eckell advised I.G. that the "supreme authority" wanted the second plant.[61] He added that the problem of financing would be solved "over the heads" of the army and the Ministry of Economics. Schacht's days as an influence in Nazi Germany were numbered. By the end of 1937, he had lost all his official positions, and by 1944 he was interned in a concentration camp.

The year 1937 marked a drastic change in the character of I.G. That year it became completely Nazified. Membership in the Nazi party was opened up, and almost all of the members of the I.G. managing board who did not already belong now joined up, including Carl Krauch, Fritz ter Meer, Georg von Schnitzler, Max Ilgner, Otto Ambros, Friedrich Jaehne, Christian Schneider, Karl Wurster, Carl Lautenschlaeger, and Ernst Buergin. (Hermann Schmitz, Heinrich Hoerlein, Wilhelm Mann, Fritz Gajewski, and Hans Kuehne already were members.[62]) Of no little significance, in 1937 all Jewish officials of I.G. were removed, including a third of the supervisory board—Carl von Weinberg, Arthur von Weinberg, Otto von Mendelssohn-Bartholdy, Richard Merton, Ernst von Simson, Alfred Merton, Wilhelm Peltzer, and Gustaf Schlieper.[63] The outspoken Bosch was no longer active head of I.G.; in 1935 Hermann Schmitz had become chairman of the managing board, and Bosch had assumed the relatively inactive honorary post of chairman of the supervisory board. Bosch, however, still retained the respect of a number of key figures in German national life. When Hitler issued a secret directive to the Wehrmacht to prepare for an attack on Czechoslovakia by October 1, 1938, two of Germany's top commanders, General Walther von Brauchitsch, commander in chief of the armed forces, and General Ludwig von Beck, chief of the army, sought Bosch out as the only German industrial leader who did not fear to speak his mind. They asked him whether German industry was ready for war. Bosch replied that industry was *not* ready and that a war was impracticable. Brauchitsch and Beck then asked whether Bosch would be willing to communicate this fact to the highest levels of the Third Reich. Bosch agreed to do so.

Bosch decided that the man to see was Goering, and he talked to Krauch about the best way to get this message to him. Krauch went to Goering's deputy, Paul Koerner, state secretary in the office of the four-year plan, and relayed Bosch's request. He was very careful to tell Koerner what was on Bosch's mind. Two days later Bosch was advised that Goering would not receive him.[64]

Despite Goering's rebuff of Bosch, Krauch himself was on the rise in Goering's office of the four-year plan. The preceding December Koerner had noticed certain disparities in the four-year plan figures prepared by General Loeb's office of raw materials and synthetics and had checked with Krauch about the Loeb office estimates on synthetic oil production. Krauch said that Loeb's figures were far too conservative and could not possibly answer the purposes of the four-year plan. Krauch was ready with an alternative plan that called for a crash program entailing an enormous expansion of I.G. production. Koerner submitted Krauch's proposal to Goering. Loeb was furious about Krauch's criticism and Koerner dropped the matter, but he did tell Krauch to report to him personally if any discrepancies arose in the future.[65]

In mid-1938 Krauch renewed his attack on Loeb's figures. He had come across Loeb's 1938–1939 projections for the production of synthetic gasoline, Buna, and gunpowder. "I know they are wrong,"[66] he told Koerner. He thought it would be disastrous to use these figures as the basis for making a military decision.

Koerner immediately took Krauch's warnings to Goering. The next day Goering summoned Krauch, who repeated his criticism of Loeb's figures in devastating detail. Goering was sufficiently impressed to take the matter up with General Wilhelm Keitel, chief of the High Command. The general assured Goering that Loeb's figures were correct. Krauch refused to retreat. He pointed out, for example, that Germany's nitric acid capacity was too low to meet the production levels of explosives and gunpowder called for in Loeb's plan.[67] Who would know the production figures for nitric acid better than Krauch: despite his official position, he was still head of the I.G. division that produced almost all of Germany's nitric acid.

A personal confrontation between Krauch and Loeb was inevitable. It finally took place at Goering's palatial estate, Karinhall. Koerner later recalled the dramatic discussion between Goering, Krauch, and Loeb:

> Krauch presented his views in greatest detail, logically and objectively, and clearly proved that Loeb was wrong. Goering said to me after this meeting that Krauch had made an excellent impression on him and [he] wanted to give him extensive powers for construction of the chemical sector.[68]

After this meeting, a more confident Krauch directed his staff to revise Loeb's program. Krauch's plan called for greatly accelerated expansion in synthetic oil and rubber and light metals as well as explosives, gunpowder, and poison gas. In mid-July Goering gave his official sanction to this program, which came to be known as "the Krauch plan,"[69] a measure of Krauch's growing influence and status in the war economy.

Up to this point, Army Ordnance had been in complete control of all explosives production. Under the Krauch plan, all explosives manufactured for the four-year plan would be transferred to Krauch's control. Since General Becker of Army Ordnance would obviously object to a civilian's securing such responsibility, Koerner suggested to Krauch that it might be good politics to pay a visit to the general. As Koerner anticipated, Becker objected strenuously to the delegation of this authority to Krauch. He told Koerner that although he found Krauch himself "objective and cooperative," he foresaw complete confusion if Army Ordnance and Krauch each had a production plan for explosives. In Becker's view gunpowder was strictly a military product and control of its production should not be in the hands of civilians.[70] Krauch countered with a secret memorandum to Koerner.[71] The production of explosives, gunpowder, and poison gas was an inextricable part of the chemical industry and therefore the entire chemical sector must be under the control of a single agency with ties to industry.

On August 13 Krauch followed up with what he termed the "rapid plan," which called for even greater increases in productive capacity for these chemical military products.[72] But Army Ordnance continued its opposition to civilian domination over matters that were so clearly military. With the invasion of Czechoslovakia imminent, Goering resolved the dispute. On August 22 he put Krauch in charge of the entire chemical production of the four-year plan with the title of Plenipotentiary General for Special Questions of Chemical Production.

War was avoided in the fall of 1938 by the signing of the Munich agreement. The delay gave Krauch another year to consolidate his power. With war a certainty in 1939, he withdrew at last from his day-to-day duties at I.G. However, he did retain his key position as a member of the I.G. managing board and no matter what his role or duties were in the Nazi hierarchy, he was first and last an I.G. man.

By now I.G.'s leadership in the industrial preparation for war was undisputed. Its factories and laboratories were working overtime for the coming onslaught on the world by Hitler. Making "the four-year plan an I.G. plan" proved its worth for Germany and for I.G. Even a partial list of the products I.G. produced for German rearmament demonstrates clearly that I.G. was indispensable: it produced almost all of the synthetic oil (direct and by license), synthetic rubber, poison gases, magnesium, lubricating oil, explosives, methanol, sera, plasticizers, dyestuffs, nickel, and thousands of other items necessary for the German war machine.

Krauch became the symbol of I.G.'s contribution to Germany's military strength. At a birthday party in his honor, a grateful Goering approached Schmitz: "I thank you very much that you have given me Krauch." When war finally came and the Wehrmacht overran Europe, Hitler himself bestowed upon Krauch a decoration reserved for heroes—"Knight of the Iron Cross"—calling him "one who won marvelous victories on the battlefield of German industry."

Never before in the history of warfare had an industrialist and an industrial concern occupied such a crucial place in the military planning and preparation for a great war. It was a military-industrial partnership at its purest.

Schlieffen was truly dead.

4

The Marriage of I.G. and Standard Oil under Hitler

Shortly before Krauch demolished Loeb and assumed the post of chemical czar of the four-year plan, he was approached by the Air Ministry on a matter of the highest priority. The Luftwaffe did not have sufficient tetraethyl lead, a vital gasoline additive, should Hitler miscalculate in his planned thrust into Czechoslovakia in the fall of 1938 and find himself in a general war. Unfortunately, Germany's own tetraethyl lead plants were not scheduled to be ready until late 1939, more than a year away. The Air Ministry, fully aware of I.G.'s relationship with Standard Oil, requested Krauch to use his position in I.G. to borrow 500 tons of the desperately needed gasoline additive from its American partner.

Probably more than the officials of any other private institution, the I.G. executives understood the Air Ministry's problem. To conduct modern war "without tetraethyl lead," one of them noted, "would have been impossible."[1] Immediately, three of I.G.'s senior officials, Krauch, Schmitz, and Knieriem, traveled to London to negotiate the loan. There they met with officials of the Ethyl Export Corporation, a Standard Oil affiliate, taking great care not to mention that the tetraethyl lead was for the Luftwaffe. Yet, despite the delicacy with which the I.G. men handled the deal, they were not quite sure that their attempt at concealment could be successful. Considering the timing of the request, who else but the armed forces would require such large amounts of tetraethyl lead in such a hurry? In this connection, Knieriem later pointed out, "It is quite unusual for I.G. to purchase oil in the amount of 20 million dollars. Our business is to make oil by the hydrogenation process and not to purchase gasoline."[2] In any event, I.G. accomplished its mission for the Luftwaffe without mishap. It informed the Air Ministry on July 8 that the Ethyl Export Corporation would begin shipping the tetraethyl lead within the month.[3] The delivery was completed before the Czech invasion, materially strengthening Hitler's hand in the confrontation with Chamberlain and Daladier.

Some years earlier an American concern, the Ethyl Gasoline Corporation (owned fifty percent each by Standard Oil and General Motors), had become the principal developer of the technology of tetraethyl lead and its foremost if not exclusive producer. In the middle thirties, when the Nazi rearmament effort was gaining momentum, it became obvious to I.G. that Germany must have a tetraethyl lead capacity of its own. Without it the Luftwaffe would be seriously handicapped. Through the good offices of its cartel partner, Standard Oil, I.G. approached the Ethyl Gasoline Corporation with the suggestion that they enter into a partnership to build tetraethyl plants in Germany. The Ethyl Corporation was receptive and before long negotiations got under way. Apparently there was no great fear that the U.S. War Department would object to the transfer of the tetraethyl know-how to Germany. Instead, it was left to the Du Pont Company, the principal stockholder in General Motors, to express opposition to the deal. Once Du Pont became aware of the negotiations between Ethyl and I.G., it made its views known to the president of the Ethyl Corporation in no uncertain terms:

It has been claimed that Germany is secretly arming. Ethyl lead would doubtless be a valuable aid to military aeroplanes. I am writing you this to say that in my opinion, under no condition should you or the Board of Directors of the Ethyl Corporation disclose any secrets or "know-how" in connection with the manufacture of tetraethyl lead in Germany.[4]

The Du Pont warning was ignored and the negotiations went on. At its conclusion Ethyl and I.G. entered an agreement to form a jointly owned company, Ethyl GmbH, to build and operate the tetraethyl lead plants in Germany. After studying the matter, the U.S. War Department expressed no objection and the joint enterprise was put into operation. These plants were not quite ready when Hitler was preparing his move into Czechoslovakia—hence the need to acquire the tetraethyl lead through Standard.

While the Nazi government encouraged I.G. to exploit its cartel arrangement with Standard to acquire technical know-how and other benefits for Germany, it kept a careful watch that the flow of information as far as possible travel only in one direction. With this in mind, the Reich Air Ministry in June 1935 reviewed the hydrogenation contracts between Standard and I.G. It noted, "The I.G. is bound by contract to an extensive exchange of experience with Standard. This position seems untenable." It then added quite pointedly, "Therefore the Reich Air Ministry will soon conduct an extensive examination of applications for patents of the I.G."[5] The trouble caused by I.G.'s international cartel agreements, especially those with Standard Oil, led I.G. to make a determined effort to clarify the situation for the benefit of the German authorities.

That fall Knieriem and Carl Krauch raised the issue with Colonel Thomas of the High Command. They acknowledged that in the interests of national defense leakage of technical information abroad had to cease. However, Knieriem pointed out that the solution was not an easy, clear-cut one.

It would certainly be a simple thing to insist on secrecy in the interest of national defense in all cases where there is any doubt. But the consequences of such an action would be very serious. ... To begin with, it would mean that other countries would not share their know-how with us any more. But for us, too, this know-how of other countries sometimes carries decisive weight.

In support, Knieriem cited the extraordinary benefits of the tetraethyl lead contract with the Ethyl Gasoline Corporation: "In this affair ... the War Department in Washington after lengthy deliberation granted permission for this process, which is so important for the conduct of the war, to be made available by American heavy industry to I.G. Farbenindustrie in Germany."[6] Later, when the war was going badly for Germany and it appeared that serious consequences for I.G. might result from its contractual relations with Standard Oil, Knieriem once again sought the protection of the tetraethyl lead experience. "Without tetraethyl lead," he wrote in defense of I.G.'s relations with Standard, "the present method of warfare would have been impossible. The fact that since the beginning of the war we could produce tetraethyl lead is entirely due to the circumstances that shortly before, the Americans presented us with the production plans, complete with their know-how."[7]

Despite I.G.'s argument that secrecy pressed too far could be self-defeating, the German government was inflexible. It forced I.G. to take strong measures to insure the maintenance of secrecy in its own plants and to adopt stringent safeguards against leakage of technical information. In a memo circulated to all employees working on inventions, secret patents, and experimental and developmental work for the army or for the four-year plan, I.G. warned that they were subject to the penalties of the penal code introduced by the Nazis. This warning was necessary "not only for efficient protection against espionage and treason, but also ... for the protection of the I.G. employees concerned against eventual legal prosecution for negligence."[8] With death

99

the penalty for violations the matter was at the very least disquieting.

Since oil and rubber were the keys to German rearmament, the I.G. Farben-Standard Oil agreements were elevated to a matter of highest official concern. To be absolutely certain that secrecy would not be compromised, representatives of Goering's Air Ministry met with I.G. executives in July 1937. The Air Ministry wanted to be sure that Standard was not being informed of the work done by I.G. toward the large-scale production of synthetic oil. They set forth guidelines to be followed by I.G. with its American partner:

In consideration of its exchange of know-how agreements I.G. Farbenindustrie is permitted to inform its partners in the agreements, in a cautious way, shortly before the start of large-scale production, that it intends to start a certain production of iso-octane and ethylene lubricant. *The impression is, however, to be conveyed that this is a matter of large-scale experiments. Under no circumstances may statements on capacity be made* [emphasis added].[9]

In late 1937, with war seeming more certain, Standard Oil began to recognize the fact that its cartel arrangements with I.G. could pose serious trouble with the United States government. Should war break out, the problem of synthetic rubber would prove an especially sensitive matter. Standard began to request I.G. to supply it with the rights and know-how for making Buna rubber even though both sides agreed that I.G. was not obligated to do so under the Jasco agreement. On the other hand, Standard was required to turn over to I.G. the patent rights and know-how for a promising new synthetic rubber called Butyl since the original I.G.-Standard agreement assigned all rights in the chemical field to I.G.

In March 1938, immediately after Hitler's troops invaded Austria and war was a step closer, Frank Howard was in Berlin to talk to ter Meer about Buna. He pleaded for the Buna know-how. Ter Meer explained that until his government gave permission, he could not honor Standard's request, but he convinced Howard that it would be to their mutual advantage for Standard to turn over to I.G. all know-how on Butyl. In return, ter Meer promised, I.G. would continue to try to secure Nazi government "consent" to make available the know-how on Buna. Howard, sympathetic to I.G.'s problem, explained ter Meer's difficulties in a letter to Standard officials in New York.

> Certain difficulties still exist which prevent our I.G. friends from giving us full technical information and proceeding in the normal manner with the commercial development [of Buna] in the United States. It is to be hoped that these difficulties will be surmounted in the near future and we here desire to do everything possible to bring about the result.
>
> In view of the very genuine spirit of cooperation which Dr. ter Meer displayed, I am convinced that it is not only the right thing to do, but the best thing from every standpoint to pass on to them full information on [Butyl] at this time. I do not believe we have anything to lose by this which is comparable with the possible benefit to all of our interests.[10]

And so Standard turned over the Butyl know-how without getting the Buna information in return. It is unfortunate that Howard could not have been present at a top secret meeting a few days later at which ter Meer reviewed the status of the American rubber program with German officials.[11] He would have gained a shocking insight into ter Meer's "genuine spirit of cooperation." Present were Brigadier General Loeb of the four-year plan; Botho Muelert, fuel expert in the Ministry of Economics; Johannes Eckell; and ter Meer himself. The purpose of the meeting, as stated in ter Meer's file note, was *"to halt the development in the U.S.A.* [emphasis added]" of a synthetic rubber capacity.

In this connection, there was a long discussion as to whether further American developments in synthetic rubber could be delayed by withholding information on the Buna process. Ter Meer argued that it was unrealistic to try to maintain secrecy for long. In many respects American rubber manufacturers were at least as familiar with the technology of synthetic rubber as German manufacturers. He insisted that "an attempt to hold back the development of things in the U.S.A. by affecting secretiveness could mean nothing else but indulging in illusions." Nevertheless, he said, I.G. had been doing its part to delay rubber progress in the United States. It had been holding meetings with Standard Oil, Goodyear, and Goodrich with the "sole object of easing the minds of American interested parties and possibly to prevent an initiative on their own part." I.G. had been treating the license requests of the American firms "in a dilatory way so as not to push them into taking unpleasant measures." But ter Meer did not believe a holding operation could be continued for any length of time: "We are under the impression that one cannot stem things in the U.S.A. for much longer without . . . the risk of being faced all of a sudden by an unpleasant situation." If the American rubber companies were stalled too long, they would begin a program of their own without the benefit of I.G. or its patents. The American government could not be expected to allow itself to be strangled by its own patent system.

Ter Meer apparently convinced the German government representatives of the merits of his reasonable approach to the problem. Muelert endorsed ter Meer's "cooperative" stall and General Loeb even indicated that he might agree to ter Meer's proposal to consider initiation of negotiations in the United States for the fall of 1938.

In line with the decision reached at this conference, ter Meer wrote on April 9, 1938, to Howard. After thanking him for "the detailed information" about Butyl, he reported on his meeting with Loeb and Muelert.

In accordance with our arrangements in Berlin, I have meanwhile taken up negotiations with the competent authorities in order to obtain the necessary freedom of action in the U.S.A. with regard to rubber-like products. As anticipated, those negotiations have proved to be rather difficult and the respective discussions are expected to take several months before the desired result is obtained. I will not fail to inform you about the result in due course.[12]

Howard replied on April 20, wishing ter Meer "early success in your negotiations" with the German government. Howard hoped, however, that

without waiting for final conclusions on all the questions involved, you may be able to grant us the authority to proceed in a preliminary way with the rather lengthy discussions here which must be had with the various interested rubber companies preparatory to organizing them into a cooperative group. . . . My view is that we cannot safely delay the definite steps looking toward the organization of our business in the United States . . . beyond next fall—and even to obtain this much delay may not be too easy.[13]

In the spring of 1938, the Goodyear Rubber Company and the Dow Chemical Company, intent on developing a synthetic rubber capacity, pressed Standard for licenses under I.G.'s Buna patents. Standard, unable to get I.G.'s permission, resorted to the same stalling technique with the American rubber companies that I.G. was using with Standard. Standard was not yet in a position to give licenses but at the same time did not want to force the companies to strike out on their own. As Howard wrote to Friedrich H. Bedford, Jr., an important, long-time Standard Oil director and the president of a Standard subsidiary that sold rubber products, *Our primary objective in our talk with the Goodyear and Dow people was to convince them of our good*

103

faith and our willingness to cooperate with them in order to avoid having them proceed prematurely with an independent development [emphasis in original]."

At the bottom of Standard's rubber problems, of course, was I.G.'s failure to act: "The thing that is really holding us up," explained Howard, "is . . . the inability of our partners [I.G.] to obtain permission of their government to proceed with the development in the United States. Until they obtain this permission, it is not possible for us to make any commitment at all."[14] A few days later Howard wrote to Bedford assuring him that he would continue to press I.G. for permission at least to hold informal talks with the rubber industry about synthetic rubber.

Until we have this permission, however, there is absolutely nothing we can do, and we must be especially careful not to make any move whatever, even on a purely informal, personal, or friendly basis, without the consent of our friends. We know some of the difficulties they have, both from business complications and interrelations with the rubber and chemical trades in the United States, and from a national standpoint in Germany, but we do not know the whole situation—and *since under the agreement they have full control over the exploitation of this process, the only thing we can do is to continue to press for authority to act, but in the meantime loyally preserve the restrictions they have put on us* [emphasis added].[15]

The first week in October 1938, immediately after Germany invaded the Sudetenland and war was another step closer, Howard was again in Berlin to negotiate with ter Meer about synthetic rubber. Ter Meer promised to proceed to the United States as soon as he was free; first, however, he would have to finish several important matters concerning "the expansion" of I.G., a reference to the newly acquired Sudeten properties. A few days later he wrote Carl Duisberg's son Walter in New York that it would probably be the middle of November before he could get to the United States.

> The annexation of the Sudetenland brings up certain new problems for us. . . . If you explain it to [Standard] in the right manner, I am convinced that our American friends who are counting on my coming to the United States will understand the situation, especially if you mention that I am even prepared to sacrifice Christmas in Germany in order to place a Buna tire under the American Christmas tree.[16]

At last, on Thanksgiving Day of 1938, ter Meer arrived in the United States. At a high level conference, he and Howard met with the executive committee of Standard. Since ter Meer had not yet obtained permission from his government to resolve the Buna problem, it was agreed that ter Meer, rather than Standard, would deal with the five leading American tire companies (U.S. Rubber, Firestone, Goodyear, Goodrich, and General). According to the committee memorandum on the meeting, "The Committee felt that [ter Meer] should contact the tire companies on Jersey's behalf as sponsor for the process, it being intimated to the tire companies that negotiations between I.G. and Jersey Company have not yet been crystallized, but that they are in process of development."[17] Nothing would be said about the Nazi government's refusal to grant permission. Ter Meer then made his tour of the five rubber companies and advised them that negotiations between I.G. and Standard would soon be completed although he could not give a specific date. The stall continued.

By August 1939 it was obvious that war in Europe could not be averted. Should the conflict lead to war between the United States and Germany, the consequences to Standard and I.G. could be serious. The I.G. interest in both the Standard-I.G. Company and in Jasco would surely be seized by the U.S. alien property custodian as enemy owned assets. With this concern in mind Walter Duisberg, after returning from conferences with I.G. in Germany, suggested to Walter Teagle that action be taken to dispose of I.G.'s ownership in both of the jointly owned companies to American citizens.[18] Teagle agreed and suggested to some of Standard's top officials that "in view of the unsettled conditions" it might be desirable for Standard itself to acquire the I.G. interest. Negotiations, he added, would have to be conducted with Duisberg since he was now "the German I.G.'s sole representative in the country."[19]

The pressure of events in Europe moved negotiations to a swift conclusion. Within days, Standard agreed to purchase I.G.'s twenty percent interest in the Standard-I.G. Company for $20,000 and Duisberg himself, now a naturalized American citizen, acquired I.G.'s fifty percent share of Jasco for a mere $4000. The Standard negotiators expressed no concern that Duisberg, the son of the founder of I.G., was a peculiar choice to immunize I.G.'s property from possible seizure by an alien property custodian. To the contrary, they pointed out naïvely that Duisberg's purchase of I.G.'s Jasco shares would "prevent their being seized by an Alien Property Custodian because [Duisberg] is an American citizen and prepared to purchase the shares with his own funds." They noted further that when Duisberg bought the stock, it was planned that he would execute an option in favor of Jasco "so as to insure that these shares will not fall into unfriendly hands in the event of his death."[20]

The next day, September 1, just as Germany was invading Poland and World War II had officially begun, the executive committee of Standard met hurriedly to approve the action of its negotiators. The negotiators, in their report to the committee, were quite candid: "Of course, what we have in mind is protecting this minority interest in the event of war between ourselves and Germany, as it would certainly be very undesirable to have this twenty percent in Standard-I.G. pass to an Alien Property Custodian who might sell it to an unfriendly interest."[21] As soon as the executive committee voted approval, a cable was sent to the I.G. Berlin office offering to buy I.G.'s stock interest in Standard-I.G. for $20,000.[22] I.G. immediately cabled its acceptance.

Two unresolved questions still remained in the relationship between Standard and I.G. The first concerned the critical problem of how to protect the worldwide patent holdings of I.G. to which the Standard-I.G. Company and Jasco had rights but which remained in I.G.'s name. The second was Standard's repeated and almost desperate request to I.G. for the rights to the Buna rubber patents and the know-how to use them. The outbreak of war seriously complicated the possibility of an affirmative answer.

When war erupted on September 1, Howard was in France. This would probably be the last opportunity to work out a solution to the problem of transferring I.G.'s foreign patents to the Standard-I.G. Company and Jasco and to get the Buna know-how. Howard cabled William Farish, Teagle's successor as president of Standard, suggesting that he be permitted to delay his return to the United States in order to meet with I.G. officials.[23] Since the state of war between France and Germany prevented Howard from communicating directly with I.G., he arranged for the New York Standard office to set up a meeting in neutral Holland.[24]

Knieriem assigned Fritz Ringer, a young engineer familiar with the patent problem, to confer with Howard at The Hague. Before Ringer could negotiate such a matter, however, permission had to be obtained from the proper German authorities, in this case the High Command because military products were involved.

Buetefisch conferred on the matter with the officials of the High Command on September 13. He advised them of Standard's proposal by which I.G. would transfer its foreign patents to the Standard-I.G. Company and Jasco. These patents, he warned, were in imminent danger of being seized by enemy governments if ownership remained in I.G.'s name. I.G., he explained, anticipated "substantial advantages from a speedy transfer" and he assured the High Command that "German in-

107

terests would not be prejudiced." Finally, Buetefisch gave assurances that I.G. "would be able to resume at any time, without hindrance, the relationships existing now."[25] For these reasons Buetefisch urged that I.G. be granted permission to proceed with these transactions. It was simply a matter of camouflaging I.G.'s interest for the duration of the war.

At the close of the conference, the High Command officials present gave I.G. the go-ahead for the proposed meeting at The Hague. Relying on this verbal assurance, I.G. got word to Howard, who was waiting in England, that Ringer would meet him at The Hague on September 22, bringing the patent assignments.

While waiting in England, Howard had second thoughts and called at the American Embassy to inquire about the legality of meeting with an I.G. representative in Holland. Herschel V. Johnson, then counselor at the American Embassy, expressed serious doubts as to the propriety or wisdom of an American citizen's going to Holland from England to talk to England's enemies.[26] Howard tried to convince Johnson that the English and the Americans had much to gain if the patent rights to valuable processes that had originated in Germany could be transferred to Standard. As matters stood, only the Germans could derive any military benefit from this situation. A doubtful Johnson referred Howard to the Ambassador, Joseph P. Kennedy. Unlike his counselor, Ambassador Kennedy saw nothing questionable in Howard's proposal, nor any reason for the British to object. He promptly secured for Howard the necessary clearance from the British Foreign Office.[27]

The meeting having been cleared by their respective governments, the two men met at The Hague on September 22. Almost three weeks had passed since the outbreak of war, an uncomfortable fact that dominated the conference. Ringer arrived at the meeting with blank assignments for approximately 2000 patents that I.G. was prepared to turn over to Jasco and the Standard-I.G. Company, presumably all the foreign patents covering the products and processes within the fields of operation of each of these concerns. There was one significant omission. Howard noted with disappointment that the Buna patents were not included. With the war now under way in Europe, it would only be a matter of time before the United States became aware that the spread of the conflict to the Pacific would make its supply of natural rubber vulnerable. Without the Buna patents or know-how, Standard was being placed in a very uncomfortable position. It is understandable that Howard pressed Ringer hard on the subject of Buna. The United States government at any moment might take a jaundiced view of the I.G.-Standard arrangement. Ringer replied that although he did not have the Buna patents with him, he could assure Howard that I.G. fully intended to adhere to its unwritten commitment to include the Buna patents in the new Jasco arrangement.

In discussing the change with regard to I.G.'s interest in Jasco, both men were appalled by the sale to Duisberg, agreeing that the transfer was a first-class blunder. Ringer assured Howard that this would be rectified and that Duisberg would follow whatever course I.G. asked him to take.[28] Duisberg did exactly as I.G. wished. He sold the fifty percent interest in Jasco to Standard at the same price he paid I.G.[29]

At their meeting Howard and Ringer then got down to the business of accommodating the relations of Standard and I.G. to the new circumstances caused by the war. Broadly stated, they agreed that Standard would receive U.S. and Allied countries as exclusive territory for the exploitation of the products and processes covered by the Jasco patents, with the rest of the world reserved for I.G.[30] Iraq was included in the territory assigned to Standard on the mistaken assumption that it had declared war on Germany.[31] To keep matters flexible, if the workings of the agreement should result in an unfair financial distribution, the basic division of territory could be recast at any time in the future.

To Howard's partial satisfaction, the new agreement gave Jasco rights to I.G.'s Buna patents. But the patents were only part of the story. The know-how, which I.G. did not include, was even more important to Standard. Just as the final meeting between the two men was coming to a close, Howard brought up the subject of Buna again. Was there any chance, he asked, that I.G. would provide Standard with the know-how for making Buna? Without this technical information, Standard would be at a great disadvantage. Ringer, of course, did not have the authority to give an answer. In his report back to I.G., however, Ringer noted that Howard anticipated a refusal "since in the event of war, the United States would be dependent on the importation of crude rubber."[32] Therefore, Ringer concluded, Howard did not condition Standard's approval of the revised Jasco agreement on I.G.'s furnishing the know-how. In Ringer's view, Howard did not expect the German government to permit the know-how on Buna to be made available to a potential enemy who might need it in case it lost access to natural rubber, such as might happen in a war with Japan, Germany's Axis partner.

On September 25, Ringer and Howard finished their business and departed for home, each carrying a copy of the "Hague memorandum," a draft agreement for the consideration and approval of their respective companies. I.G.'s problem now was to get the approval of the German government. Ter Meer and Buetefisch paid a visit to General Thomas of the High Command and Ministerial Director Muelert of the Ministry of Economics to present I.G.'s application for government permission to sign the Jasco readjustment agreement. Ter Meer again stressed the compelling need to get the foreign Buna patents out of I.G.'s name as quickly as possible in order to avoid possible enemy seizure. With the assignment to Jasco, they would be under the control of Standard, a concern that I.G. could trust to resume friendly relations after the war.

Thomas and Muelert were agreeable but made it plain that they would grant permission to I.G. to make the transfer only on the condition that there would be no transmission of Buna know-how. Ter Meer and

110

Buetefisch assured them that this prohibition would be respected absolutely.[33]

By October 12 both the German High Command and the Ministry of Economics had given I.G. written permission for the assignment of the Buna patents to Standard. With all the necessary government permits in order, I.G. cabled the Standard Oil Development Company on October 16 that it agreed in principle with the Jasco arrangement outlined in the Hague memorandum. The wording of the cable was identical with that in the draft tentatively prepared three weeks before except for one additional sentence: "Re article two of the Hague Memorandum we ask that Jasco assign also Iraq to I.G."[34] This was designed to correct the mistake Ringer had made when he allocated Iraq to Standard under the incorrect assumption that Iraq was at war with Germany. Obviously, I.G. did not intend to relinquish any territory it did not have to.

I.G. also sent a second cable to Standard Development, settling the Buna question: "As agreed we will assign Buna patents for Jasco field. Documents are being prepared. . . . Referring to your question with respect to technical information about Buna we have to inform you that under present conditions we will not be able to give such information."[35]

Upon receipt of the two cables from I.G., Howard immediately wrote a memorandum for the executive committee of the Standard board explaining the reason for the Jasco arrangement. After noting the basic outlines of the Hague agreement, he commented:

I believe this arrangement, when coupled with the provision for future readjustments, is entirely equitable, and that without regard to the possibility of legally enforcing the readjustment provision, it should be satisfactory in substance to us, as it is to the I.G. An attempt to put this provision in a form which would be fully legally enforceable might result in many difficulties, and (speaking for myself and the I.G. negotiators) it was not our in-

111

tention to provide any legally enforceable clause of this character in our arrangements.

He added one note of caution.

We will probably have some legal difficulties in both England and France in connection with establishing our right to these I.G. inventions, but since we believe we can establish an equitable title antedating the war (and in any case we certainly have all the technical information, without which it would be difficult to proceed), this situation is not too bad.[36]

On the morning of October 18, the executive committee, with Howard present, approved the Jasco readjustment and Howard then cabled I.G. in Berlin agreeing "in principle to arrangement outlined in your cable October 16."

In December an afterthought struck Howard. He proposed to I.G. that the Jasco agreement be dated retroactively to September 1, 1939,[37] two days before Great Britain and France officially declared war on Germany. Technically, the new date made the Hague memorandum into a prewar document.

By the summer of 1940, the last of the Buna patents, about fifty assignments, were officially transferred by I.G. to Jasco. However, as understood by the parties, the know-how was not turned over. And by the end of 1941 this lack proved a personal tragedy for Howard, Teagle, and Farish and a corporate disaster for Standard. Worst of all, it was a major military setback for the United States.

On December 7, 1941, Japan attacked Pearl Harbor, and the United States was suddenly faced with a monumental rubber crisis. It was blocked from its main source of natural rubber in Southeast Asia—just as Germany had been blocked from its source of saltpeter in Chile during World War I. Desperate measures were called for, and rubber was soon tightly rationed. A campaign was started by patriotic citizens to collect rubber goods of all kinds for possible recycling into tires. It was a futile if laudable enterprise. These enthusiasts learned, to their dismay, that rubber bathmats could generally be turned into new rubber bathmats but not into tires. The United States would have to rely on synthetic rubber for tires. However, the American rubber and chemical companies were completely unprepared to mass-produce a synthetic.

While feverish work was going on among the rubber and chemical companies to develop a synthetic rubber out of which to make tires, there seemed to be no prospect for immediate success as far as Buna was concerned. I.G. had successfully kept the know-how for its production from reaching the United States. For the United States and for Standard the results were calamitous.

Since early 1941, the Antitrust Division of the Department of Justice had been investigating the I.G.-Standard cartel, and by the end of the year, spurred by the attack at Pearl Harbor, the government was getting ready to indict the Standard Oil companies, I.G. Farben, and their principal officers for a conspiracy to restrain trade and commerce in the oil and chemical industries throughout the world, including synthetic rubber and synthetic gasoline.

Standard protested to the War Department that the defense of such a lawsuit would divert the energies of many of its executives from the war effort. The War Department, more concerned with war production than prosecution under the antitrust laws, agreed. However, the Department of Justice, with the backing of several powerful senators and administration officials, insisted that the only effective way to eliminate the restrictions of the I.G.-Standard cartel and open up the development and manufacture of synthetic rubber was by enforcement of the antitrust laws. On March 20, 1942 Assistant Attorney General Thurman Arnold, Attorney General Biddle, Secretary of War Stimson, and Secretary of the Navy Knox signed a memorandum to President Roosevelt recommending suspension of pending antitrust investigations and lawsuits that might interfere

113

with the war effort. They argued that lengthy court actions would "unavoidably consume the time of executives and employees of those corporations which are engaged in war work."[38] Roosevelt approved this policy, but as a concession to Arnold and his Antitrust Division staff he agreed to ask for congressional action to extend the statute of limitations on the antitrust cases affected so that postwar prosecution would be possible.[39]

It was generally recognized that the I.G.-Standard antitrust case precipitated the change of policy. However, Standard did not elect to postpone resolution of the case until after the war. Instead, the parties agreed that Antitrust would file criminal charges against Standard and its principal officers and that all the Standard defendants would plead nolo contendere (no contest). It was also agreed that the Justice Department would file a civil complaint, to which Standard would enter a consent decree agreeing to abandon all contracts and practices to which the government objected.

When the parties met on March 24 in Assistant Attorney General Arnold's office to forge a formal agreement, one problem remained. Arnold wanted the court to assess fines totaling over $1.5 million, one of the largest financial penalties in the history of antitrust actions. The fine would be divided among a large number of defendants—Standard Oil (New Jersey), several Standard subsidiaries, and all the directors of the parent company. John W. Davis, counsel for Standard, rejected this suggestion as absolutely unacceptable. Such a huge fine would call into question the patriotism of Standard. Instead, he made a counteroffer: fines totaling $50,000 to be divided among the defendants any way Arnold chose. Arnold retorted that equal division of a fine that small would mean individual fines of only $600 to $700, an absurd figure in view of the serious nature of the charges. With the papers due to be filed in court the next day—and it was already approaching midnight—Arnold finally capitulated, at least for the time being. The number of defendants was reduced to ten so that the individual fines amounted to $5000.

As the meeting was breaking up, Arnold made a

114

brief statement to the opposing counsel and some of the proposed defendants who were present: "Of course, you understand that I am under subpoena to appear the day after tomorrow before the Truman Committee [the U.S. Senate War Investigating Committee] to tell them all the facts about the case." Davis replied wearily, "Mr. Arnold, that is a matter of utter indifference to us."

The next day, March 25, 1942, was a black one for Standard Oil. What Standard and I.G. had been frantically trying to avoid since they first realized that war was inevitable had happened. The new U.S. alien property custodian, Leo T. Crowley, issued his first vesting order, seizing the interests of I.G. Farben, "an enemy corporation," in the stock, patents, and contracts of Jasco and Standard Catalytic Company. (In the fall of 1940, the Standard-I.G. Company had been changed to the Standard company whose name bore the I.G. initials.)

Two hours after Crowley vested the alleged interest of I.G. Farben in Jasco and Standard Catalytic, the Department of Justice filed a massive action against the Standard Oil Company (New Jersey), six subsidiaries, and Walter C. Teagle, William S. Farish, and Frank A. Howard. I.G. Farbenindustrie was named an unindicted co-conspirator.[40] According to the compromise worked out two nights earlier, the ten defendants in the criminal action pleaded no contest and were fined $5,000 each.

The antitrust complaint detailed the history of Standard's relations with I.G. Farben. The section that gained the most careful attention by the press, quite naturally, concerned synthetic rubber. The complaint implied that the current rubber crisis could be traced, at least in part, to the I.G.-Standard cartel.

To remedy matters, the consent decree required Standard to sever all relations with I.G. and to make available to all United States applicants all patents by which Standard and I.G. had monopolized trade in the chemical and petroleum fields, furnishing technical know-how as well.

As an interesting sidelight, the alien property custodian joined in the case as the legal representative of I.G.'s interests. His primary role was to provide Standard with a defense in case I.G. Farben brought suit in the future for nonperformance under the agreements.

Arnold, who traditionally issued lively public statements, put out a brief and uninformative press release: "Because members of the Antitrust Division have been subpoenaed to appear before the Truman Committee tomorrow to present a detailed explanation of both the complaint and the decree, such details are omitted from this announcement."[41] Standard Oil also issued a press release, mainly to explain why it chose not to contest the case.

> The company realizes that to obtain a vindication by trying the issues in the courts would involve months of time and energy of most of its officers and many of its employees. Its war work is more important than court vindication. Nor has the company any desire to remain in a position which the Department of Justice considers in any way questionable.[42]

The release pointed out that agreements between Standard and I.G. had actually advanced the progress of American industry and its ability to meet the war emergency.

The next day Thurman Arnold appeared before the Senate Special Committee to Investigate the National Defense Program, headed by Harry S. Truman. Arnold set forth in full detail the history of Standard Oil's relations with I.G. Farben before and during Hitler's regime. All the facts were supported by documents from Standard Oil's own files. The effect on the senators and press was electrifying.

Scripps-Howard's Thomas L. Stokes, a Pulitzer Prize-winning reporter, described the atmosphere in the committee room.

> Members of the Senate Defense Committee sat grim and visibly shocked as Thurman Arnold . . . testi-

116

fied. . . . [Truman] was particularly indignant about a memorandum by Frank Howard . . . made at The Hague, Netherlands, October 12, 1939, after the outbreak of war, in which Mr. Howard said "representatives of I.G. Farbenindustrie delivered to me assignments of some 2,000 foreign patents and we did our best to work out complete plans for a modus vivendi which would operate through the term of the war whether or not the U.S. came in." . . . That last phrase sent a shudder through the committee room.

Stokes went on to discuss the evidence on which Arnold's testimony was based: 40,000 documents reviewed by the Department of Justice investigators.

Thurman Arnold dumped exhibit after exhibit on the committee table as he went through his prepared statement of twenty-seven pages to prove his underlying contention that the use of buna rubber was delayed in this country "because the Hitler government did not wish to have this rubber exploited here for military reasons."[43]

Farish and Howard testified before the committee a few days later. Farish told the committee,

I wish to assert with conviction that whether the several contracts made with I.G. did or did not fall within the borders set by the Sherman Act, they did inure greatly to the advance of American industry and more than any other thing they have made possible our present war activities in aviation gasoline, toluol and explosives and in synthetic rubber itself.[44]

He then presented letters from the War and Navy departments confirming Standard's contribution to the war effort.

Standard's ordeal in Congress did not end with the Truman committee hearings on the rubber crisis. On

April 13, the Senate Committee on Patents, under the chairmanship of Senator Homer T. Bone, began hearings on the role of patents in the national defense program. Hardly had the committee convened when Senator Robert M. La Follette of Wisconsin embarked on an attack on international cartels generally and the I.G.-Standard arrangement specifically.

Recently, Standard Oil of New Jersey was found by the Antitrust Division of the Department of Justice to be conspiring with I.G. Farben . . . of Germany. I.G. Farben, through its maze of international patent agreements, is the spear-head of Nazi economic warfare. By its cartel agreements with Standard Oil of New Jersey, the United States was effectively prevented from developing or producing any substantial amount of synthetic rubber.

The penalty administered on Standard Oil for its part in this obstructionist arrangement was a court "consent decree" which provided a $50,000 fine and a temporary—strictly temporary—and only partial suspension of the monopoly patent privileges which estopped full United States use of granted patents. . . .

It seems to me that the Standard Oil of New Jersey consent decree is a real victory for Standard Oil Co. . . . All the consent decree does . . . is to guarantee that Standard Oil will hold those patents for I.G. Farben . . . until the day when Standard Oil can render an accounting to I.G. Farben, and return the patents.[45]

The adverse effect of congressional inquiries and the escalation of bad publicity convinced the Standard board that the situation was critical. The matter soon reached such serious proportions that it engaged the attention of John D. Rockefeller, Jr., the largest stockholder in Standard. Rockefeller was particularly disturbed by a series of open letters addressed to him by I. F. Stone in the newspaper *PM*. The letters called for

Rockefeller to use his influence in forcing the dismissal of Teagle, Farish, and Howard.

> After the teapot dome scandal, you stepped in and forced the resignation of Col. Robert Stewart as Chairman of the Board of Standard Oil Company of Indiana. . . . We think you owe it to your good name and your company and your country to take similar action at the scandal which has broken around the parent Standard Oil Company itself. You bear an inescapable personal responsibility for Standard Oil policies. . . . Whatever the intentions which lay behind these policies, the effect was to make Standard Oil an ally of Hitler, an economic enemy agent within the U.S.A. . . . We think it your duty to remove Walter C. Teagle as Chairman of the Board and William S. Farish as President and Frank A. Howard as Vice President of the Standard Oil Company and radically to change the policies which put them in the position of acting as international economic collaborators of the Third Reich.[46]

After the appearance of these letters, Rockefeller emphatically challenged the board of directors to improve Standard's image with the public.[47]

Robert T. Haslam was chosen by the board to seek a solution to the problem. He had been serving as general manager of the ESSO Marketeers and had recently warned the board that his organization could not deliver a satisfactory sales performance unless something were done to improve Standard's public image. Standard hired Elmo Roper's organization to survey public opinion. Roper's conclusion was that the company was currently suffering from the effects of an acute attack of Arnolditis and that the public believed that Standard had let Germany best it in business.[48]

The board of directors decided to assert tighter control over Standard's affairs. They declared that too often in the past critical decisions had been made and acted upon without the board's being informed. For example, in the many years during which Frank Howard had conducted negotiations with I.G. Farben, he had frequently informed the Standard board only after action had been taken. In the future the board was determined to take charge itself.

Howard remained with the Standard Oil Development Company for two more years, but the board's action left him with only a shadow of his former influence and authority. In November 1942, the two other Standard officials named as defendants in the antitrust case, Teagle and Farish, disappeared from the Standard picture. Teagle resigned from the board, and less than a week later Farish died of a heart attack.

5

The Rape
of the
European Chemical Industry

In the five years since Bosch made his compact with Hitler to prepare Germany for war I.G.'s descent into the theory and practice of Nazi morality moved with accelerating speed. During that time I.G. had become the leading industrial-financial backer of the Nazi party; it cleansed itself of identifiable Jewish directors and executives; and the Aryan officials who remained joined the Nazi party and some the dreaded S.S. I.G. proclaimed the inviolability of Nazi doctrine as corporate policy. But I.G. had not even begun to plumb the depths of Nazi depravity.

In the spring of 1938 Hitler's program of military conquest took a great leap forward. Action was ready to replace rhetoric; the time for talk was over; the drive for territorial expansion by force was about to become reality. Terrified by Hitler's diplomatic onslaught, his opponents scattered in retreat. As country after country collapsed in the face of Hitler's "Operation Terror," I.G.'s embrace of the Nazis became progressively more passionate. As country after country fell to the Wehrmacht's assault, I.G. played the jackal to Hitler's lion.

Despite Hitler's apparent invincibility, I.G. continued to calculate the odds and prepare for all contingencies. The acquisitions, no matter how brutal, were inevitably accomplished with the color of legality, a charade designed to protect I.G.'s interests in the improbable event that Germany lost the war. But this veneer of lawfulness could not conceal the terror I.G.'s methods evoked in its victims. And those in I.G. who would challenge the wisdom of such a course were silenced not only by a fear of Nazi retribution but also by I.G.'s great success.

The invasion of Austria on March 11, 1938, marked the beginning of Hitler's policy to move beyond the borders of Germany by force. I.G. was ready within days after the troops started to march. It presented the Nazi occupation officials with a memorandum entitled "New Order for the Greater Chemical Industry of Austria."[1] Essentially, the "new order" plan was a request for government permission for I.G. to take over Skoda Werke Wetzler, the largest chemical concern in Austria. I.G. made sure to clothe its plea with the rhetoric of German national interests. The erstwhile Jewish company was now ready to goose-step with Hitler. The absorption of the Austrian concern, I.G. promised, would aid in the pursuit of the aims of the four-year plan as well as promote the elimination of Jewish influence in Austrian industry. Skoda Werke Wetzler was dominated by the Jewish Rothschilds, and I.G. made the most of this fact.

The Rothschilds were not naïve. Even before the Anschluss, they had recognized I.G.'s intentions. Through the general manager of Skoda, Isador Pollack, they tried to thwart I.G.'s acquisitive plans.[2] To this end, Pollack explored the possibility of merger with two other European chemical organizations, Montecatini of Italy and Aussiger Verein of Czechoslovakia. But I.G. proved too formidable, and the mergers were never seriously entertained by either the Czech or the Italian company.

Hitler's move into Austria left terror in its wake, and the chemical industry was no exception. Immediately after the Anschluss, all the top Jewish personnel of Skoda were dismissed by government decree. I.G. filled the breach by supplying Aryan technicians.[8] However, to protect the takeover against possible future legal challenges, I.G. entered into negotiations with Josef Joham, the personal representative of the Rothschilds.[4] Joham, also a Jew and therefore personally vulnerable, was hardly in a position to oppose I.G.'s demands. These kept enlarging as the so-called negotiations proceeded. When necessary, I.G. was not reluctant to use the anti-Semitic threat to squeeze out the terms it considered suitable. After a series of annoying difficulties posed by the Nazi bureaucracy in Austria, I.G. finally in the fall of 1938 claimed Skoda as its own.[5] By that time Joham had fled the country[6] but Pollack, not so fortunate, was literally stomped to death by Nazi Storm Troopers before he could make his escape.[7]

Czechoslovakia was next on Hitler's schedule. Anticipating another industrial meal, I.G. prepared a special study of the chemical plants of the Czech Sudetenland.[8] Particularly coveted by I.G. were two plants owned by Aussiger Verein, the largest chemical company in Czechoslovakia, a participant in the European dyestuff cartel dominated by I.G., and a respected member of the world's chemical community.[9] Once again I.G. looked forward to exploiting a special advantage in dealing with Aussiger Verein. Under the formula applied by the Nuremberg laws, Aussiger could be classified as a Jewish company.[10] Twenty-five percent of its directors were non-Aryan.

By the summer of 1938, the demands of Hitler upon Czechoslovakia with regard to the Sudetenland were becoming so outrageous that a general war seemed imminent. A terrified British prime minister, Neville Chamberlain, with the assistance of Edouard Daladier of France, forced Czechoslovakia to capitulate to Hitler's terms. The humiliation of the democracies was certified on September 29 with the signing of the Munich agreement and the immediate occupation of the Sudetenland by German troops. To soften the blow, Hitler declared that this was his last territorial demand in Europe. The next day, in a telegram of congratulations, Hermann Schmitz, now the head of I.G., let Hitler know of I.G.'s interest in the Sudetenland: "Profoundly impressed by the return of the Sudetenland to the Reich which you, my Führer, have achieved. The

I.G. Farbenindustrie A.G. puts a sum of half a million reichsmarks at your disposal for use in the Sudetenland territory."[11]

Before long I.G. was engaged in negotiations with Aussiger Verein for the "purchase" of the Sudetenland plants.[12] Just about the only defense left to the Aussiger directors was to stall the so-called negotiations as long as possible in the hope that something would turn up to rescue them. Finally, Schnitzler proclaimed to the Aussiger representatives that as the result of their inflexible attitudes and unwillingness to negotiate in good faith, he was planning to send a complaint to the German government that "unrest and a breakdown of social peace" in the Sudetenland appeared inevitable. Schnitzler did not conceal the threat that Hitler might very well use this charge as an excuse to occupy the rest of Czechoslovakia.[13]

In desperation the Aussiger directors appealed to the Czech government, which only confirmed the force behind Schnitzler's threat. The Aussiger men were advised to manage on their own as well as they could. No official help was possible. Accordingly, they decided the next day to "sell" the plants on I.G.'s terms.[14] However, it made little difference to the future of their country. A few months later, in March, Hitler's troops marched into Prague and soon occupied all of Czechoslovakia.

Poland was next on Hitler's timetable of conquest. Once again, I.G. made plans to be in on the kill. It compiled a list of prospective booty: "The Most Important Chemical Plants in Poland."[15] Three dyestuff companies in particular interested I.G.: Boruta, the largest; Wola, a small company owned by three Jews[16]; and Winnica (of which Joseph Frossard was chairman), jointly owned by I.G.'s Swiss affiliate, I.G. Chemie, and Kuhlmann of France.

On September 1, 1939, Germany invaded Poland. This time the Allied countries resisted and World War II began. Schnitzler, who personally followed right behind the troops, wired the I.G. agent in Berlin to stay close to the Reich Ministry of Economics and keep informed as to the status of the Polish chemical industry. "The factories contain considerable and valuable stocks of preliminary, intermediate, and final products," telegraphed Schnitzler. ". . . we consider it of primary importance that the above-mentioned stocks be used by experts in the interest of the German national economy. *Only the I.G. is in a position to make experts available* [emphasis added]."[17]

When Schnitzler returned to Berlin from Poland a week later, he called on the Ministry of Economics to make it clear that only I.G. was capable of operating the Polish plants.[18] The ministry, through General Hermann von Hanneken, agreed to I.G.'s provisional management of the three Polish companies. He was not, however, pleased with I.G.'s greed or methods. Undoubtedly aware of I.G.'s activities in Austria and Czechoslovakia, Hanneken warned I.G. not to expect to take over the Polish plants permanently. His words were as stern as they were unmistakable: "I expressly emphasize that there will be no changes in the condition of ownership of the concerned plants; and that also no preparations for a change in the ownership conditions are to be seen in this appointment."[19]

Hanneken's attitude shocked Schnitzler. I.G. particularly wanted to control and operate the large Boruta plants with "a certain permanence."[20] Schnitzler thereupon went over Hanneken's head to I.G.'s friend Hermann Goering, who had just set up an organization to confiscate and dispose of Polish property in accordance with the needs of the four-year plan.[21]

But Goering's power in Poland was under challenge by a rising star in the Nazi firmament, Heinrich Himmler, head of the S.S., who had his own ideas about the disposal of Polish property. When Goering's representative proved unable to help I.G., the reason soon emerged. I.G. discovered that Himmler's deputy in Poland, S.S. Brigadefuehrer Ulrich Greifelt, was vested with the power to veto any sale of confiscated Polish property authorized by Goering's office.

The change in political climate was not wasted on I.G.; it shifted its allegiance from Goering to Himmler and Greifelt. Greifelt was worthy of Himmler's trust and he exercised his authority in Poland with a ruthlessness that made his chief proud: among his accomplishments was the forced sterilization of Polish men and women, the kidnapping of children to be raised by the S.S., the enslavement of large segments of the population, and the mass shooting of hostages.[21a]

Schnitzler was assigned the project of cultivating Greifelt. Not long thereafter, I.G. took over the Polish plants on its own terms, proving once again its ability to prosper in the world of Nazi intrigue.[22] This time I.G.'s choice of ally would have more than an ordinary effect on its future. A fateful step in the alliance with Himmler was already taking place in the small community of Auschwitz in Polish Silesia.

As I.G. and Hitler became more indispensable for each other's goals, Bosch's physical and mental decline became more noticeable. His recurrent depressions deepened as he brooded over the thought that the war itself was the direct result of his great achievements, the creation of the vital synthetics of nitrates, oil, and rubber. He refused to see anyone from I.G. except Krauch; alcohol became his only solace.

By February 1940, Bosch could no longer bear living in Hitler's Germany. He decided to move to Sicily and took with him as his only companion an ant colony from the Kaiser Wilhelm Institute, where his name was still revered. The change gave Bosch no relief and his physical condition worsened. In April he returned to Germany with no hope of recovery. As he lay dying, he predicted the coming defeat of France. But this he told his doctor would only be an interlude. Ultimately, Hitler's lunacy would result in the destruction of Germany and the end of I.G., which for him were equal disasters.

Bosch did not live to witness the accuracy of his prediction. On April 26, 1940, two weeks before the Wehrmacht launched its attack on France, Bosch, not quite sixty-six years old, died.[23]

Without Bosch's towering reputation and personality

hovering over the company, Hermann Schmitz assumed in fact a position he already held in name, the head of I.G. At the same time Krauch was elected to succeed Bosch as chairman of the supervisory board,[24] giving up all managerial duties to spend more time as a plenipotentiary of the four-year plan. Hereafter, Schmitz would call the I.G. tune.

On May 9 Hitler mounted his assault on France, and on June 22 it was all over. Except for England and the Soviet Union, all of Europe was firmly in Hitler's grip. I.G. was ready to share in the booty. It had already prepared a "new order" plan for the chemical industry of the world that would provide for the "recovery and security of world respect for the German chemical industry."[25] I.G. spelled out in its detailed, written plans the absorption of the chemical industries of France, Norway, Holland, Denmark, Luxembourg, and Belgium.[26] But its appetite did not end there. I.G. also included in its scheme the Soviet Union, at the moment a friendly neutral; Switzerland, certainly not an unfriendly neutral; England, not yet conquered; and finally Italy, an ally. After only a brief interlude, the chemical industry of the United States, which was an unfriendly neutral, was added.

In I.G.'s view France was the key to controlling the chemical industry of Europe. Broadly stated, the "new order" plan for France recommended that I.G. and the German government enter into a partnership to own and control the French dyestuff industry, in line with the Third Reich's program of territorial and economic expansion. This offered "the best solution to bring about a uniform regulation of French production and marketing *for all time to come* [emphasis added]."[27]

I.G.'s plan for France was delivered to Gustav Schlotterer of the Ministry of Economics in early August. Schlotterer completely agreed with the necessity of restoring I.G.'s position of leadership under the so-called new order and said that in his opinion I.G.'s proposal for France was not at all excessive and would probably fit into the coming peace plans.[28]

While I.G.'s "new order" plan was under consideration, a shortage of coal and electric power brought the French dyestuff plants to a standstill.[29] The executives of the French industry realized quite early that I.G. held the key not only to the resumption of production but also to the future of the French industry. They began to press for a meeting with the I.G. officials to be arranged through the armistice commission in Wiesbaden.[30] Mistakenly, the French anticipated favorable treatment from their former cartel partner. Schlotterer, a high official in the Ministry of Economics, who agreed in principle to a meeting between I.G. and French industry officials, nevertheless suggested to I.G. that delay was in their best interests. Actual negotiations, he advised, should not begin until the French realized that they were not coming to bargain for a favorable ownership status but rather to cede "first place" to the German dyestuff industry.[31] A period of uncertainty, coupled with despair, would soften the French. Hans Hemmen, chief of the economic delegation of the German armistice commission, echoed this advice. He also counseled a policy of delay rather than premature action, specifically suggesting that I.G. should stall at least until late fall or early winter, when the situation in France would be more desperate.[32] I.G. agreed.

In the meantime, I.G. gathered intelligence from its employees in Paris about the leaders of the French industry with whom it would eventually have to deal. The most intriguing information concerned Joseph Frossard, Bosch's "trump card" at Versailles. He was now the leading figure in Kuhlmann, along with René Duchemin. Frossard, who was then in unoccupied France, with the rest of the directors of Kuhlmann told the I.G. people that he could not enter the German occupied zone because he would have to expect trouble as "a German deserter."[33] It was a strange fear for the acknowledged leader of the French chemical industry. As a Frenchman, how could Frossard be a German deserter? But neither the Germans nor the French have ever supplied an explanation for this unusual remark, which may be the clue as to why Bosch had referred to Frossard as a secret trump card.

Frossard and the other French industrialists continued to press the French armistice delegation to arrange a meeting with I.G. I.G., however, kept stalling. An I.G. official remarked, "We do not think that the time has come to initiate these negotiations—a view shared by both the government and military representatives in Paris, and by Hemmen."[34] Hemmen, acting out his role in accordance with I.G.'s scheme, informed the French armistice delegation that these negotiations would have to await the final settlement of the demarcation line beween occupied and unoccupied France.[35]

As I.G. planned, the French chemical situation continued to deteriorate. In early October Frossard sought out Hans Kramer, head of the I.G. sales agency in France. With Bosch dead, Frossard had been unable to make effective contact with I.G. Frossard beseeched Kramer to arrange a meeting between himself and a member of the I.G. hierarchy. The situation of the French chemical industry, he said, made collaboration at an early date imperative. It was absolutely clear to him that Germany would win the war and that the organization of the European economy must come under German leadership. Frossard offered the support of the entire French chemical industry in Germany's war against England.[36] In his view the end was a foregone conclusion. England was doomed.

Frossard added that he regretted the actions taken against the German chemical industry before the 1927 cartel agreement was signed, explaining that these were measures forced by French government pressure. (He was referring to Kuhlmann's efforts to keep I.G. from taking over the French dyestuff industry in 1926.) Now Frossard suggested a secret collaboration with the French industry under I.G. leadership—a clandestine "marriage" in the dyestuff and chemical fields.[37]

Frantically, Frossard pleaded with Kramer to find out whether I.G. would enter negotiations. I.G. could depend on him for anything it wished. If I.G. objected to any Kuhlmann executive, he would be dismissed.[38]

All Frossard needed was a sign and he would become a trump card ready to be played again.

In the meantime, political events of great moment were taking place. On October 24, Hitler and Pétain met at Montoire, where French collaboration with Germany was settled. According to their secret agreement, "The Axis Powers and France have an identical interest in seeing the defeat of England accomplished as soon as possible. Consequently, the French government will support, within the limits of its ability, the measures which the Axis Powers may take to this end."[39] In return, France was to be given the place in new Europe "to which she is entitled."[40]

The "collaboration" principle now was presumably to be extended to the entire private economic sphere. Hitler and Pétain agreed in essence to what Frossard had privately urged for I.G. and the French industry two weeks earlier. The German government should not confiscate French industries but rather permit German and French companies to deal with each other on a private, voluntary basis. The change in direction was welcomed by I.G. It would be free to act without entering a partnership with the Reich in the exploitation of French industry. Since I.G.'s partners would now be private French firms, it could truly assert its claim to leadership and demand a controlling ownership in the French dyestuff industry.[41]

I.G. was now ready to "negotiate" with the French. Within a week after the Montoire agreement was reached, Hemmen, with I.G.'s consent, informed the French armistice delegation that the time had come for the conference sought by the French chemical industry. In anticipation, I.G. engaged in preliminary meetings in Paris with Frossard and René Duchemin, both of whom were becoming openly known collaborationists. According to an I.G. file note on these conferences, "the situation had already been prepared and clarified to the greatest extent in line with German ideas."[42] The French dyestuff companies would be merged into a company to be called Francolor, in which I.G. would own fifty-one percent and the French forty-nine percent. Francolor would be confined to the French market and prohibited from exporting to the rest of Europe.[43]

With all the basic questions apparently agreed upon privately, it was time for official negotiations to begin. Schnitzler decided that the meeting should take place at Wiesbaden under the direct aegis of the armistice commission because "it is quite obvious that our tactical position towards the French will be far stronger if the first fundamental discussion takes place in Germany and, more particularly, at the site of the Armistice Delegation; and if our program as outlined, is presented, so to speak, from official quarters."[44]

As planned, the meeting was held at Wiesbaden on November 21, 1940. Schnitzler and ter Meer led the I.G. delegation; Duchemin represented the French. Frossard was missing; his French colleagues were informed that he was home sick in bed.[45]

Schnitzler miscalculated. Matters did not run as smoothly as the preliminary meetings in Paris with Frossard and Duchemin had promised. An I.G. official noted, "The transfer to Wiesbaden gave the French cause an opportunity for a 'change of tactics' and necessarily encouraged the hope in them of achieving something better in 'official surroundings' than what had been prepared unofficially, so to speak, in Paris."[46]

The French delegation proposed that the parties revive the Franco-German dyestuff cartel of 1927. French legal experts, they said, had advised them that the cartel agreement had not been abrogated by the outbreak of war in 1939 but was merely in temporary abeyance. With peace restored, the agreement could be put back in force. The industrialists, they pointed out, should follow the direction of the collaboration agreed to by Pétain and Hitler at Montoire. After all, they were now allies and collaborators, not victor and vanquished.[47]

The French were stunned by the German response to their proposal. Hemmen interrupted the French with a violent tirade. Pounding the table, he shouted that it was an insult to insist that the 1927 cartel agreement still was valid after the German victory in 1940: the cartel was merely the product of the Versailles treaty.

131

Hemmen forbade any discussion of such an amazing proposal. The French must come to their senses and recognize that they had lost the war and that the time had come to accept the leadership of I.G. in the chemical field. Hemmen left no doubt in the minds of the Frenchmen that I.G.'s demands were fully backed by the Reich.[48]

Schnitzler then spoke in a modulated voice but in equally hard terms. The French suggestions, he said, ignored political and economic realities. After all, France had declared war on Germany and now French industry would have to pay the price of defeat and accept I.G.'s leadership. It was, in truth, a relationship of victor and vanquished.[49]

One of the French representatives mustered the courage to ask a final question. Exactly what did I.G. "leadership" mean? Schnitzler did not equivocate. Leadership meant that I.G. would have unrestrained financial, industrial, and ownership control of the French chemical industry.[50]

Hemmen concluded the session with the announcement that the French and I.G. representatives would meet the next day without the armistice officials to work out the details of their agreement. It was the German ambassador's wish that the parties come to an agreement that would serve as a model for all German-French industrial relations.[51]

That evening Schnitzler wrote to Hermann Schmitz.

We have just returned from the first conference with the French dyestuff industrialists in Wiesbaden. Thanks to the very methodical and energetic chairmanship of Minister Hemmen, we were able to get down to business at once and shall now hear tomorrow morning what the French dyestuff industry . . . thinks of our "claim to leadership."[52]

At the scheduled meeting the next day Schnitzler pressed I.G.'s ultimatum. I.G. was to own fifty-one percent of a new Franco-German dyestuff company; the French were to abandon the export market and accept I.G.'s control of all elements of production and sales.[53] The French vigorously protested. I.G.'s terms were too severe. However, they realized that the entire French chemical industry could cease to exist at the whim of German authorities under I.G. influence. The hard attitude of Hemmen and Schnitzler underscored the reality of this alternative.[54] The French, hoping to salvage what they could, stalled, saying they would have to go home and get the advice of their government.

In Paris a few days later, Kramer again met with Frossard, who "talked fairly openly about the whole problem of the agreement."[55] Frossard assured Kramer that he himself had "the deepest understanding" of I.G.'s position. As Kramer later reported to I.G., "Not only did he think to a certain extent along German lines because of his origin and education, but he was now facing the fact that Germany had won the war. It was true that not all of his colleagues thought as he did."[56] Apparently Frossard was ready to come to an agreement. The French hesitated to accept a joint manufacturing company under I.G. control, he said, since it would mean officially abandoning the character of a "national" dyestuff industry headed by a Frenchman. Frossard suggested that an exclusive *sales* company jointly owned but under I.G. control would accomplish the same thing and still preserve French pride.

As soon as the French industrialists returned to Paris from the Wiesbaden conference, they took up I.G.'s proposals with the French government. It was agreed that many obvious difficulties would attend the German takeover of the French dyestuff industry. Plants indispensable to French national defense would be in the hands of the Germans. Moreover, a dangerous precedent would be established, and the Germans could then demand control of other French industries.[57]

The French industry representatives realized that care must be taken, however, to avoid too brusque a rejection of I.G. demands. They feared that if the negotiations were broken off, I.G. would see to it that their plants, already in a precarious state, would be com-

133

pelled to close down permanently for lack of raw materials, coal, and power. Nevertheless, despite these anxieties in December the French government emphatically rejected the German demand for a controlling, fifty-one percent interest.[58]

The French industrialists then prepared a counterproposal. They returned to the suggestion of a joint "marketing organization" or sales agent rather than a joint manufacturing company. Only forty-nine percent of the stock would be assigned to the Germans, a majority interest of fifty-one percent to the French. A president would be selected who would be agreeable to both the French and the Germans. Each group would have the right to select an equal number of directors. With French government approval, it was agreed that the new plan be submitted to I.G.[59]

Duchemin met with Kramer and others at the headquarters of the German occupation forces. He tentatively presented the French counterproposal. The Germans stated that it was absolutely unacceptable.[60] Duchemin, with a surprising show of backbone, replied that so long as negotiations between the German and French industries continued on a free, voluntary basis, the French would never consent to a fifty-one percent participation by the Germans: "I would rather see my hand cut off than sign such an agreement."[61]

Under these circumstances, Kramer said, there was no point to further negotiations. He pointed out, however that breaking off negotiations could have "detrimental" consequences. Then, changing his tune, Kramer introduced a new element into the discussion. He would use the carrot rather than the stick. Would the French industrialists change their mind if I.G. offered some sort of compensation? Duchemin was intrigued. In that case, he replied, the transaction might be more bearable.[62] For the moment the kind or the amount of the compensation was not specified.

Kramer hardened his appearance of reasonableness with the warning that Duchemin and his associates avoid any instructions from the French government restricting their freedom to act. This would keep the negotiations within the area of "private enterprise." Otherwise, he added sternly, the matter would go back to the armistice commission and the "mercies" of Ambassador Hemmen.[63]

Negotiations were resumed on January 20 in Paris. Despite Kramer's warnings to Duchemin, the French once again pressed their counterproposal of a joint sales company in which the French would hold a majority interest. They claimed that they would make no further concessions.[64] I.G. continued to demand that only a majority interest would be acceptable. At this point, the I.G. representatives officially offered their "carrot" hinted at by Kramer to Duchemin. I.G. would turn over to the French industrialists one percent of I.G.'s stock.[65]

I.G.'s "generosity," however, was coupled with a very meaningful threat. Duchemin was told that if he was not willing to accept the I.G. plan, Kuhlmann would be classified as a Jewish concern and all of its plants would be confiscated by the Germans. The fact that Raymond Berr, a Jew, had been a managing director of the Kuhlmann plants before the German occupation was sufficient to have it so classified.[66] In the face of pressures that were becoming progressively uglier and more intense, the resistance of the French industrialists began to crumble. They reluctantly agreed in principle to I.G.'s demand for a joint manufacturing company, still protesting, however, I.G.'s demand for a majority of the stock. They declared that the French government would have to approve that concession.[67]

All protestations were in vain, however. At a "peace conference" on March 12, it was officially revealed that a new company, Francolor, was to be formed for which I.G. would compensate the French with one percent of its stock; in return, I.G. would receive a controlling interest of fifty-one percent in Francolor. To reassure the French government that this agreement would not become an example to pave the way for German takeovers of other French industries, it was agreed that the Francolor case was to be regarded as a special circum-

135

stance and not as a precedent for future German action.[68]

Both I.G. and the French shareholders would have the right to nominate an equal number of administrative officials. And, in what on its face appeared to be a major concession, I.G. agreed that the president of Francolor would always be a Frenchman.[69]

By May, however, the Germans began to realize that French capitulation would not be quite as easy as they had been led to believe. The French were complicating their surrender with a number of counterproposals. Kramer complained to Schnitzler, "The French are going back on practically all matters which are essential for us. . . . Thus, in our next meeting, we will have to tackle anew these problems." Duchemin himself admitted to Kramer that the French were stiffening their position.[70]

Once again Kramer sought out Frossard. At their meeting Frossard explained apologetically that the various countersuggestions from his French colleagues did not represent his views. He went on to describe the difficulty of his position. Less flexible elements in the French chemical industry, particularly within Kuhlmann, Frossard said, had "gained momentum." From what Frossard told Kramer, the resistance of the French chemical industry was going to be somewhat more formidable than the March 12 understanding indicated.[71]

Despite the fact that I.G. could exercise an ultimate power to break French intransigence, the negotiations dragged on. Nevertheless, Frossard assured I.G. that as far as he was concerned, the establishment of Francolor was a reality and that he would not engage in any important transactions without the approval of I.G.[72]

To prove his devotion, Frossard now involved himself in the Aryanization of the French plants as Duchemin himself temporarily assumed the duties of Raymond Berr, the highest ranking Jewish victim.[73] Even in this performance Frossard remained an ambiguous figure. He made a real effort to prevent "miscarriages of justice" caused by faulty or mistaken information as to who was Jewish. In at least two cases Frossard made strong protests to the Nazis on behalf of two Kuhlmann employees accused of being Jews. One was Serge de Kap-Herr, whose son had married the daughter of the French writer André Maurois (whose name, Frossard volunteered, was really Herzog).[74] Frossard insisted that Kap-Herr was Aryan. The Germans were convinced, and Kap-Herr was not dismissed from his job. The other case involved Frossard's long-time associate and close personal friend M. Rhein. Like Frossard, Rhein was born in Alsace when it was part of Germany. Unlike Frossard, he had remained in Germany as a chemist for BASF before and during World War I. After the war, as an Alsatian, he chose to become a French citizen and joined Frossard in the government-owned Compagnie Nationale Française. Rhein had been with the French dyestuff industry ever since.

Frossard told I.G. that Rhein's father was not a Jew, as had been charged, but a Christian clergyman from Hamburg and he insisted that Rhein had "no Jewish blood at all in his veins and is in no way affected by the laws concerning Jews."[75] Frossard's efforts were fruitless, however, and Rhein was dismissed.[76]

By mid-summer of 1941, the resistance of the French dyestuff men was broken and most of the details of a final agreement were worked out. I.G. was to assume majority control of the dyestuff plants in France and of all the French company's foreign properties that were in German-occupied territory.[77] This included the French interest in Winnica, the Polish dyestuff plant, which Frossard headed as chairman of the board. Although I.G. agreed to surrender one percent of its stock to the French, even this concession carried a severe condition. The stock was so restricted that it could not be sold to any buyer outside the French dyestuff group and could never be pledged as collateral.[78]

One last problem remained to be resolved. I.G. objected to the French version of the preamble to the Francolor agreement because it emphasized "the fact that the French Government surrendered participation

in the French dyestuff industry . . . under pressure."[79]
In the unlikely event that Germany failed to win the
war, I.G. was concerned that "the preamble as it now
stands might . . . prove of great disadvantage to us."[80]
It could provide the basis for the French to "annul the
convention" when a "change in conditions" arose.[81] To
avoid the possibility that the French might "demand
the termination of the convention" sometime in the
future on the ground of duress, the I.G. lawyer insisted
upon wording that indicated consent by the French
government. The preamble as finally agreed upon satisfied I.G. It included the sentence: "The French Government is to recognize the legality . . . of the present
contract, which may be contrary to present or future
laws of France."[82]

During one of the last conferences at which the details of the agreement were being worked out, ter Meer
unconsciously expressed the atmosphere of the negotiations. On a folder titled "France, 1940–41: German-
French Dyestuff Discussion," he doodled a line from a
ditty popular in Germany, "For in the woods there are
robbers."[83]

On November 18, 1941, one year after the Wiesbaden conference, the Francolor agreement was signed
in Paris by Schnitzler and ter Meer for I.G. and by
Duchemin, Thesmar, and Frossard for the French dyestuff industry.[84] Frossard was elected president of Francolor by agreement of both contracting parties. This
was expected. Schnitzler had already proclaimed earlier: "Of course, there cannot be any doubt that Frossard would be president."[85]

As agreed, too, the supervisory board of Francolor
was equally divided between French and Germans:
Schnitzler, ter Meer, Ambros, and Hermann Waibel
from I.G.; Frossard, Duchemin, and two other Pétain
collaborators from the French industry.[86]

The signing of the agreement was celebrated at a
luncheon for about a dozen or so key participants, both
French and German. Ter Meer, who was present, reported that

Frossard got up and made a speech which, in my opinion, exceeded the form of mere politeness, for he was visibly touched and strongly impressed personally. He said then that he wanted to express his personal gratitude for the fine confidence and trust that was placed in him by appointing him president of the new firm.[87]

In Frossard's opinion, the Francolor contract could be called ideal.

The annual meeting of Etablissements Kuhlmann, at which the agreement was to be ratified, took place in Vichy. When a stockholder rose to protest the surrender of the fifty-one percent stock interest in Francolor to I.G., it was explained to him that the transfer of a majority interest to the Germans was counterbalanced by the selection of a Frenchman, Frossard, as president.[88] The stockholders thereupon voted to approve the agreement, although a surprising 50 stockholders voted nay and another 406 abstained from voting.[89] The new order for the French chemical industry now had legal sanction.

I.G. was at the zenith of its power. From the Barents Sea to the Mediterranean, from the Channel Islands to Auschwitz, it exercised control over an industrial empire the likes of which the world had never before seen.

Frossard, the "trump card" played by Bosch with such success at Versailles, continued his special role for Krauch and I.G. In the summer of 1942, with Hitler's dreaded two-front war depleting the German labor supply, Nazi eyes turned to the conquered countries of Europe. In his post as plenipotentiary, Krauch tried to recruit foreign labor in France. At first this effort was a miserable failure. Of the expected 350,000 French workers, only 36,000 were sent to Germany.[90] To correct matters, Krauch called upon his successful experience in rebuilding the Oppau plant after the explosion of 1921. At that time, it will be recalled, he prevailed upon companies all over Germany to send complete units of workers to help reconstruct the destroyed plant.

In a letter to Schnitzler, Krauch, wearing the hats of both an I.G. official and a Nazi plenipotentiary, noted that the decision to invoke the "closed unit" system would increase the supply of workers from French factories for German industry.[91] He explained that the French workers "would remain employees of the French mother company and return to France after their work [was] completed."[92] He was delighted that Frossard approved the new approach.

> Out of the negotiations which took place up to now I have learned that Mr. Frossard is entirely of the opinion . . . that the use of closed units is the right way to bring . . . French workmen [into] the German works on a broad basis. Mr. Frossard has, therefore, used his own initiative for the conclusion of the first unit work contract with the I.G. Ludwigshafen. I hope therefore that further workmen of Francolor will be sent to Germany.[93]

Schnitzler replied that Frossard could be relied upon to help fulfill Germany's need for labor: "You can be convinced that General Director Frossard handles the question of sending workmen in closed units to works of the I.G. with just as much understanding as goodwill."[94]

The French workers soon learned that "closed units" was a euphemism for forced labor. In a nasty bit of gallows humor, an I.G. official referred contemptuously to those Frenchmen with whom the company dealt in the recruiting of such labor battalions as "slave traders."[95] The crime of slave labor was now being committed with greater refinement and efficiency and in far greater numbers than it had been during World War I. But that was only the beginning. This practice was soon to reach proportions that the world could neither believe nor comprehend.

6

Slave Labor
and
Mass Murder

In August 1942 the office of the World Jewish Congress in Lausanne, Switzerland, received the first report that the Third Reich had embarked on a course that could only be described as insane. A German industrialist reported, at the risk of his life, that for the past eight months the German government had been "solving the Jewish problem" by an organized scheme of mass murder. Its goal was to exterminate the entire Jewish people. Killing centers had been erected in Poland, he said, where hundreds of thousands of Jews had been asphyxiated by a lethal gas in sealed chambers designed for the singular purpose of killing them.

In the following months, increasing evidence began to surface of Germany's extraordinary program to destroy the Jews. At the end of August 1943, an Allied report of Axis war crimes was released to the public. The report accused Germany and its satellites of "carrying out with increasing tempo a deliberate program of wholesale theft, murder, torture and savagery unparalleled in world history."[1] It charged that Germany had deliberately exterminated 1,702,500 human beings. Incredible as the figure appeared at the time, it was a gross understatement.

German war crimes soon became a matter of major concern to the Allied leaders. On November 1, 1943, Roosevelt, Churchill, and Stalin, at their Moscow summit meeting, jointly drafted "The Declaration of German Atrocities."[2] The Germans were put on notice that they would be held responsible for their crimes, tried in appropriate courts, and punished.

The Moscow declaration was delivered to the German people, their satellites, and the occupied countries by all means available—continuous radio broadcasts, leaflets dropped by planes, and underground newspapers. The warning was unequivocal and blunt.

At the time of the granting of any armistice to any government which may be set up in Germany, those German officers and men and members of the Nazi party who have been responsible for, or have taken a consenting part in . . . atrocities, massacres, and executions, will be sent back to the countries in which their abominable deeds were done in order that they may be judged and punished according to the laws of these liberated countries and of the free governments which will be created therein. Lists will be compiled in all possible detail from all these countries having regard especially to the invaded parts of the Soviet Union, to Poland and Czechoslovakia, to Yugoslavia and Greece, including Crete and other islands, to Norway, Denmark, the Netherlands, Belgium, Luxembourg, France and Italy.[3]

The Moscow declaration proved no deterrent at all; in fact, the pace of the Reich's program of extermination accelerated.

On March 24, 1944, therefore, President Roosevelt issued his own warning to the German nation:

In one of the blackest crimes in all history—begun by the Nazis in the day of peace and multiplied by them a hundred times in time of war—the wholesale systematic murder of the Jews of Europe goes on unabated every hour. . . . It is therefore fitting that we should again proclaim our determination that none who participate in these acts of savagery shall go unpunished. . . . All who share the guilt shall share the punishment.[4]

By November 1944, millions had been killed in Hitler's deliberate destruction of the Jews. John Pehle, executive director of the War Refugee Board, decided to make public the reports of two prisoners who had escaped from Auschwitz, the largest of all the killing complexes. Pehle released these reports to the newspapers, vouching for the reliability of the information. The reports described in great detail the organization of Auschwitz, the concentration camps, the terrible conditions under which the inmates lived and died, the brutality of the German authorities, the immense gassing buildings in which victims were asphyxiated by the thousands every day, the crematoria where their bodies were disposed of—almost all the terrible facts of the Nazi program of extermination.[5]

Elmer Davis, head of the Office of War Information, demanded that Pehle recall the reports, which had not yet been published because of a ten-day "hold." Davis argued that publicizing these reports would be counterproductive. The American public, he said, would not believe them but would regard them as mere atrocity stories like those circulated during World War I.

Pehle had great regard for Davis and appreciated his opinion; yet, he believed that the desperate situation demanded that these reports be made known to the public. Convinced that only by exposure was there any hope of saving the remaining Jews of Europe, Pehle refused to withdraw the reports, and the public learned of the gruesome details of Auschwitz for the first time.

Among the extraordinary facts disclosed by the reports was the existence at Auschwitz of an enormous industrial establishment owned and operated by I.G. Farben. The men who had written the reports had been inmate workers in the Buna division of this installation, and the details they supplied showed how far I.G.'s compact with Hitler had progressed.

We worked in the huge Buna plant, to which we were herded every morning about 3 A.M. At midday our food consisted of potato or turnip soup and in the evening we received some bread. During work we were terribly mistreated. As our working place was situated outside the large chain of sentry posts, it was divided into small sectors of 10×10 meters, each guarded by an SS man. Whoever stepped outside these squares during working hours was immediately shot without warning for having "attempted to escape." Often it happened that out of pure spite an SS man would order a prisoner to fetch some given object outside his square. If he followed the order, he was shot for having left his assigned place. The work was extremely hard and there were no rest periods. The way to and from work had to be covered at a brisk military trot; anyone falling out of line was shot. On my arrival about 3,000 people, of whom 2,000 were Slovak Jews, were working on this emplacement. Very few could bear the strain and although escape seemed hopeless, attempts were made every day. The result was several hangings a week.[8]

In the American business community, especially in companies that had had prewar dealings with I.G., these disclosures met with disbelief. Nevertheless, the reports of I.G.'s involvement were only too true. I.G. was building enormous synthetic oil and rubber factories at Auschwitz.

Pehle, who as chairman of the War Refugee Board was responsible for saving tens of thousands of Jewish lives, was the first official anywhere to urge consideration of the bombing of the industrial installations and mass extermination equipment at Auschwitz. He wrote to the U.S. War Department in this regard. In reply, the War Department explained that a bombing attack against Auschwitz was an unwarranted diversion of planes needed elsewhere. Pehle replied that Auschwitz was an important producer of war matériel. The War Department still refused.

By embarking on the Battle of Britain in the late summer of 1940, twenty-six years almost to the month after the decisive Battle of the Marne, Germany miscalculated again. Despite assurances from Hermann Goering that the Luftwaffe would break the English will to resist within weeks, if not days, Britain refused to be subdued. The British Isles remained as an "unsinkable aircraft carrier" aimed at the heart of Germany.

Hitler, ignoring Germany's tragic experience with a two-front war, refused to let the British setback change his timetable of conquest. His plans to attack his ally, the Soviet Union, remained fixed. Certain of the invincibility of his military power and the inviolability of his military judgment, he ordered his generals to prepare for an early attack. Hitler's generals were not so sanguine. Once again the problem was the shortage of raw materials. They informed Hitler that the battles of Poland, France, and Britain had seriously exhausted the supply of munitions and such basic raw materials as oil and rubber. Any attack against the Soviets would be imprudent until additional facilities to produce synthetic rubber and oil were built and the reserves replenished. The size of such a conflict would demand amounts never even contemplated before. A reluctant Hitler agreed to wait but ordered that the attack on Russia begin in the spring.

With Hitler's personal views on military raw material autarky acting as a goad, the war planners began at once to prepare for the construction of the necessary synthetic rubber facilities to fulfill the enormous requirements projected for the Soviet invasion. The Ministry of Economics immediately summoned Fritz ter Meer and Otto Ambros to a top secret, high priority conference. At the meeting, the I.G. officials were informed that there must be "an increase in Buna production with the greatest possible speed."[7] To reach the projected production demanded by the ministry required the construction of two new plants. These installations, when added to the existing plants at Huels and Schkopau, would bring the Buna capacity of I.G. to a healthy

150,000 tons annually, enough to mount the Russian invasion.

The I.G. officials were assured that the German government was prepared to support the expansion in every way. They were given further assurances that the irritations of the past with the army would be eliminated. This was underscored by the High Command's promise of "all suitable assistance."[8] Speed was crucial and Krauch, acting in his government role of plenipotentiary general for special questions of chemical production, ordered the immediate construction of one of the new plants, which was to operate in conjunction with the existing I.G. high-pressure plants at Ludwigshafen. Construction of the second plant, he noted, would begin as soon as a suitable site was chosen. At the moment, Krauch was considering Norway and Polish Silesia.

Krauch assigned Ambros, one of I.G.'s most talented Buna chemists, to survey Silesia. Ambros had joined I.G. in 1926, at which time he was sent to Sumatra for a year to study the chemistry of natural rubber. By 1935 he was I.G.'s leading synthetic rubber expert. Ambros's expertise was formally recognized by Bosch, who placed him in charge of the construction and operation of the first large-scale Buna plant at Schkopau.

Ambros was an unusual figure. He was the I.G. expert on both Buna and poison gas. Moreover, in 1932 he had conceived the underlying theories which ultimately led to the modern magnetic tape technology. In view of Ambros's later fate it is worth noting that he was a protégé of Nobel laureate Richard Willstaetter, under whom he wrote his Ph.D. thesis. Even after Willstaetter was driven out of Germany to become a stateless Jew, Ambros continued to correspond with him.

In evaluating the Polish Silesian area Ambros made a personal and detailed exploration of the proposed sites. The one he finally recommended was particularly suited for the installation. A coal mine was nearby and three rivers converged to provide a vital requirement, a large source of water. Together with these three rivers, the Reich railroad and the autobahn afforded excellent transportation to and from the area. These were not decisive advantages, however, over the Norwegian site. But the Silesian location had one advantage that was overwhelming: the S.S. had plans to expand enormously a concentration camp nearby. The promise of an inexhaustible supply of slave labor was an attraction that could not be resisted.[9]

Krauch wholeheartedly accepted Silesia over Norway, where the population was already in ferment over the brutality of the German occupation. The historic nature of Krauch's choice could never have crossed his mind. *The name of the Polish village he selected for the Buna site was Auschwitz!*[10]

Once the project and site were formally approved by the Reich, the I.G. management, enthusiastic about expanding its operations, assigned the name "I.G. Auschwitz" to the new division, hereafter the official designation in I.G.'s meticulously ordered table of corporate organization.

Technologically and economically it was only natural that a synthetic oil plant be built as a companion to the rubber factory. For Bergius and Buna, high pressure chemistry was the common ground. Accordingly, a large hydrogenation plant to convert coal into oil with a capacity of 778,000 tons a month was also begun.

The I.G. directors selected Ambros for the rubber installation and Heinrich Buetefisch for the gasoline plant at Auschwitz. For the two youngest members of the managing board of directors, both still under forty, these appointments represented an important step upward in the I.G. hierarchy. After all, it gave Ambros and Buetefisch authority over the largest synthetic rubber and oil installation in the world. With Hitler and I.G. marching together, the future appeared to be without limit.

It was at this point that I.G. made another crucial, even fateful decision. With the U.S.S.R. about to be attacked, I.G. began to contemplate the enormous opportunities for expansion to the east. The possible rewards appeared boundless. Everything about the Auschwitz project indicated that it was heaven-sent.

147

The Soviet Union and Asia represented a potential market to challenge even the commercial imagination of I.G.'s directors. For I.G., Hitler's "Drive to the East" promised to open a vast new area for profitable exploitation. Indeed, so great did I.G. regard the post-war potential of the Auschwitz project that it decided to make an unusual gamble on its future. Rather than let the German government finance the building of the installations, the I.G. directors voted to put up the funds to make I.G. Auschwitz a privately owned I.G. enterprise and to assume the entire risk. With almost no opposition, they committed more than 900 million Reichsmarks, over $250 million,[11] to the building of the single largest project in the I.G. system. With such an enormous risk, officials of I.G. carefully watched over their huge investment.

There were other factors supporting the risk and indicating the prudence of such an investment. The I.G. Auschwitz projects were so vital to Germany's military plans that I.G. was able to marshal the aid of the most powerful figures in the Nazi government. Krauch, in a top secret letter to Ambros, wrote:

> In the new arrangement of priority stages ordered by Field Marshal Keitel, your building project has first priority. . . . At my request, [Goering] issued special decrees a few days ago to the supreme Reich authorities concerned. . . . In these decrees, the Reich Marshal obligated the offices concerned to meet your requirements in skilled workers and laborers at once, even at the expense of other important building projects or plans which are essential to the war economy.[12]

Krauch was already taking steps to insure an adequate labor supply for the construction of the I.G. Auschwitz plants. He had arranged for Goering to write Himmler on February 18, 1941, asking that "the largest possible number of skilled and unskilled construction workers . . . be made available from the adjoining concentration camp for the construction of

148

the Buna plant."[13] Between 8000 and 12,000 construction and assembly workers were needed. Goering requested Himmler to inform him and Krauch "as soon as possible about the orders which you will issue in this matter."[14] Acting on this request, Himmler ordered the S.S. inspector of concentration camps and the S.S. economic and administrative main office "to get in touch immediately with the construction manager of the Buna works and to aid the . . . project by means of the concentration camp prisoners in every possible way."[15] After Himmler issued this decree, Krauch wrote to Ambros, "These orders are so far-reaching that I request you to apply them to the widest extent as soon as possible."[16]

So that there would be no misunderstanding of the urgent priority of the I.G. Auschwitz project, Himmler delegated S.S. Major General Karl Wolff, chief of his personal staff, to be liaison officer between the S.S. and I.G.[17] On March 20, General Wolff met with Buetefisch to discuss "the details of the ways and means in which the concentration camp could assist in the construction of the plant."[18] Buetefisch was chosen to deal with General Wolff not only because of his eminence as a synthetic fuel authority but also because of his rank as a lieutenant colonel in the S.S. At the meeting it was agreed that I.G. would pay the S.S. three Reichsmarks a day for each unskilled concentration camp inmate and four Reichsmarks for skilled inmates.[19] Later, the S.S. agreed to furnish children at one and a half Reichsmarks.[20] These payments were for the S.S.; the inmates, of course, received nothing. Wolff guaranteed that the payment would include "everything such as transportation, food, et cetera and [I.G.] will have no other expenses for the inmates, except if a small bonus (cigarettes, etc.) is given as an incentive."[21] Both parties realized, in calculating the rate of payment, that a concentration camp inmate could not be as productive as a free, normal, well-fed German worker; thus, it was estimated at the meeting that a seventy-five percent efficiency was all that could be expected.[22]

A week after this preliminary conference, a meeting

was held at Auschwitz among various I.G. technical men, including Duerrfeld, chief engineer in charge of construction at I.G. Auschwitz, his senior engineer, Max Faust, and the Auschwitz concentration camp commandant, S.S. Major Rudolf Hoess.[23] Duerrfeld, in his summary of the conference, assured his superiors, Ambros and Buetefisch, that "the concentration camp showed its willingness to assist in the construction of the plant as far as it could."[24] One big problem, however, troubled him. This, he reported, was the procurement of Capos, "straw bosses" with "special talents" recruited from among concentration camp inmates. However, Commandant Hoess told Duerrfeld that I.G. would have a priority in obtaining those inmate-leaders whose special talent was sadism. "These Capos," reported Duerrfeld, "are being selected from amongst the professional criminals and are to be transferred from other concentration camps to Auschwitz."[25] Every twenty inmates, it was estimated, would require a Capo.

A few weeks later Himmler himself, on an inspection tour of I.G. Auschwitz, gave assurances of his personal support to I.G.'s project. He guaranteed I.G. an immediate labor supply of 10,000 concentration camp inmates.[26] Ambros wrote ter Meer, "Our new friendship with the S.S. is proving very profitable."[27]

Soon that tune changed. With the personal blessing of such Nazi luminaries as Hitler, Himmler, Goering, and Keitel, I.G. Auschwitz should have been a tremendous success. Despite the cooperation of the Nazi hierarchy, especially the S.S., however, the project continually was disrupted by shortages, breakdowns, and delays. As the difficulties began to pile up fears began to mount correspondingly that the rubber and gasoline works would never be completed in time to help the German war effort. Some malign influence seemed to be affecting the entire operation.

The I.G. executives on the spot laid most of the blame on the S.S. According to them, the leaders of the S.S. at Auschwitz did not seem to understand "the working methods of . . . free enterprise."[28] Their treatment of the concentration camp inmates, by far the largest segment of I.G. Auschwitz labor, was proving counterproductive. These complaints were detailed in the weekly I.G. Auschwitz reports sent back to I.G. headquarters in Frankfurt. The report of August 3–9, for instance, include the following doleful note:

> We have ... drawn the attention of the officials of the concentration camp to the fact that in the last few weeks the inmates are being severely flogged on the construction site by the Capos in increasing measure, and this always applies to the weakest inmates who really cannot work harder. The exceedingly unpleasant scenes that occur on the construction site because of this are beginning to have a demoralizing effect on the free workers [Poles], as well as on the Germans. We have therefore asked that they should refrain from carrying out this flogging on the construction site and transfer it to ... the concentration camp.[29]

A few months later the I.G. Auschwitz weekly report began exhibiting greater appreciation of the difficult problems faced by the S.S.

> The work, particularly of the Poles and inmates, continues to leave much room for improvement. ... Our experience so far has shown that only brute force has any effect on these people. ... As is known, the Commandant always argues that as far as the treatment of inmates is concerned, it is impossible to get any work done without corporal punishment.[30]

The delays and construction problems continued and the report ended on a note of concern for the economic consequences confronting the I.G. management. The combination of all the difficulties encountered "will increase costs considerably."[31]

A greater appreciation of S.S. methods, however, did not solve I.G.'s problems. At an I.G. Auschwitz construction conference attended by technical personnel including Ambros, Duerrfeld, and Faust, a variety of troubles were reviewed.[32] Among the problems were bottlenecks in housing, transportation, fuel, and plumbing facilities and late deliveries of all kinds of necessary supplies. The overburdened railroad station and the shortage of motor vehicles added to the delays. Faust reported that the free Poles were only half as efficient as German workers and concentration camp inmates were not even a third as efficient.

Life at Auschwitz was not all beatings, shortages, inefficiencies, and other problems. The weekly reports at the close of 1941, for example, ended on a happier note: "On December 20 representatives of the I.G. took part in a Christmas party of the Waffen S.S. which was very festive and which ended up alcoholically gay."[33] Moreover, although the failures of the Auschwitz project kept mounting, cordial relations between the I.G. management and the S.S. officials were not affected. Duerrfeld and the commandant went on hunting parties together and, with their wives, frequently exchanged visits. The difficulties in building the rubber and oil facilities continued, however, and the progress at the Buna works fell further behind schedule. I.G. viewed the performance of the first year at Auschwitz as far from satisfactory—in fact, as nearly disastrous.

Inmate labor proved the most vexing problem in the construction of the I.G. Auschwitz installation. The labor details were marched more than four miles from the main Auschwitz camp to the I.G. construction site through the extreme summer heat and winter cold. The lack of guards caused security problems. The result was that "the inmates can only march out in daylight and must return to the camp in daylight. If it is foggy in the morning, the inmates are also not permitted to leave the camp."[34]

Sickness, malnutrition, the work tempo, and sadistic S.S. guards and Capos also took their toll. It was an unsettling sight for I.G. officials to witness work details carrying their dead back and forth so that all inmates could be accounted for at roll call when the work day began and when it ended. It was a strange way to run a business.

I.G. Auschwitz was approaching a financial and technical crisis. With the investment of almost a billion Reichsmarks in jeopardy, the I.G. managing board of directors decided on a drastic solution. It made a further and dramatic descent into the Nazi hell. In July 1942, just after Hitler had begun his second year of troubles in the Soviet Union, the I.G. managing board voted to solve its Auschwitz labor problems by establishing its own concentration camp. The initial appropriation was five million Reichsmarks,[35] a modest amount to protect its investment of almost a billion Reichsmarks. For a private company to set up its own concentration camp to insure a supply of labor may have been an odd undertaking, but the problem called for imagination and audacity, especially since the size of the investment and the certain consequences of Hitler's wrath made abandonment of the project unrealistic. The managing board of directors, without any recorded opposition, felt that economically and politically I.G. had no other choice.

On the other hand, under the circumstances an I.G. concentration camp had obvious advantages to recommend it. Inmates would not be drained of their already limited energy by the long marches from the main concentration camp to the construction site. Security would improve and fewer of the scarce S.S. guards would be required. Discipline and punishment would be more effective, and I.G. would also have greater and more immediate control over the use of the inmates. Of no small consequence, costs would be reduced.

The site chosen for I.G.'s concentration camp was called Monowitz. In the operation of this unique facility I.G. was to be responsible for the housing, feeding, and health of the inmates; the S.S. was charged with the security, punishment and supply of inmates.

Monowitz was completed in the summer of 1942. Although it belonged to I.G., Monowitz had all the equipment of the typical Nazi concentration camp—watchtowers with searchlights, warning sirens, poised machine guns, armed guards, and trained police dogs.

The entire camp was encircled with electrically charged barbed wire. There was a "standing cell" in which the victim could neither stand upright, kneel, nor lie down.[86] There was also a gallows, often with a body or two hanging from it as a grim example to the rest of the inmates. Across the arched entrance was the Auschwitz motto, "Freedom through Work."

In the administration of Monowitz, I.G. adopted the principle enunciated by Fritz Saukel, plenipotentiary for labor allocation of the four-year plan: "All the inmates must be fed, sheltered and treated in such a way as to exploit them to the highest possible extent, at the lowest conceivable degree of expenditure."[87]

The complete Auschwitz installation was now comprised of four entities: Auschwitz I, the original and vast concentration camp with hundreds of thousands of inmates; Auschwitz II, the extermination center of gassing chambers and crematory ovens at Birkenau; Auschwitz III, the I.G. Buna and synthetic fuel works; and Auschwitz IV, I.G.'s own concentration camp at Monowitz.

When I.G. took its place in the industrial labor complex of Auschwitz and accepted Himmler's offer of concentration camp labor, it embarked on a road that led ultimately to participation in the most extraordinary crime in civilized history, what Winston Churchill called the crime for which there is no name, the "Final Solution of the Jewish Question."[88]

Even before the Final Solution became the official policy of the German Reich in January 1942, Heinrich Himmler had already started an S.S. program for killing Jews. When the German armies conquered Poland, Himmler organized special S.S. squads to begin the mass slaughter. The first extermination center was set up at Chelmno, Poland, in the fall of 1939.[89] Three mobile gas vans, using the carbon monoxide from their exhausts, became the first instruments of mass murder. Primitive and inefficient as this early extermination center was, it reached a killing rate of 1000 a day.[40] Soon the methods of mass destruction of Jews were refined and killing centers with permanent gas chambers, still using carbon monoxide, were opened. One of the most notorious was at Treblinka, near Warsaw, built in early 1941.

In June 1941, Himmler instructed Commandant Hoess to begin the extermination of the Jews at Auschwitz. Hoess visited Treblinka to study the use of carbon monoxide. Hoess then set up a similar installation at the Birkenau site in Auschwitz.[41] Very soon he realized that the carbon monoxide was not sufficiently lethal and was much too slow if Himmler's goals were to be achieved.[42]

Hoess cast around for a better way. What he found was to make him the most successful mass killer in modern history. In August 1941, using 500 Russian prisoners of war as an experimental group, Hoess introduced into the airtight chambers of Birkenau a new asphyxiating agent, Zyklon B.[43] Actually, Zyklon B, whose generic name is prussic acid, was new only in its application to human beings; its traditional, commercial use was as an insecticide. The result was a revelation of efficiency.

Only one firm, Deutsche Gesellschaft fuer Schaedlings-bekampfung (German Corporation for Pest Control), known in the trade as Degesch, supplied this lethal chemical. The firm and its most valuable asset, the monopoly of Zyklon B manufacture, was owned 42.5 percent by I.G. Farbenindustrie; 42.5 percent by Deutsche Gold und Silberscheidenanstalt—known as Degussa (in which I.G. owned a third); and 15 percent by the Theo. Goldschmidt concern.[44] That I.G. dominated Degesch was general knowledge in the chemical industry. In fact, in its official corporate pronouncements Degesch described itself as an exclusive selling agent for I.G. Moreover, I.G. dominated the Degesch supervisory board: of its eleven members five were from I.G., including the chairman, Wilhelm Mann.[45]

Five months after Hoess's introduction of Zyklon B, Himmler's personal program to exterminate the Jewish people was transformed into the official policy of the Third Reich. Its formal adoption under the title of the "Final Solution of the Jewish Question" took place in the Berlin suburb of Wannsee, at a meeting presided over by Reinhard Heydrich, chief of the security police and security service of the S.S., and attended by undersecretaries from the various Reich ministries and the top officials of the S.S.[46]

At the meeting, Heyrich unfolded the details for the complete annihilation of the Jewish people. Until this program was revealed at Wannsee, only Goering, Goebbels, Himmler, and Bormann knew of Hitler's ultimate plans for the Jews.[47] Now the civil service was enlisted, and the German bureaucracy became an active party in the execution of this plan. As the preparations began for the Final Solution, the purchases of Zyklon B by the S.S. increased tremendously.

In the past the S.S. had bought moderate amounts of Zyklon B from Degesch as a vermin control in its concentration camps. When the Final Solution added Jews to the S.S. extermination plans, Degesch profits reflected the new prosperity. I.G.'s dividends on its Degesch investment for the years 1942, 1943, and 1944 were double those of 1940 and 1941.[48]

At least one top official of Degesch, Gerhard Peters, the managing director, definitely knew about the new use of Zyklon B. He had been specifically informed of the details of the Final Solution by Kurt Gerstein, the chief disinfection officer of the S.S., who did the purchasing of Zyklon B.[49]

There was still another episode that gave the officials of Degesch more than a hint of the dread purpose to which their Zyklon B was being put by the S.S. When manufactured as a pesticide Zyklon B contained a special odor, or *indicator,* to warn human beings of its lethal presence. The inclusion of such a warning odor was required by German law. When the S.S. demanded that the new, large order of Zyklon B omit the *indicator,* no one familiar with the workings of the S.S. could have failed to realize the purpose behind the strange request. The Degesch executives at first were unwilling to comply. But compassion was not behind their refusal. What troubled them was the fact that the S.S. request endangered Degesch's monopoly position. The patent on Zyklon B had long since expired. However, Degesch retained its monopoly by a patent on the warning odor. To remove the *indicator* was bad business, opening up the possibility of unwelcome competition.[50] The S.S. made short shrift of this objection and the company removed the warning odor. Now the doomed would not even know it was Degesch's Zyklon B.

I.G.'s camp at Monowitz began operations in September 1942 stocked with inmates from Auschwitz who were to work on the construction of the I.G. rubber and fuel installations. Despite the availability of workers, I.G. was still faced with a labor problem. As Jews from all over Europe were brought into Auschwitz, S.S. physicians picked inmates strong enough to work at I.G. Auschwitz. People who were considered too weak for construction work were selected for the gassing stations and crematoria of Birkenau. "Selection" was the most dreaded word in a world of dread.

It soon became apparent that the "selections" were being made without sufficient regard for the urgent demands of war production. Too many skilled and reasonably strong workers were being rushed to the ovens although months of useful labor were still in them. For example, during the early months of Monowitz, those in charge of the construction of I.G. Auschwitz were promised a carefully chosen batch of workers culled from a shipment of over 5000 Jews. However, when the transports were unloaded near the crematory ovens, the camp officials, ignoring the labor needs of I.G. Auschwitz but with punctilious devotion to the Final Solution, sent 4092 of the 5022 to the gas chambers. When objections were raised over such a high rate, the explanation offered was that the males were too frail and the females were mostly children, little girls incapable of construction work.[51] Sometime later, when the transports were reported to contain a more choice supply of skilled Jewish workers, an S.S. official in charge of labor allocation suggested a possible means of avoiding overzealous application of the selection process. He recommended that the trains be unloaded near the I.G. works instead of the "usual place" near the crematory. The improvement was noticeable. On the next shipment of 4087 Jews, only 2398 were selected for extermination; this was a lower rate than before. The complaints, however, continued: "If the transports from Berlin continue to have so many women and children as well as old Jews," an official said, "I don't promise myself much in the matter of labor allocation."[52]

From the moment the transports were unloaded at Monowitz, those fortunate enough not to be selected for gassing lived in horror of the extermination center at Birkenau. When the construction fell behind the scheduled deadlines, I.G. officials often complained that the poor physical condition of the inmates chosen to work at I.G. Auschwitz was responsible. "Consequently," observed an eyewitness,

the Labor Allocation Officer in Auschwitz went to Monowitz early in the morning when the squads left for work, posted himself near the gate, and picked out those people whom they considered sickly amongst the laborers who marched to their work in files of five. These people were sent to the gas chambers straight away.[53]

For thousands of inmates, Monowitz thus became merely a brief stop on the way to Birkenau and extermination.

Conditions were such that sickness was a pervasive fact of life among the inhabitants of Monowitz. The hospital wards built by I.G. were so inadequate that even the S.S. suggested additional wards be built. I.G. refused because of the cost.[54] Later I.G. did expand its hospital facilities but also enforced a rule that no more than five percent of the Monowitz inmates could be sick at any one time, a procrustean matching of beds and illness. The overage was disposed of by shipment to Birkenau. Even under the five percent rule, inmates confined to the hospital had to be returned to work within fourteen days. Those who failed the fourteen-day test were deemed unrecoverable. On the records that I.G. kept was added the final phrase "Nach Birkenau."[55]

Starvation was a permanent guest at Auschwitz. The diet fed to I.G. Auschwitz inmates, which included the famous "Buna soup"—a nutritional aid not available to other prisoners—resulted in an average weight loss for each individual of about six and a half to nine pounds a week. At the end of the month, the change in the prisoner's appearance was marked; at the end of two months, the inmates were not recognizable except as caricatures formed of skin, bones, and practically no flesh; after three months, they were either dead or so unfit for work that they were marked for release to the gas chambers at Birkenau. Two physicians who studied the effect of the I.G. diet on the inmates noticed that "the normally nourished prisoner at Buna could make up the deficiency by his own body for a period of three months. . . . The prisoners were condemned to burn up their own body weight while working and, providing no infections occurred, finally died of exhaustion."[56]

As for shelter at Monowitz, the inmates slept in three tiers of wooden cubicles. Each slot, barely large enough for one person to lie down, actually held three. An eyewitness reported, "As a result it was practically impossible to sleep, since if one man was in a reclining position, the others would have to sit up or lie over him."[57] The simplest comforts were denied; even tables and chairs were almost unknown. Hygienic conditions were subhuman. In the summer the heat was oppressive, almost beyond endurance, and in the winter there was no heat at all.

In cases of infractions of the rules by inmates, the I.G. foremen sent written requests to the S.S. administration for suitable punishment. The S.S. complied, recording on its own forms the details of the I.G. charge and the S.S. disposition. Typical offenses charged by I.G. included "lazy," "shirking," "refusal to obey," "slow to obey," "working too slowly," "eating bones from a garbage pail," "begging bread from prisoners of war," "smoking a cigarette," "leaving work for ten minutes," "sitting during working hours," "stealing wood for a fire," "stealing a kettle of soup," "possession of money," "talking to a female inmate," and "warming hands." Frequently reports included the I.G. foreman's recommendations of "severe punishment."[58] The response of the S.S. could be forfeiture of meals, lashes by cane or whip, hanging, or "selection."[59]

To meet the construction schedule, the I.G. management worked the inmates at an almost murderous pace. It adopted, for example, the "S.S. trot" as a work tempo so that even cement and other heavy construction materials were carried to the job at "double time."[60] I.G. plant police and foremen, as well as Capos, continuously threatened and thrashed the prisoners who did not work up to S.S. standards.

At times, the inmates were literally worked to death: "It was no rare occurrence that detachments of 400 to 500 men brought back with them in the evening 5 to 20 corpses. The dead were brought to the place of roll call and were counted as being present."[61] Two or three times a week those who died on the site and those from whom all useful life had been extracted were piled on open platforms for all to see and trucked to Birkenau. For the inmate laborer, it was a useful reminder employed effectively by I.G. foremen and S.S. guards.

The construction of I.G. Auschwitz has assured I.G. a unique place in business history. By adopting the theory and practice of Nazi morality, it was able to depart from the conventional economics of slavery in which slaves are traditionally treated as capital equipment to be maintained and serviced for optimum use and depreciated over a normal life span. Instead, I.G. reduced slave labor to a consumable raw material, a human ore from which the mineral of life was systematically extracted. When no usable energy remained, the living dross was shipped to the gassing chambers and cremation furnaces of the extermination center at Birkenau, where the S.S. recycled it into the German war economy—gold teeth for the Reichsbank, hair for mattresses, and fat for soap. Even the moans of the doomed became a work incentive, exhorting the remaining inmates to greater effort.

Krauch was satisfied with the system of labor employed at Auschwitz. He wrote to Himmler in July 1943:

> I was particularly pleased to hear ... that you may possibly aid the expansion of another synthetic factory, which I consider absolutely essential for securing rubber supplies in a similar way as was done at Auschwitz by making available inmates of your camps if necessary. I ... would be grateful if you would continue sponsoring and aiding us in this matter.[62]

Half a year later, in February 1944, Krauch was still actively sponsoring the Auschwitz approach to the labor problem. In advising how to deal with a labor shortage at an I.G. plant at Heydebreck, he wrote its officials: "In order to overcome the continuous lack of labor, Heydebreck must establish a large concentration camp as quickly as possible *following the example of Auschwitz* [emphasis added]."[63]

One can only wonder about the reason for Krauch's enthusiasm. From the bare records available, 300,000 concentration camp workers passed through I.G. Auschwitz of whom at least 25,000 were worked to death.[64] The plants when completed were so enormous that they used more electricity than the entire city of Berlin. But in the final tally, I.G. Auschwitz was a miserable failure. Despite the investment of almost 900 million Reichsmarks and thousands of lives, only a modest stream of fuel and not a single pound of Buna rubber was ever produced.[65]

7

I.G. Loses the War

May 12, 1944, was a fateful day for Germany and for I.G. On that day the United States Eighth Air Force sent 935 bombers over Germany to attack its synthetic oil industry; 200 bombers concentrated on I.G.'s Leuna plant alone. This attack marked the beginning of what the U.S. strategic bombing survey called "the Battle of Leuna," classifying it as "one of the major battles of the war."[1]

The next day Albert Speer, Reich minister for armaments and war production, toured the wreckage of Leuna with Buetefisch. What he saw convinced him that "the technological war was decided. . . . It meant the end of German armament production."[2] For Speer it was the turning point in the war. He immediately flew to Hitler's headquarters at Obersalzburg to report on the extent and meaning of the disaster: "The enemy has struck us at one of our weakest points," he told the Fuehrer. "If they persist at it this time, we will soon have no fuel production worth mentioning. Our one hope is that the other side has an air force general staff as scatterbrained as ours!"[3]

Hitler then summoned four of the top fuel experts from I.G., including Krauch and Buetefisch, for a discussion about the consequences of the May 12 air raid. Goering and Speer accompanied them to the meeting. Before the group went in to see Hitler, Speer advised

162

the four fuel experts to tell "the unvarnished truth." However, Goering insisted that they not be too pessimistic. "He was probably afraid that Hitler would place the blame for the debacle chiefly on him," Speer wrote later.[4] Krauch was determined to follow Speer's advice. He told Hitler that Germany's position was hopeless if the enemy air raids on the synthetic oil plants continued. To support his grim forecast, he presented Hitler with an impressive array of facts and figures.

Goering, full of rage at what he regarded as gross insubordination, turned on Krauch in front of Hitler. The success of the Allied air raids was all Krauch's fault, he fumed, since planning for air raid protection was Krauch's responsibility.[5] By this time Goering had lost his influence with Hitler, who ignored his tirade against Krauch. For Hitler there was a more fundamental reason for the terrible effectiveness of the Allied air raids directed against the German productive centers: "In my view the fuel, Buna rubber and nitrogen plants represent a particularly sensitive point for the conduct of the war."[6] Because of I.G.'s monopoly, these vital war materials were concentrated in too few plants.[7]

But it was too late for Hitler to invoke a German Antitrust Act. The only thing to do was to try to put the plants back in operation as quickly as possible and then protect them with a heavy defensive air cover. Speer gave the restoration project the highest priority for men and matériel; 350,000 workers were assigned to the task of restoring German oil production. At Leuna the effort succeeded in bringing the facilities back to partial operation within ten days. But, on May 28, the Eighth Air Force resumed the battle of Leuna. The result was another crippling blow, which reduced German fuel production by half.

By now Goering acknowledged the seriousness of the situation. He promised Krauch and other German fuel experts that a significant part of Germany's new aircraft production would be designated solely to protect the oil plants and would never be diverted to the front.[8] But the Allied invasion of the continent on June 6 forced Goering to renege on that promise. The planes and anti-aircraft guns promised by Goering to protect the oil plants were diverted to meet the more immediate danger. At the end of June, a desperate Speer wrote to Hitler for help.

> Our aviation gasoline production was badly hit during May and June. The enemy has succeeded in increasing our losses of aviation gasoline up to 90 percent by June 22. Only through speedy recovery of damaged plants has it been possible to regain partly some of the terrible losses. In spite of this, however, aviation gasoline production is completely insufficient at this time.
>
> ... If it is not possible for us to protect these plants we will be forced to curtail the flow of supplies to the Army in September, which will mean that from that time on there will be a terrible bottleneck which may lead to the most tragic consequences....
>
> I regret having to inform my Fuehrer of these tragic developments and I beg you to issue all the necessary orders for this additional protection of these plants.[9]

The course of the Battle of Leuna became the gauge for the state of German oil production. By early July the resourceful I.G. technicians were able to restore Leuna to seventy-five percent operating capacity. However, the Eighth Air Force returned on July 7, again bombing the plant to a halt. Two days later the plant started operating again and by July 19 had reached fifty-three percent of capacity.[10] And so the cycle of bombings and reconstruction continued. But the total effect on German fuel production was nothing less than catastrophic. Krauch concluded that the only way fuel installations could be rebuilt after each raid was to cannibalize other installations. Under this plan to prevent the total cessation of oil production, Germany's productive capacity diminished with each recuperation. By September, oil production had dropped to fifteen percent, a condition from which Germany was never to recover.[11]

The intensive bombing of Leuna led to a curious confrontation between Buetefisch, who was in charge of Leuna, and Paul Harteck, a leading nuclear scientist working on Germany's atomic bomb project. Part of Leuna was devoted to the manufacture of heavy water, a necessary component of atomic energy. After the first bombs fell on Leuna, Buetefisch informed Harteck that the heavy water installation must be abandoned. He claimed that the massive bombing could not have been aimed at fuel production since there was a "gentlemen's agreement" between heavy industry in Germany and abroad that I.G.'s synthetic gasoline plants would not be bombed. The only explanation for the raids against Leuna, therefore, was the heavy water facility.[12]

Stories of such agreements between Allied and German concerns became part of the war's mythology. Except for this extraordinary statement by Buetefisch, which was confirmed by Harteck, not a scintilla of credible evidence ever has been uncovered to support any of them. Moreover, the removal of the heavy water installation did not halt the Allied bombings, which continued until Leuna became inoperative.

At about the same time, Buetefisch had another, more personal concern. The *Petroleum Times* in its December 23, 1943 issue published in detail a lecture by Robert T. Haslam of Standard Oil. In the article, Haslam claimed that United States technical warfare would not have been effective if I.G. had not supplied Standard with valuable information before the war. In fact, said Haslam, the success of the U.S.S.R.'s military campaigns was the result of the "technical achievements" the Soviet Union gained from I.G. via Standard.[13] Buetefisch, who had been personally charged by General Thomas with the responsibility for seeing that there were no leaks of technical information to Standard, was terrified by the *Petroleum Times* article. He took the matter up with Knieriem, apparently the most level-headed person still in I.G. Knieriem immediately realized that "this was a dangerous situation and we had

165

to recognize the possibility that we might be attacked for treason."[14] This would never have been a pleasant contemplation at any time in Nazi Germany, but during the Allied bombings it had awesome implications. "Imagine," said Knieriem, "the situation of a German firm in 1944 before the People's Court."[15]

As quickly as possible the I.G. executives prepared a point-by-point refutation of Haslam's lecture in the event the German government delved into the matter. But the Nazis were preoccupied with other troubles, and no such inquiry was ever undertaken. Had the Nazis learned of Haslam's defense of the Standard-I.G. agreements, Buetefisch, ter Meer, and probably other I.G. officials might conceivably have been placed in the most serious jeopardy.

By the fall of 1944, the German military situation had become so desperate that Bormann, Goebbels, and Ley—three of the most dedicated and ruthless Nazis in the Third Reich—began to pressure Hitler to attack enemy strongholds and cities with Tabun, a nerve gas so deadly that a drop on the skin killed a victim in minutes by attacking the nervous system.[16] Tabun, as well as Sarin, a companion nerve gas, had been discovered during I.G. research and development on pesticides and became one of Germany's most closely guarded military secrets, referred to in documents only by the code name "N-Stoff."

This was not the first time this trio had pleaded with Hitler to employ I.G.'s Tabun against the enemy. In May 1943, after the debacle of Stalingrad, they had urged its use on the Russian front. At that time Hitler called a conference at his headquarters in East Prussia to weigh this proposal. Speer, who was strongly opposed to the introduction of Tabun, flew Otto Ambros, I.G.'s authority on poison gas as well as synthetic rubber, to the meeting. Hitler asked Ambros, "What is the other side doing about poison gas?"[17] Ambros explained that the enemy, because of its greater access to ethylene, probably had a greater capacity to produce mustard gas than Germany did. Hitler interrupted to explain that he was not referring to traditional poison gases:

"I understand that the countries with petroleum are in a position to make more [mustard gas], but Germany has a special gas, Tabun. In this we have a monopoly in Germany."[18] He specifically wanted to know whether the enemy had access to such a gas and what it was doing in this area. To Hitler's disappointment Ambros replied, "I have justified reasons to assume that Tabun, too, is known abroad. I know that Tabun was publicized as early as 1902, that Sarin was patented, and that these substances appeared in patents."[19]

Ambros was informing Hitler of an extraordinary fact about one of Germany's most secret weapons. The essential nature of Tabun and Sarin had already been disclosed in the technical journals as far back as 1902, and I.G. had patented both products in 1937 and 1938. Ambros then warned Hitler that if Germany used Tabun, it must face the possibility that the Allies could produce this gas in much larger quantities.[20] Upon receiving this discouraging report, Hitler abruptly left the meeting. The nerve gases would not be used, for the time being at least, although they would continue to be produced and tested.*[21]

However, Hitler did not give up his interest in such

---

* Guinea pigs and white rats, animals traditionally used for testing purposes, were deemed inadequate for measuring the effect of the nerve gases on humans. Early in the war, it was decided to substitute apes, whose biological reactions to such gases were believed to be more like those of human beings. However, apes were not readily available in Germany, and Speer's office supplied 200,000 Swiss francs, a precious foreign currency, to buy them in Spain. They were transported to Germany with great difficulty; many died before the experiments were concluded (TWC I, p. 351, Brandt Document Book 12, Defense Exhibit 11). Eventually it was decided to experiment on concentration camp Jews.

It is suspected that the testing of I.G.'s poison gases on humans was known in the highest echelons of I.G. After the war, Georg von Schnitzler swore that Ambros, Schmitz, and ter Meer were aware of these activities. According to British intelligence, one of them was reported to have "justified the experiments not only on the grounds that the inmates of concentration camps would have been killed anyway by the Nazis, but also on the grounds that the experiments had a humanitarian aspect in that the lives of countless German workers were saved thereby" (Hearings before a Subcommittee of the Committee on Military Affairs, U.S. Senate, 79th Congress, 1st Session (1945), pursuant to S. Res. 107 and 146, *Elimination of German Resources for War*, part X, p. 1276).

a weapon entirely. After the Allied invasion of the continent in June 1944, Hitler became disenchanted with Army Ordnance tests of "N-Stoff." He informed Speer that he intended to transfer the "responsibility for the production and tests of N-Stoff to the S.S."[22] Speer objected, apparently shocked by the award of such decisive power to the S.S. Moreover, I.G. was too important to the program to be removed at this time. Speer convinced Hitler to limit the S.S. authority to testing the nerve gas while permitting I.G. to retain control over production and development.[23]

Hitler was persuaded and issued an order to this effect. On July 7, 1944, Speer received a teletype message from General Keitel:

> The Fuehrer has ordered that the Reichsfuehrer S.S. [Himmler] immediately continue experiments with "N Stoff." . . . To this end, the Army Ordnance Office will immediately submit to the Reichsfuehrer S.S. all reference material and know-how gathered up to now about "N Stoff" and will support him in his endeavors with all possible means.[24]

After the issuance of Hitler's order, Speer sought to clarify his position in a letter to Himmler. It would be a mistake, explained Speer, for the S.S. to take over the production of N-Stoff when, after all, only I.G. had the qualified specialists. Speer regretted that no competitive firm to I.G. Farben had been established within the framework of the four-year plan when it could easily have been done: "Nowadays we are entirely dependent on the work of I.G. Farben for chemical progress."[25] Himmler, apparently satisfied, replied that the S.S. would devote all its energy to the testing of N-Stoff and leave production to I.G.[26]

When the suggestion to use Tabun was made again in the fall of 1944, Hitler was still concerned about retaliation. He inquired once again of Speer about the possibility that the enemy possessed an equivalent weapon. Speer checked with Ambros and was told that nothing had changed and no defense against the nerve gas had been developed. Hitler again forbade its use.[27]

Ambros's estimate of the Allies' chemical warfare capability proved wrong. The Allies had nothing comparable to I.G.'s nerve gases with which to retaliate. It is terrifying to speculate on the holocaust that would have resulted had Hitler known this and ordered a massive nerve gas attack on London, Moscow, or Washington. Or worse, Hitler might have found the weapon to win the war.

The subject of Tabun surfaced for one more brief moment before the war was over. In order to end the war more quickly, Speer conceived the idea in February 1945 of using the gas to kill Hitler.[28] He planned to induce Tabun into the ventilating system of the Chancellery bunker. But the technical problems proved insuperable, and Speer abandoned the scheme. The war continued for another three months.

On May 8, 1945, Germany surrendered unconditionally. By August war crimes trials were being organized, and by November the first of the trials against the major war criminals had begun.

I.G. officials acted as though they had a premonition of what the future had in store. As early as September 1944 ter Meer and Ernst Struss, secretary of the managing board, were planning for the destruction of the files of I.G. in the event that the American forces occupied Frankfurt. The next spring, when Frankfurt was about to fall to the American army, a massive burning and shredding of files was undertaken—some fifteen tons of paper. Most of the records at Auschwitz were also destroyed before the Soviet army arrived. When the Allies began to try to piece together the I.G. record from the Nazi period, there were enormous gaps. More than one observer has suggested that I.G.'s record would have been far more incriminating had these files been available. What remained for the Allies to capture was horrible enough.

8

I.G. at Nuremberg

On August 8, 1945, the representatives of the governments of the United States, Great Britain, the Soviet Union, and France met in London to establish an International Military Tribunal to try the war criminals of Germany.[1] Prominent jurists from the four major powers were selected to serve as judges and a committee of chief prosecutors was appointed to draft an indictment.

On October 6, the formal indictment was completed and filed with the International Military Tribunal.[2] Indicted were the leaders of Nazi Germany still alive. They were charged with three basic war crimes: planning, preparing, and waging aggressive war; plunder and spoliation of the property of conquered countries; and slavery and mass murder.

It had been planned to include among those indicted a prominent industrialist who typified the complicity of German business in Hitler's programs. Gustav Krupp von Bohlen und Halbach, head of the Krupp steelworks, was chosen to fill this role. Although I.G. had been far more important to Germany's military-economic war preparations, Krupp was the individual most associated by reputation with the war-making power of Germany.

When James H. Rowe, Jr., a prominent American lawyer representing the International Military Tribunal, tried to serve the indictment upon the steel baron, he discovered that the aged Krupp was mentally and phys-

Members of the I.G. managing board in 1937 (left to right): Lautenschlaeger, Knieriem, Schmitz, Kuehne, Krauch, ter Meer, Hermann Abs (member of the Supervisory Board), Schnitzler, and Gajewski.

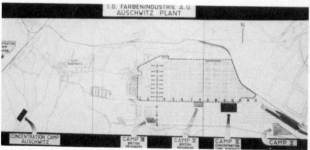

Plan for Auschwitz plant.

Himmler, flanked by Duerrfeld and other I.G. representatives, in his March 1941 inspection of the Auschwitz plant. Courtesy of the YIVO Institute for Jewish Research.

Auschwitz, the extermination center where four million human beings were destroyed in accordance with the "Final Solution of the Jewish Question," was chosen by I.G. as the site for the plant for its unlimited reservoir of death camp laborers. Courtesy of the YIVO Institute for Jewish Research.

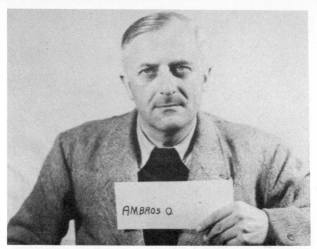

Otto Ambros, expert on poison gas and synthetic rubber and member of the I.G. managing board, sentenced to imprisonment for eight years for slavery and mass murder.

Heinrich Buetefisch, chemist and member of the I.G. managing board, sentenced to imprisonment for six years for slavery and mass murder.

Fritz ter Meer, the highest ranking scientist on the I.G. managing board, being sentenced to seven years' imprisonment for his part in the Auschwitz operation.

Across the arched entrance to Auschwitz was the motto "Work Makes You Free." Courtesy of the YIVO Institute for Jewish Research.

A German postcard portraying a group of slave laborers at work. Courtesy of the YIVO Institute for Jewish Research.

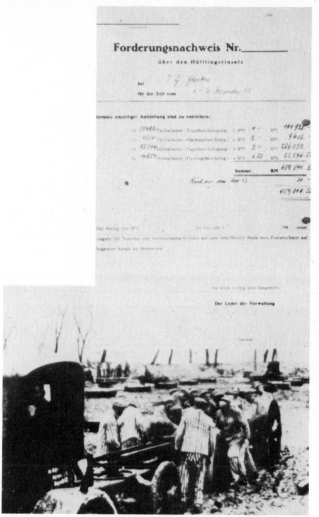

Slave laborers at work and a settlement of accounts made between the S.S. and I.G. Farben for the work of concentration camp inmates (see p. 149).

Carl Krauch, Nazi plenipotentiary for chemical production, who praised the efficiency of the Auschwitz solution of the labor problem, being sentenced at the Nuremberg trials.

(Left to right): Bosch, Schmitz, Adolf Haeuser (member of I.G.'s Supervisory Board), and Schnitzler in 1937—the year I.G. was "Nazified"—at a party in the Petersberg Hotel.

Krauch, Schmitz, Ilgner, Schnitzler, Gajewski, Gattineau, and Von der Heyde at the Nuremberg trials.

The tracks to Birkenau, the camp where Zyklon B was first introduced and where extermination of "selected" prisoners took place. Courtesy of the YIVO Institute for Jewish Research.

Zyklon B, the lethal gas manufactured by an I.G. dominated company and made for use at Auschwitz without the **indicator,** a warning odor.

ically unable to defend himself.[3] It was agreed that he would therefore have to be dropped as a defendant. The chief prosecutors, determined to include a German industrialist among the major war criminals, filed a motion to substitute Gustav Krupp's son Alfried. The motion was denied by the Tribunal,[4] and the trial began on November 20, 1946, without an industrialist as a defendant.* To assuage public opinion in the Allied countries, the French and British issued a joint declaration that in the future a number of leading German industrialists would be indicted as war criminals and tried before another International Military Tribunal.[5]

On April 5, 1946, with the trial nearing its end, the committee of chief prosecutors revived the plan to try a number of leading German industrialists before a second International Military Tribunal.[10] It was agreed that the list of the industrialist defendants must be held to a manageable number, preferably six but not to exceed eight. That Alfried Krupp was to be one of these defendants was a certainty. As it turned out, only four other industrialists were selected. The United States nominated Hermann Schmitz and Georg von Schnitzler of I.G. Farben. The French chose Hermann Roechling, the coal and steel magnate of the Saar. (Roechling's trial was to be a repeat performance: a quarter of a century earlier, after World War I, he had been tried and convicted as a war criminal in absentia by the French.) The British nominated Kurt von Schroeder, the Cologne banker. The Russians reserved the right to designate two defendants but never did so.

However, the plans for conducting a second trial be-

---

* At the conclusion of this trial on August 31, 1946, the following were sentenced to death: Hermann Goering, Joachim von Ribbentrop, Wilhelm Keitel, Alfred Rosenberg, Ernst Kaltenbrunner, Hans Frank, Wilhelm Frick, Julius Streicher, Fritz Sauckel, Alfred Jodl, Arthur von Seyss-Inquart and Martin Bormann (in absentia).[6] All were hung except Goering, who committed suicide on the morning of the executions, and Bormann, who was never apprehended.[7] Rudolf Hess, Walter Funk, and Erich Raeder were sentenced to life imprisonment. Albert Speer and Baldur von Schirach received twenty years' imprisonment;[8] Konstantin von Neurath, fifteen years; and Karl Doenitz, ten years. Hjalmar Schacht, Franz von Papen, and Hans Fritsche were acquitted on all counts.[9]

fore an International Military Tribunal collapsed. The experiences of the trial of the major war criminals convinced the prosecutors that a court made up of the four Allied powers was too unwieldy. Instead, a trial of industrial war criminals was to be left to each of the Allies in its own occupation zone of Germany.[11]

The United States proved the most energetic of the Allies in this connection and promptly initiated plans to proceed with a series of war crimes trials against the leading executives of the I.G., Krupp, and Flick concerns.[12] Judges were recruited from the state and federal judiciaries and from the faculties of law schools to preside over the trials. Staffs were organized to collect facts, draft indictments, and generally make the necessary preparations for the trials.

The chief of the prosecution staff for the I.G. case was Josiah E. DuBois, Jr., a deputy to Brigadier General Telford E. Taylor, who succeeded Justice Jackson as chief U.S. provost of the war crimes trials. After months of gathering evidence, examining witnesses, and organizing thousands of documents, the prosecution staff filed an indictment on May 3, 1947, on behalf of the United States.[13] Twenty-four I.G. executives were indicted: Carl Krauch as chairman of I.G.'s supervisory board; Hermann Schmitz as chairman of the I.G. managing board; all the other members of this board (Georg von Schnitzler, Fritz Gajewski, Heinrich Hoerlein, August von Knieriem, Fritz ter Meer, Christian Schneider, Otto Ambros, Max Brueggemann, Ernst Buergin, Heinrich Buetefisch, Paul Haefliger, Max Ilgner, Friedrich Jaehne, Hans Kuehne, Carl Lautenschlaeger, Wilhelm Mann, Heinrich Oster, and Karl Wurster); and four other important I.G. officials (Walter Duerrfeld, Heinrich Gattineau, Erich von der Heyde, and Hans Kugler).

The indictment, a document of over sixty pages, consisted of five separate counts into which was poured the record of I.G.'s involvement with the Nazi machine. The major counts were "Planning, Preparation, Initiation and Waging of Wars of Aggression and Invasions of Other Countries"; "Plunder and Spoliation"; and "Slavery and Mass Murder."

Under the aggressive warfare count, the indictment listed a wide range of offenses: alliance of I.G. with Hitler and the Nazi party; synchronization of all I.G.'s activities with the military planning of the German High Command; participation in the four-year plan preparations and direction of Germany's economic mobilization for war; participation in creating and equipping the Nazi military machine for aggressive war; procuring and stockpiling critical war materials for the Nazi offensive; participation in weakening Germany's potential enemies; carrying on propaganda, intelligence, and espionage activities; preparation for and participation in the planning and execution of Nazi aggressions and reaping of spoils therefrom; and participation in plunder, spoliation, slavery, and mass murder as part of the invasions and wars of aggression.

In the plunder and spoliation count, the indictment charged that "I.G. marched with the Wehrmacht and played a major role" in Germany's program for acquisition by conquest: "To that end, it conceived, initiated, and prepared detailed plans for the acquisition by it, with the aid of the German military force, of the chemical industries of Austria, Czechoslovakia, Poland, Norway, France, Russia, and other countries."

The charge of slavery and mass murder was the crucial count in the indictment, without which it is even doubtful that there would have been any war crimes trial at all.

All of the defendants, acting through the instrumentality of I.G. . . . participated in . . . the enslavement of concentration camp inmates . . . the use of prisoners of war in war operations . . . and the mistreatment, terrorization, torture, and murder of enslaved persons. In the course of these activities, millions of persons were uprooted from their homes, deported, enslaved, ill-treated, terrorized, tortured, and murdered.

173

In effect the indictment was a catalogue of Nazi inhumanities in which the I.G. defendants played a part, particularly in the most notorious of all extermination centers, Auschwitz.

Farben, in complete defiance of all decency and human considerations, abused its slave workers by subjecting them, among other things, to excessively long, arduous, and exhausting work, utterly disregarding their health or physical condition. The sole criterion of the right to live or die was the production efficiency of said inmates. By virtue of inadequate rest, inadequate food (which was given to the inmates while in bed at the barracks), and because of inadequate quarters (which consisted of a bed of polluted straw, shared by from two to four inmates), many died at their work or collapsed from serious illness there contracted. With the first signs of a decline in the production of any such workers, although caused by illness or exhaustion, such workers would be subjected to the well-known "Selektion." "Selektion," in its simplest definition, meant that if, upon a cursory examination, it appeared that the inmate would not be restored within a few days to full productive capacity, he was considered expendable and was sent to the "Birkenau" camp of Auschwitz for the customary extermination. The meaning of "Selektion" and "Birkenau" was known to everyone at Auschwitz and became a matter of common knowledge.

The working conditions at the Farben Buna plant were so severe and unendurable that very often inmates were driven to suicide by either dashing through the guards and provoking death by rifle shot, or hurling themselves into the high-tension electrically-charged barbed wire fences. As a result of these conditions, the labor turnover in the Buna plant in one year amounted to at least 300 percent. Besides those who were exterminated and committed suicide, up to and sometimes over 100 persons died at their work every day from sheer exhaustion. All depletions occasioned by extermination and other means of death were balanced by replacement with new inmates. Thus, Farben secured a continuous supply of fresh inmates in order to maintain full production.

Farben's conduct at Auschwitz can be best described by a remark of Hitler [sic; should be Himmler]: "What does it matter to us? Look away if it makes you sick."[14]

The possible verdicts ranged from acquittal to death.

From the outset the legality of the war crimes trials had been challenged by a number of legal scholars and politicians who contended that such trials represented victors' justice. Among the most prominent of those who joined in the debate were Chief Justice Harlan F. Stone, Justice William O. Douglas, and Senator Robert A. Taft.

Justice Douglas wrote,

No matter how many books are written or briefs filed, no matter how finely the lawyers analyzed it, the crime for which the Nazis were tried had never been formalized as a crime with the definiteness required by our legal standards, nor outlawed with a death penalty by the international community. By our standards that crime arose under an ex post facto law. Goering et al. deserved severe punishment. But their guilt did not justify us in substituting power for principle.[15]

Chief Justice Stone was even more emphatic. In a private letter, he wrote, "Jackson is away conducting his high-grade lynching party at Nuremberg. I don't mind what he is doing to the Nazis, but I hate to see the pretense that he is running a court and proceedings according to common law."[16]

Senator Taft said, "In these trials we have accepted the Russian idea of the purpose of trials—government policy and not justice—with little relation to Anglo-Saxon heritage. By clothing policy in the forms of legal procedure, we may discredit the whole idea of justice in Europe for years to come."[17]

By the time the prosecution of the I.G. officials began in 1947, a new element had been added to the objections of war crimes trials. The cold war had begun. Germany, the wartime enemy, had become a sought after ally; the U.S.S.R., the former ally, was now regarded as the enemy. Congressman John E. Rankin of Mississippi declared on the floor of the House of Representatives:

> What is taking place in Nuremberg, Germany, is a disgrace to the United States. Every other country now has washed its hands and withdrawn from this saturnalia of persecution. But a racial minority, two and a half years after the war closed, are in Nuremberg not only hanging German soldiers but trying German businessmen in the name of the United States.[18]

Representative George A. Dondero of Michigan continued the attack in the House, charging that ten communist sympathizers had infiltrated key positions in the American military government in Germany. He specifically attacked Josiah DuBois, the deputy chief counsel of the prosecution staff in the I.G. case, as a "known left-winger from the Treasury Department who has been a close student of the Communist Party line."[19] DuBois challenged Dondero to repeat his charges off the floor of Congress so that he would not be immune from a libel suit, but Dondero refused to do so.[20]

The trial opened on schedule on August 27, 1947, in the Palace of Justice at Nuremberg. Selected as judges to conduct the trial were Curtis Grover Shake, formerly a judge of the Supreme Court of Indiana, who was to preside; James Morris, justice of the Supreme Court of North Dakota; and Paul M. Hebert, dean of the Law School of Louisiana State University. Clarence F. Merrell, an Indiana lawyer who was a friend of Judge Shake's, was to serve as alternate judge.[21]

The large courtroom was filled to capacity. Members

of the public occupied all 300 seats allocated to them and the press section was filled to overflow. The twenty-three defendants (Brueggemann was declared too ill to stand trial) were attended by more than sixty lawyers, among the best of the German bar, and another twenty accountants and other specialists. The prosecution staff consisted of a dozen lawyers and experts. There were also clerks, stenographers, police, and military guards, as well as technicians and simultaneous translators required to make an electronic, bilingual trial possible.

General Telford Taylor set the tone of the prosecution's case in his opening statement.

> The indictment accuses these men of major responsibility for visiting upon mankind the most searing and catastrophic war in human history. It accuses them of wholesale enslavement, plunder and murder. These are terrible charges; no man should underwrite them frivolously or vengefully....
>
> The defendants will, no doubt, tell us that they were merely overzealous, and possibly misguided patriots. We will hear it said that all they planned to do was what any patriotic businessman would have done under similar circumstances. . . . As for the carnage of war and the slaughter of innocents, these were the regrettable deeds of Hitler and the Nazis, to whose dictatorship they, too, were subject.[22]

Taylor correctly divined one of the main defense strategies—to make the defendants out to be ordinary businessmen like those the world over. However, the way the prosecution began to develop the case seemed to play into the hands of the defense. The prosecution introduced organizational charts, cartel agreements, patent licenses, correspondence, production schedules, and corporate reports, as is done in antitrust cases, not at a trial of war criminals charged with mass murder.

Judge Morris finally voiced his irritation with the proceedings.

Mr. Prosecutor, this organization, so far as records show here, was simply a big chemical, commercial and business concern, the like of which there are many throughout the world. . . . I am at a complete loss to comprehend where documents of this kind are of the slightest materiality to the charges. This trial is being slowed down by a mass of contracts, minutes and letters that seem to have such slight bearing on any possible concept of proof in this case.[23]

Emanuel Minskoff of the prosecution staff appealed to his chief, Josiah DuBois, to change the order and direction of the prosecution case. It would have been more effective, he argued, to have opened with the charge of slavery and mass murder: "We should have started with Auschwitz on the first day." Because the prosecution failed to do so, "the court just can't believe these are the kind of men who would be guilty of aggressive war." DuBois replied that it was too late to adopt such an approach. Minskoff perservered, "But I still say you should argue Auschwitz; then they will see what kind of men they are trying and they'll understand the rest of it."[24] It was too late to adopt Minskoff's recommendation, much as DuBois would have liked to. The trial moved along according to the sequence of the counts in the indictment.

It was not until the prosecution staff reached the charge of slavery and mass murder that the critical point of the trial was reached. No longer did the procedures resemble those of an antitrust suit. The prosecution, in order to support these charges, introduced scores of eyewitnesses who had been in I.G. Auschwitz, including prisoners of war, Jewish and foreign inmates, physicians, and I.G. officials troubled by conscience, all of whom told stories that were incredible but still had the ring of truth. An effective prosecution witness was Norbert Jaehne, the son of defendant Friedrich Jaehne, and a certified engineer at I.G. Auschwitz from January 1943 to the end of the war. The elder Jaehne had made several trips to visit his son at the camp. Norbert

Jaehne's position at I.G. Auschwitz and his blood relationship with a defendant gave added force to his description of what went on at Auschwitz.

Of all the people employed in I.G. Auschwitz, the inmates received the worst treatment. They were beaten by the Capos, who in their turn had to see to it that the amount of work prescribed them and their detachments by the I.G. foremen was carried out, because they otherwise were punished by being beaten in the evening in the Monowitz camp. A general driving system prevailed on the I.G. construction site, so that one cannot say that the Capos alone were to blame. The Capos drove the inmates in their detachments exceedingly hard, in self-defense, so to speak, and did not shrink from using any means of increasing the work of the inmates, just so long as the amount of work required was done.[25]

Hardly less compelling was the testimony of the secretary of the I.G. managing board, Ernst A. Struss, who had visited I.G. Auschwitz several times.

COUNSEL: "The chief engineer of the Buna plant with whom you spoke in 1943, did he specifically tell you that people were being burned at Auschwitz?"

STRUSS: "Yes, I think he also told me that before the burning, they were gassed. . . ."

COUNSEL: "And in the summer of 1943 you knew that people were being burned and gassed?"

STRUSS: "Yes."

COUNSEL: "And to your best recollection you told that to Ambros and ter Meer?"

STRUSS "Yes."[26]

Through former Auschwitz inmates, the prosecution presented a graphic picture of conditions at I.G. Auschwitz and Monowitz. Typical was the testimony of Robert Elie Waitz, a professor at the University of Stras-

179

bourg, an inmate who was also a physician with an international reputation. He worked in the Monowitz hospital and, because of his renown and demeanor, was a forceful witness.

I found out very soon that Monowitz was an extermination camp. On account of the severe living conditions, the prisoners were exposed to that slow process of physical and mental dissolution which terminated in most cases in the gas chambers. The final aim was unmistakable: the dehumanization and eventual extermination of the prisoners employed in the I.G. plant at Auschwitz. I heard an S.S. officer in Monowitz saying to the prisoners, "You are all condemned to die, but the execution of your sentence will take a little while." Until that time, the S.S. and I.G. in common exploited the prisoners beyond what they could bear.[27]

From witness Rudolf Vitek, also both a physician and an inmate, came the following appraisal:

The prisoners were pushed in their work by the Capos, foremen, and overseers of the I.G. in an inhuman way. No mercy was shown. Thrashings, ill-treatment of the worst kind, even direct killings were the fashion. The murderous working speed was responsible for the fact that while working many prisoners suddenly stretched out flat, turned blue, gasped for breath and died like beasts. . . .

It was no rare occurrence that detachments of 400 to 500 men brought back with them in the evening five to twenty corpses. The dead were brought to the place of rollcall and counted as being present.[28]

A Czechoslovakian inmate swore that

The directors of I.G. Farben knew about the selections. . . . The employees of I.G. Farben indirectly occasioned the selections. . . . The master craftsmen complained to the management . . . and from there the complaints were forwarded to the management, Dr. Duerrfeld, and from there to the S.S. Consequently, the Labor Allocation Officer in Auschwitz went to Monowitz early in the morning, when the squads left for work, posted himself near the gate and picked out those people . . . whom they considered sickly; these people were sent to the gas chambers straight away. Those written complaints came from I.G. I myself have seen such reports.[29]

Very dramatic was the appearance for the prosecution of a group of British prisoners of war. Their testimony was especially impressive.

The condition of the concentration camp inmates was deplorable. I used to see them being carried back at night, dead from exposure, hunger, or exhaustion. The concentration camp inmates did heavy manual labor, such as carrying steel girders, pipes, cables, bricks, and sacks of cement weighing about 100 lbs. As a rule the inmates weighed less than the cement sacks. I have seen the inmates shuffle, trying to make it in double time, but unable to do it, and I have seen them collapse.

. . . We would see the chaps hanging up in the gate of Lager IV, and the prisoners had to walk underneath them. I saw those bodies myself; working parties passed under the gate while walking to work.[30]

Cross-examination did not help the defendants' cause.

Q. "Did you see personally how prisoners were hanged in camp IV [Monowitz]?"
A. "I saw three men hanging in the gate of camp IV approximately in February 1944."
Q. "Do you know why these prisoners were hanged?"
A. "I didn't know there had to be a reason."[31]

Another British prisoner of war testified:

I was at Auschwitz nearly every day. The population at Auschwitz was fully aware that people were being gassed and burned. On one occasion they complained about the stench of burning bodies. Of course, all of the Farben people knew what was going on. Nobody could live in Auschwitz and work in the plant, or even come down to the plant without knowing what was common knowledge to everybody.[32]

In an attempt to overcome the deadly impact of the prosecution's witnesses, the defense introduced into evidence some 386 affidavits. The prosecution challenged fifteen of them, which came from former inmates of Monowitz and I.G. Auschwitz. They were called as witnesses for cross-examination by Emanuel Minskoff of the prosecution staff. He was unusually successful in breaking down the credibility of the witnesses. One example reflects the general atmosphere Minskoff was able to create.

Q. "Now, Mr. Witness, isn't it a fact that during the winter days as many as twenty inmates at a time were carried away from the Farben site back into Monowitz because they couldn't walk by themselves any more?"

A. "Yes."

Q. "And could you say what the average weight of the inmates would be?"

A. "100 to 120 pounds."

Q. "Now, Mr. Witness, is it not a fact that the I.G. Farben foremen used to write evaluation sheets each night?"

A. "Yes."

Q. "And isn't it also true that if the Farben foremen reported the battalion under 70 percent, the inmates would be punished with twenty-five strokes each?"

A. "If he reported it—yes, that is true."

182

Q. "And wasn't the whipping post at Monowitz?"

A. "I don't know that."

Q. "Mr. Witness, you speak of there being no instruments of torture at Monowitz. Now isn't it a fact that there was a standing cell in Monowitz?"

A. "Yes."

Q. "Were there gallows in Monowitz?"

A. "Yes."

Q. "And didn't you often pass those gallows when an inmate had been hanged?"

A. "Unfortunately."

Q. "Now, Mr. Witness, you state at the end of your affidavit that you survived I.G. Auschwitz for three years. Isn't it a fact that you were what was known as an 'old inmate,' and that because of that and particularly because of the fact that you were aryanized while you were at the camp, you were in a completely different position from the other inmates?"

A. "That is correct."[33]

When Minskoff concluded, the witness was a broken man, crying uncontrollably.

A major point in the defense strategy to counteract such damaging testimony was the introduction of affidavits detailing the efforts of the I.G. defendants to protect Jewish employees from the Nazis. Especially interesting in this connection were the attempts to protect Carl and Arthur von Weinberg. Affidavits from Richard von Szilvignyi, the son-in-law of Carl von Weinberg, and Count Rudolf von Spreti, son-in-law of Arthur von Weinberg, established that Schmitz, Krauch, Schnitzler, and ter Meer attempted to save the Weinbergs from the Nazis. Schmitz, for example, supplied Spreti with money to pay a large sum to a high Nazi official so that Arthur von Weinberg would not have to wear the yellow "Jewish star." When Weinberg was later arrested and incarcerated in the dreaded concentration camp at Theresienstadt, Schmitz and Krauch intervened with Himmler. An agreement was reached for

Weinberg's release, subject to two relatively minor conditions: that he live with his only daughter, Princess Charlotte Lobkowicz, at Serrahn for the rest of his life and that this arrangement be approved by the local *Gauleiter* of Mecklenburg. However, before the approval of the *Gauleiter* of Mecklenburg could be secured, Weinberg died. Weakened by hunger, he failed to survive a gall bladder operation.[34]

Carl von Weinberg was more fortunate than his brother. With the aid of I.G. officials, he fled to Italy, where he was supported by payments from an I.G.-controlled company in Milan. All during the Nazi regime, he received his I.G. pension of 80,000 Reichsmarks, at great risk to the top members of the I.G. hierarchy who approved this payment.[35]

Testimony and affidavits from Jewish witnesses, however, did not always achieve the desired effect. Gerhard Ollendorff, a retired deputy member of the I.G. managing board, supplied an affidavit on behalf of defendant Fritz Gajewski. Ollendorff had been arrested in February 1939 during what he thought was a Nazi roundup of Jews. Gajewski went immediately to the chief of the Gestapo of the area and succeeded in effecting Ollendorff's release. In Ollendorff's affidavit, he recounted this event and added other information to show Gajewski's anti-Nazi sentiments and his help to Jewish employees.

The cross-examination of Gajewski by Morris Amchan of the prosecution staff, however, cast a different light on his relationship to Ollendorff's arrest.

Q. "Now, Dr. Gajewski, is it not a fact that when your colleague of the [I.G. managing board], Dr. Ollendorff, came to you as a friend and told you very confidentially that because of his Jewish ancestry, he was going to emigrate from Germany, having told you that in confidence, that you thereupon informed the Gestapo to arrest him and search his house—is that not a fact?"

A. "No. May I explain that? It was like this. Dr.

184

Ollendorff did not tell me that in confidence. It was generally known that he was going to emigrate. I talked to . . . Bosch about it. He said to me, 'Be careful. See to it that no "know-how" gets into other countries in this way or you will be in trouble.' We said, 'There has to be a search of Dr. Ollendorff's house, so that we are safeguarded in that respect.' That was all we did."

Q. "Now I show you [a document] and I ask you whether that does not refresh your recollection that on the same day when Ollendorff told you that he was going to emigrate from Germany, you wrote the Gestapo and told them to arrest the man and search his house? Does that refresh your recollection?"[36]

Amchan then handed the witness a letter that Gajewski had written to the Gestapo about Ollendorff.

Dr. Ollendorff has informed the Reich Office for Economic Development that he intends to go abroad. We wish to inform you that according to our interpretation Dr. Ollendorff has knowledge of secret matters and that, therefore, it would serve the general interest of the economy not to permit Dr. O. to go abroad for the time being. Since Dr. Ollendorff may still be in possession of papers, we would consider it advisable to have his home searched as a precautionary measure and any documents sent to us for study and analysis.

We request that this matter be treated in absolute confidence.

Heil Hitler![37]

Q. "One more question. Did you ever tell Ollendorff that you reported him to the Gestapo and ordered his arrest?"
A. "No, I didn't."[38]

Another relatively unsuccessful ploy of the defense was the attempt to show a lack of knowledge by the defendants of what I.G. Auschwitz really was. The prosecution had demonstrated that in the three and a half years of Auschwitz's existence Ambros visited the compound eighteen times, Buetefisch seven, Jaehne twice, ter Meer twice, and Krauch, Knieriem, and Schneider once each. Duerrfeld lived on the site during its entire existence. In addition, both the I.G. managing board and the technical committee were supplied with complete reports on the amount, character, and disposition of the various types of labor in I.G. Auschwitz and I.G. plants in Germany where slave labor was also used. These figures were reduced to multicolored charts and hung in the appropriate meeting room. Beginning in 1941, as the problem of labor supply became more acute, new classifications began to appear on the charts. The I.G. leaders were now aware that more than half I.G.'s "employees" were prisoners of war, foreign loan workers, convicts of the Wehrmacht, and concentration camp inmates. In the face of such evidence, the testimony of the defendants that the facts of the slave labor program and the atrocities of Auschwitz were unknown to them was hardly credible. Anyone visiting Auschwitz could not doubt its true function as an extermination center. The smell of death poured from its chimneys and polluted the atmosphere for miles around. Attempts to describe conditions as clean and good were palpably ridiculous.

A much more effective legal strategy was the "defense of necessity." The defense emphasized the compulsion under which German industrialists performed during the Nazi period. So far-reaching were the Reich's regulations and so stringent was their enforcement that refusal to comply exposed an industrialist to imprisonment and even death. Under the duress of the Nazi terror, the defendants committed some of the acts charged in the indictment. In order to survive, it became necessary to obey even the most hideous demands of the Hitler government; hence the phrase "defense of necessity."[89]

The defense called two important witnesses in this connection. Field Marshal Erhard Milch, who himself had been convicted and sentenced to life imprisonment for participation in Germany's slave labor program, was asked what the consequences would have been if a German businessman had refused to employ concentration camp inmates or prisoners of war allocated to him for war production. Milch replied that he would have been put under arrest immediately and would have faced the People's Court for "undermining the fighting spirit"—"That was a very well known and dreaded paragraph. It normally led to the death sentence."[40]

The other witness who testified about the "defense of necessity" was Friedrich Flick, head of the Flick concern, who had been convicted and sentenced to seven years' imprisonment for slave labor, plunder and spoliation, and membership in the S.S. Counsel for defendant Schnitzler asked whether a prominent industrialist could have refused to attend the February 1933 meeting that Goering had called to raise election funds for the Nazis and that Schnitzler had attended.

A. "He could do that, if he did not consider the consequences, but naturally, he would have regretted it."[41]

Some of the judges were impressed by the attempt of the defense to equate the I.G. defendants with their industrial counterparts in the United States and other countries as God-fearing, decent, and vigorously opposed to communism. This tactic proved most effective: "Replace I.G. by I.C.I. [Imperial Chemical Industries] for England, or Du Pont for America, or Montecatini for Italy," said Krauch's lawyer to the court, "and at once the similarity will become clear to you."[42] Essentially, the defendants were peacetime businessmen and the transformation of their activities into the defense effort of their country should not be interpreted as participation in the preparation for, or the waging of, aggressive war.

The prevailing atmosphere of the cold war, reflected in the remarks and attitudes of some of the judges, was put to advantage by the defense counsel. To explain away the evidence of their clients' enthusiastic endorsement and participation in Nazi policies and practices, they cited Hitler's opposition to communism. Krauch's counsel especially hammered the theme that his client, like any good American businessman, feared the expansion of the communist threat. Hitler's speeches on foreign policy made a deep impression on him. Through all these speeches "like a red thread runs the profession of the love of peace" and the "fear of the Bolshevist danger." Then, appealing to the passions of the cold war, incredible as it may seem, Krauch's counsel cited Hitler approvingly as a prophet. "How right Hitler was in this outline of his policy . . . might be confirmed by the political situation which has developed in recent months in Europe."[43] This sounded a grimly revealing note upon which to rest the defense of the "Father of I.G. Auschwitz."

The trial finally ended on May 12, 1948, after having exhausted all concerned in 152 trial days. There had been 189 witnesses. The transcript was almost 16,000 pages long. Over 6000 documents and 2800 affidavits had been introduced into evidence.[44] In addition, there had been a multitude of briefs, motions, rulings, and other legal instruments incidental to such a proceeding.

An intellectually divided and emotionally drained court faced the task of carving from the huge record a legally valid and historically meaningful decision. On July 29, 1948, almost a year after the trial began, the court convened to read its opinion, render its verdict, and sentence the guilty. Judge Hebert, apparently supported by Alternate Judge Merrell, requested from Judges Shake and Morris additional time to complete and file both a concurrent and dissenting opinion. This was denied.

Before proceeding with the main business of the court, Presiding Judge Shake referred to a matter that had been reported in the newspapers that morning. A mysterious explosion had destroyed the high-pressure hydrogenation plant at Ludwigshafen, in the French zone of occupation, killing almost 200 workers and injuring thousands more,[45] a ghostly reminder of the unsolved explosion at Ludwigshafen in 1921. Reflecting on the tragedy, Judge Shake commented, "The Tribunal has received unofficial information of the terrible tragedy that occurred last evening at Ludwigshafen, and I am sure that I speak for the Tribunal, as well as for all who are assembled in this room, when we express our sympathy for the deceased and pay a tribute to their memory, as well as to the families of those who have suffered in this unfortunate incident." The court record then noted, "The assemblage rose in silent tribute."[46]

Rudolf Dix, counsel for Hermann Schmitz, acting as spokesman for the defense, was granted permission to respond: "May I express to you and to this Tribunal our heartfelt thanks, and the most heartfelt thanks in the name of these men here, in the name of the defense, and in the name of the unfortunate sufferers."[47]

After this brief and poignant ceremony, the court began to read its opinion. Relying on the decision in the trial of the major war criminals (October 1946), the court quickly disposed of counts one and four charging the defendants with the preparation and waging of aggressive warfare and conspiracy.

To the extent that the activities of the defendants . . . contributed materially to the rearmament of Germany, the defendants must be charged with knowledge of the immediate result. . . . The prosecution, however, is confronted with the difficulty of establishing knowledge on the part of the defendants, not only of the rearmament of Germany but also that the purpose of rearmament was to wage aggressive war. In this sphere, the evidence degenerates from proof to mere conjecture.[48]

On counts one and four the court acquitted all the defendants.

On the second count, spoliation and plunder, the court set the guidelines for guilt or innocence.

We deem it to be the essence of the crime of plunder or spoliation that the owner be deprived

of his property involuntarily and against his will
. . . when action by the owner is not voluntary
because his consent is obtained by threats, intimi-
dation, pressure, or by exploiting the position and
power of the military occupant under circumstances indicating that the owner is being induced
to part with his property against his will, it is clearly
a violation of the Hague regulations.[49]

Within this framework, nine of the defendants, including such principal members of the I.G. managing board
as Hermann Schmitz, Georg von Schnitzler, Fritz ter
Meer, Friedrich Jaehne, and Max Ilgner, were adjudged
guilty. The remaining fourteen were acquitted.[50]

Count three, charging the defendants with slavery and
mass murder, was the distinctive element of the trial,
and it remained so in the opinion of the court. Taking
note of the undisputed facts of the terror practiced by
the Nazis, even on their own citizens, the court recognized the truth of the consequences confronting those
who disobeyed the decrees of the Nazi state. Therefore,
the court was "not prepared to say that these defendants
did not speak the truth when they asserted that in con-
forming to the slave-labor program, they had no other
choice than to comply with the mandates of the Hitler
government."[51] By refusing to become an oppressor,
I.G. could have become a victim itself.

There can be but little doubt that the defiant refusal of a Farben executive to carry out the Reich
production schedule or to use slave labor to achieve
that end would have been treated as treasonous
sabotage and would have resulted in prompt and
drastic retaliation. Indeed, there was credible evidence that Hitler would have welcomed the opportunity to make an example of a Farben leader.[52]

The question that remained, therefore, was under
what circumstances could the defendants avail themselves of the defense of necessity. In its answer, the
court stated quite succinctly that

190

an order of a superior officer or a law or governmental decree will not justify the defense of necessity unless, in its operation, it is of a character to deprive the one to whom it is directed of a moral choice as to his course of action. It follows that the defense of necessity is not available where the party seeking to invoke it was, himself, responsible for the existence or execution of such order or decree, or where his participation went beyond the requirements thereof, or was the result of his own initiative.[53]

Having thus set the limits of the defendants' main defense, the court went on to outline with relative brevity the facts surrounding Auschwitz. Nevertheless, at times during the reading of the opinion, the facts evoked a passion that even a judicial manner could barely restrain.

The plant site was not entirely without inhumane incidents. Occasionally beatings occurred by the plant police and supervisors who were in charge of the prisoners while they were at work. Sometimes workers collapsed. No doubt a condition of undernourishment and exhaustion from long hours of heavy labor was the primary cause of these incidents.

. . . Rumors of the selections made for gassing from among those who were unable to work were prevalent. Fear of this fate no doubt prompted many of the workers, especially Jews, to continue working until they collapsed. In camp Monowitz, the S.S. maintained a hospital and medical service. The adequacy of this service is a point of sharp conflict in the evidence. Regardless of the merits of the opposing contentions on this point, it is clear that many of the workers were deterred from seeking medical assistance by the fear that if they did so they would be selected by the S.S. for transfer to Birkenau. The Auschwitz construction workers

191

furnished by the concentration camp lived and labored under the shadow of extermination.[54]

Despite the fact that the court made it perfectly clear that "Farben did not deliberately pursue or encourage an inhumane policy with respect to the workers."[55] it nevertheless was impressed by the facts disclosed at the trial of the direct responsibility of Ambros, Buetefisch, and Duerrfeld for taking the initiative in procuring slave labor and "to some extent, at least, they must share the responsibility for mistreatment of the workers with the S.S. and the construction contractors."[56] Moreover, the court found that I.G. Auschwitz and Fuerstengrube, a nearby I.G. coal mine where slave labor was used,[57] were wholly private projects

> operated by Farben, with considerable freedom and opportunity for initiative on the part of Farben officials connected therewith. . . . The use of concentration camp labor and forced foreign workers at Auschwitz with the initiative displayed by the officials of Farben in the procurement and utilization of such labor, is a crime against humanity and, to the extent that non-German nationals were involved, also a war crime, to which the slave-labor program of the Reich will not warrant the defense of necessity.[58]

The court wasted little time in convicting the defendants most directly involved in the operation of I.G. Auschwitz.

> Our consideration of Auschwitz and Fuerstengrube has impressed upon us the direct responsibility of the defendants Duerrfeld, Ambros, and Buetefisch. It will be unnecessary to discuss these defendants further in this connection, as the events for which they are responsible establish their guilt under count three [slavery and mass murder] beyond a reasonable doubt.[59]

192

Although there were no qualifications or reservations expressed by the court about the guilt of Ambros, Buetefisch, and Duerrfeld on count three, the language concerning Krauch and ter Meer was more circumspect.

The evidence does not convince us that Krauch was either a moving party or an important participant in the initial enslavement of workers in foreign countries. Nevertheless, he did, and we think knowingly participate in the allocation of forced labor to Auschwitz and other places where such labor was utilized within the chemical field. The evidence does not show that he had knowledge of, or participated in, mistreatment of workers at their points of employment. In view of what he clearly must have known about the procurement of forced labor and the part he voluntarily played in its distribution and allocation, his activities were such that they impel us to hold that he was a willing participant in the crime of enslavement. . . .[60]

We reach the ultimate conclusion that Krauch, by his activities in connection with the allocation of concentration-camp inmates and forced foreign laborers, is Guilty under count three.[61]

Ter Meer, the highest ranking scientist on the I.G. managing board and chairman of the technical committee, was also held guilty on the charge of slavery and mass murder. Two visits to Auschwitz and the fact that Ambros reported to him were the factors compromising ter Meer.

The captured documents . . . established beyond question that the availability of concentration-camp labor figured in the planning of the Auschwitz construction. Ambros played a major role in this planning. His immediate superior with whom he had frequent contact and to whom he made detailed reports was ter Meer. The over-all field of new construction was one in which ter Meer was both active and dominant. It is indeed un-reasonable to conclude that, when Ambros sought the advice of and reported in detail to ter Meer, the conferences were confined to such matters as transportation, water supply, and the availability of construction materials and excluded that important construction factor, labor, in which the concentration camp played so prominent a part. Ter Meer's visits to Auschwitz were no doubt as revealing to him as they are to this Tribunal. . . . We are convinced beyond a reasonable doubt that the officials in charge of Farben construction went beyond the necessity created by the pressure of governmental officials and may be justly charged with taking the initiative in planning for and availing themselves of the use of concentration camp labor. Of these officials ter Meer had the greatest authority. We cannot say that he countenanced or participated in abuse of the workers. But that alone does not excuse his otherwise well established Guilt under count three.[62]

The rest of the defendants were acquitted under this count.[63]

As its final act, the court handed down its sentences of the guilty.[64]

Otto Ambros, guilty of count three, slavery and mass murder, sentenced to imprisonment for eight years.

Walter Duerrfeld, guilty of count three, slavery and mass murder, sentenced to imprisonment for eight years.

Fritz ter Meer, guilty of count two, plunder and spoliation, and count three, slavery and mass murder, sentenced to imprisonment for seven years.

Carl Krauch, guilty of count three, slavery and

mass murder, sentenced to imprisonment for six years.

Heinrich Buetefisch, guilty of count three, slavery and mass murder, sentenced to imprisonment for six years.

Georg von Schnitzler, guilty of count two, plunder and spoliation, sentenced to imprisonment for five years.

Hermann Schmitz, guilty of count two, plunder and spoliation, sentenced to imprisonment for four years.

Max Ilgner, guilty of count two, plunder and spoliation, sentenced to imprisonment for three years.

Heinrich Oster, guilty of count two, plunder and spoliation, sentenced to imprisonment for two years.

Paul Haefliger, guilty of count two, plunder and spoliation, sentenced to imprisonment for two years.

Friedrich Jaehne, guilty of count two, plunder and spoliation, sentenced to imprisonment for one and one-half years.

Hans Kugler, guilty of count two, plunder and spoliation, sentenced to imprisonment for one and one-half years.

The prosecution staff was outraged by the court's verdict and the sentences of the guilty. Chief prosecutor Josiah DuBois regarded the sentences as "light enough to please a chicken thief." As he left the courtroom he exploded, "I'll write a book about this if it's the last thing I ever do."[65] Within four years DuBois's book appeared: *The Devil's Chemists: 24 Conspirators of the International Farben Cartel Who Manufacture Wars.* It is a grimly passionate account of a unique moment in the history of commerce, warfare, and jurisprudence.

Almost five months after the verdict, Judge Hebert filed his concurring opinion on the charges of crimes against the peace (the preparation, planning, and waging of aggressive war) and his dissent on the charge of slavery and mass murder. Despite its concurrence on counts one and five, the 124-page opinion is nothing less than a castigation of the majority for their misreading of the record "in the direction of a too complete exoneration and an exculpation even of moral guilt to a degree which I consider unwarranted."[66] To the contrary, the mass of the evidence presented during the long trial constitutes an "ugly record" revealing that I.G. went far beyond the activities of normal business "in its sympathy and identity with the Nazi regime."[67]

Judge Hebert, far more than his colleagues, stressed the historic mission of the trial: "It is important not only to pass judgment upon the guilt or innocence of the accused, but also to set forth an accurate record of the more essential facts established by the proof."[68] This Hebert did, in careful detail. However, even though the action of the defendants in aiding the Nazis to prepare and wage aggressive war and their "relationship to the crimes against peace"[69] could not be condoned or minimized, Hebert nevertheless felt he had to acquit the defendants on counts one and five. This acquittal had to stand, said Hebert, regardless of how much the defendants' support "of the Nazi regime contributed first, to making the war possible from the viewpoint of production and, secondly, to prolonging the war after it had been launched."[70]

On the charge of slavery and mass murder, Judge Hebert dissented bitterly from his colleagues. In his judgment, all the defendants were guilty.

On the facts proven in this record, I am convinced that the defendants who were members of the [managing board of I.G.] were accessories to and took a consenting part in the commission of war crimes and crimes against humanity as alleged in count three of the indictment.[71]

. . . In my view, the Auschwitz project would not have been carried out had it not been authorized and approved by the other defendants, who participated in the corporate approval of the project knowing that concentration-camp inmates and other slave labor would be employed in the construction and other work. . . .[72]

Having accepted a large-scale participation in the utilization of concentration-camp inmates at Auschwitz, and, acting through certain of its agents, having exercised initiative in negotiating with the S.S. to obtain more and more workers, Farben became inevitably connected with the inhumanity involved in the utilization of such labor. . . . The evidence establishes that the conditions under which the concentration-camp workers were forced to work on the Farben site at Auschwitz were inhumane in an extreme degree. It is no overstatement, as the prosecution asserts, to conclude that the working conditions indirectly resulted in the deaths of thousands of human beings. . . .[73]

In summary, it is established that Farben selected the Auschwitz site with knowledge of the existence of the concentration camp and contemplated the use of concentration-camp inmates in its construction; that these matters necessarily had to be reported to and discussed by the [managing board] and the T.E.A. [Technical Committee]; that Farben initiative obtained the inmates for work at Auschwitz; that the project was constantly before the members of the T.E.A. for necessary appropriation of funds; that the T.E.A. had to have information on the labor aspects of the project to properly perform its functions; that the condition of the concentration camp inmates was brought to the attention of the T.E.A. and [managing board] members in various discussions and reports; that a number of the defendants were actually eyewitnesses to conditions at Auschwitz

197

because of personal visits to Auschwitz; that the defendants Krauch, von Knieriem, Schneider, Jaehne, Ambros, Buetefisch, and ter Meer were all shown to have visited the I.G. Auschwitz site during occurrences of the nature generally described above; that the conditions at Auschwitz were so horrible that it is utterly incredible to conclude that they were unknown to the defendants, the principal corporate directors, who were responsible for Farben's connection with the project.[74]

Not only Ambros, Duerrfeld, ter Meer, Buetefisch, and Krauch but every member of the I.G. managing board should have been found guilty of slavery and mass murder, according to Hebert. One can be certain that if he were passing sentences they would not have "pleased a chicken thief." Yet by the time Hebert wrote his dissent, the interest of the press and the public in the punishment of war crimes had almost disappeared, and the cold war was rapidly heating up.

9

I.G. Wins the Peace

What to do about the future of I.G. became a matter of major Allied concern almost immediately after the defeat of Germany. I.G.'s crucial role in making it possible for Hitler to wage the greatest war in history for over five and a half years did not go unnoticed by the Allied leadership. Even before Germany surrendered officially, General Eisenhower ordered an investigation of I.G.'s place in Germany's war effort. After a detailed analysis of every facet of I.G.'s operations, from the creation and production of synthetic oil and rubber to its international cartel agreements, the investigating team concluded that I.G. was indispensable for the German war effort. Without it Hitler could never have embarked on the war or come so close to victory.[1]

The report made a deep impression on Eisenhower. He decided that I.G.'s strategic position in the German economy must be broken as "one means of assuring world peace."[2] Eisenhower's specific recommendations would have warmed the heart of Marshal Foch, his predecessor as commander in chief of the Allied forces in World War I:

1. make I.G. plants and other assets available for reparations;
2. destroy I.G. plants used exclusively for war making purposes;

3. break up I.G.'s monopoly control by dispersing ownership of the remaining plants;
4. terminate I.G.'s interest in international cartels;
5. take over I.G.'s research programs and facilities.[3]

The same day Eisenhower's recommendations were released to the papers, the United States Army announced plans to dynamite three I.G. plants in the American zone devoted to the manufacture of smokeless powder and nitrocellulose. These factories would be "the first of many hundreds of plants . . . designated for actual destruction."[4]

By November 1945, the Allied Control Council enacted a law "to ensure that Germany will never again threaten her neighbors or the peace of the world . . . taking into consideration that I.G. Farbenindustrie knowingly and prominently engaged in building up and maintaining the German war potential."[5] All plants and other assets of I.G. in Germany were to be seized and legal title vested in the Control Council. Control officers were to be appointed for each zone of occupation to administer the seized plants and implement Control Council policies. The objectives set forth were exactly those recommended by Eisenhower, including destruction of I.G. plants used for war purposes and dispersion of the remaining plants.

Despite the strong words of the Control Council German speculators did not seem to take the new law or the Allied plan seriously. In the three months between October 20, when Eisenhower's recommendations about I.G. were made public, and January 20, the price of I.G. shares doubled on the Munich stock exchange. General William H. Draper, director of the economics division of the office of Military Government, was asked at a press conference about the skyrocketing price of the stock. He smiled wryly and remarked that the speculators must be "buying a piece of the Control Council"[6] since the council now held legal title to all I.G. assets.

A few days later, the American Military Government

took a more serious view of the matter and ordered an end to all trading of I.G. securities. Any violator could receive five years in prison or a fine of $10,000. It was hoped that this move would convince German speculators that the dissolution of I.G. was to be permanent.[7]

In late February 1947 the American Military Government promulgated a law that was to serve as the legal vehicle for the dissolution of I.G. in the American zone. The "Prohibition of Excessive Concentration of German Economic Power"[8] was a sweeping antitrust law designed to prevent monopoly practices. It provided for the investigation of all German firms employing more than 10,000 persons; if any of these firms were found to represent an "excessive concentration of economic power, they were to be reorganized and broken up into a number of economic units."[9]

The first target of this law—and, as it turned out, the only one—was I.G. Farben. On June 17, U.S. Military Government decartelization chief Phillip S. Hawkins announced that the I.G. facilities in the American zone had been broken up and established as forty-seven independent units to be run by German trustees until the final disposition of the plants.[10] By any standard, the breakup of I.G. into forty-seven parts was quite a dissolution.

Most of the German trustees had already been appointed and they had been briefed as to widespread German business practices that were now outlawed by the new antitrust law. Prohibited were price fixing, boycotts, discrimination against any manufacturer or distributor, division of markets or field of industry, suppression of technology or invention whether patented or not, fixing of quotas, and other devices or practices in restraint of trade or production.[11]

It was not long before all this fine sermonizing turned out to be too good to be true. By the middle of 1947, American foreign policy was taking a direction that was drastically to affect the decartelization program in Germany. The new point in view was expressed in a report by fourteen top American businessmen appointed by the War Department to review the U.S.

Military Government's industrial policies in Germany. The committee of businessmen specifically attacked the decartelization law, charging that it embodied

a series of controls and regulations, many of which represent economic principles quite new to the German mind and to the past industrial development of the country. Since we are now confronted with the urgent necessity of bringing about as rapidly as possible recovery of the economic life of a starving people—it is our belief that too strict adherence to the law in its administration will seriously retard this primary objective.[12]

In keeping with the new attitude of the cold war, the breakup of I.G. was suspended. Nothing further happened for the duration of the Allied Control Council's existence. However, when the four-power military control of Germany ended in June 1949 and was replaced by the Western Allied High Commission (composed of civilians from the United States, Great Britain, and France), the stockholders of the old I.G. went into action. They formed a stockholders protective committee and demanded that instead of forty-seven separate units operated by trustees, the I.G. plants should be consolidated into three companies: Bayer, BASF, and Hoechst. The stockholders committee further demanded that all the stock of the old I.G. Farbenindustrie be converted pro rata into the stock of the proposed three successor companies. The large stockholders of each company would be the same. To the skeptical this appeared to be an ingenious scheme for maintaining common control of each of the three companies[13] by the erstwhile major stockholders of I.G. Farben.

The stockholders committee embarked on a powerful lobbying and propaganda campaign to secure Bonn government support of their plan. During 1950 nothing was done to dispose of the I.G. units. A High Commission spokesman explained that a new, three-power Allied High Commission law must be enacted to take the place of the old, four-power Allied Control Council law before any action on I.G. could be taken. He added that previous plans for a vast liquidation program for I.G. would have to be scrapped; the program to sell individual plants was "dead as a doornail." The spokesman did not need to point out that the emphasis was on the cold war and the industrial recovery of Germany and not on the deconcentration of excessive economic power and demilitarization.

The new Allied High Commission Law, No. 35, "Dispersion of Assets of I.G.," was issued in August 1950. It declared that "the Allied High Commission shall take such action as it considers necessary to accomplish the winding up of I.G. Farbenindustrie A.G. and to extinguish its juristic personality." The company's assets in the American, British, and French zones were to be "dispersed among such a number of economically sound and independent companies as will ensure dispersion of ownership and control and promote competition in the German chemical and related industries." The number of companies was not specified. An I.G. Farben liquidation committee of German nationals was to be appointed by the Allied High Commission to put the new law into effect. Any convicted war criminal was to be barred from participating either directly or indirectly in the management of any of the proposed new companies; this edict barred such prominent I.G. figures as Krauch, Schmitz, Schnitzler, ter Meer, Jaehne, Ambros, and Buetefisch. The provisions of the new law definitely gave the impression that the old order of I.G. control had been effectively terminated.

By mid-January 1951, the Allied High Commission finally agreed to a plan for the dispersion of ownership. The 159 I.G. plants in the western zone were to be divided among nine companies: the Big Three (Bayer, BASF, and Hoechst) and six smaller firms, including Agfa, Kalle, Cassella, and Huels.

Those in Allied countries who had demanded the dissolution of I.G. "as one means of ensuring world peace" were bitterly disappointed. However, the I.G. stockholders committee also was not satisfied with the

203

proposal. The stockholders were still insisting on the Big Three formula. In this demand they were supported by the German trustees of the I.G. plants—some of them I.G. officials from the old days—and by the Bonn government. The result was protracted negotiation between the Western Allies and the Germans. Time was on the side of the stockholders committee. Before long the Allies would be leaving.

By late 1951 the question of what to do with the smaller companies had not yet been resolved. However, there was no dispute that the Big Three should resume their pre-1926 corporate identities. In fact, these firms were being reestablished while negotiations continued between the Allied High Commission and the Germans as to what other companies were to be formed. In December the names of the boards and officials of the Big Three companies were announced. Included were many former I.G. executives, but for the time being there were no convicted war criminals among them.[14]

Some Allied officials who had been involved in the decartelization program began to say openly that control seemed to be slipping from the Allies and returning to former I.G. men. They speculated that the Big Three might return to their old ways once the Allies left Germany. They also found another matter disquieting. The stock in the newly formed Big Three companies would be available to former I.G. stockholders on a priority basis. This raised the possibility that the Big Three would be owned by the same stockholders.[15] Nevertheless, no one was much inclined to prevent this situation.

Still, the Allies refused to capitulate on one point, the German demand to register the stock in the new companies only to "bearer." They insisted that every share be registered in the name of the actual owner in order to insure against secret control. The Germans responded that registering all shares was too difficult and too expensive. But on this issue, the Allied High Commission refused to compromise. Bearer shares were prohibited.

In March 1953, the Allied High Commission finally produced a plan for the disposition of the remaining I.G. assets in West Germany. Most of the assets were transferred to the Big Three. Bayer ended up with 100 percent of Agfa.[16] Of all the smaller units, only Cassella and Huels were to survive as independent companies. The shareholders of the dissolved I.G. were to receive shares in the five successor companies in exchange for their old stock.[17]

A year and a half later, in October 1954, treaties were signed in Paris terminating the occupation regime in West Germany. With the ratification by the signatory nations, the Federal Republic of Germany would soon become a sovereign and equal member of the Western Alliance.[18] Chancellor Konrad Adenauer wrote the U.S. high commissioner, James B. Conant, affirming the determination of the Federal Republic of Germany to follow the antitrust policy that had been pursued by the Allied occupation regime.[19]

But not all of the occupation officials were sanguine about the effectiveness of this transfer of authority. According to a *New York Times* dispatch: "United States officials acknowledge that they cannot be certain the Germans will not soon reverse the trend by reconstituting the Farben empire and other enterprises that wielded vast political and economic power in pre-war Germany."[20]

On May 5, 1955, the Federal Republic of Germany became a sovereign government, and the Allied occupation forces left. Three weeks later, 450 stockholders of the old I.G. Farben met, for the first time since the defeat of Germany, to receive a report on the past decade. They were informed by the I.G. liquidators that the formal dissolution of I.G. would not take place "for many years to come."[21] Numerous claims on I.G.'s assets had been filed, including demands for compensation from slave laborers who had worked in the I.G. plants during the war. Moreover, the disposition of I.G.'s assets in the Soviet zone, including the huge Leuna works, had to await the reunification of East and West Germany, an uncertain and distant possibility.

In the spring of 1955 the I.G. successor companies held their first annual stockholders meeting without the benefit of Allied supervision. Bayer, exercising its new freedom, promptly revised its bylaws to permit bearer shares. Henceforth, the owners of Bayer could be anonymous.[22] This action was soon repeated by the other companies.

Moreover, the successor companies did not intend to be bound by the Allied High Commission law barring convicted war criminals from executive posts. Friedrich Jaehne, a war criminal who had been sentenced at Nuremberg to a year and a half in prison, became a member of the supervisory board of Hoechst in June 1955. In September he was elected chairman.[23] In 1956 Fritz ter Meer, the only war criminal who had been convicted of both plunder and slavery, was elected chairman of the supervisory board of Bayer.[24]

Prosperity was returning to the Big Three. Their profits already outstripped those of their monolithic I.G. predecessor. All three raised their annual stock dividends from nine to ten percent in 1956. The combined value of BASF, Bayer, and Hoechst stock represented over fifteen percent of the value of all stock listed on the West German stock exchange.[25]

At the beginning of 1956 Bayer more than tripled its capitalization.[26] Three months later it acquired twenty-eight percent of Huels. According to the *New York Times,*

> one of the Farben successor companies has now become part owner of another part of the old German chemical empire. . . .
>
> It appears then that the forces of economics are starting to draw pieces of the shattered Farben empire together.
>
> To many observers here, last week's developments, along with others like them in recent months, point to a coming rebirth of the cartel, the huge, monolithic industrial enterprises that

dominated German business before World War II.[27]

Soon the last piece, Cassella, was absorbed by Bayer. The Big Three once again merited the name. In 1977, Hoechst, BASF, and Bayer were among the thirty largest industrial companies in the world. Hoechst is the largest company in Germany. Hoechst and BASF are each larger than Du Pont; Bayer is only slightly smaller.[28] Each one is bigger than I.G. at its zenith.

10

Corporate Camouflage

Corporate camouflage, the art of concealing foreign properties from enemy governments, has a special place in the history of I.G. Unlike I.G.'s involvement in mass murder and slave labor, which was a wartime aberration, I.G.'s program of camouflage long predated and outlived the war. Its political effects will persist for years to come.

Because I.G.'s corporate camouflage was conceived and conducted in secrecy, its details largely escaped the prosecutors at Nuremburg. As a result, the description of I.G.'s cloaking campaign in the indictment was limited to a few obscure paragraphs of uncertain accuracy, less a reflection on the adequacy of the prosecution than on I.G.'s skill. In any event, the indictment charged that beginning in 1937 I.G.

> embarked upon an intensive program to camouflage and cloak its foreign holdings to protect them from seizure in the coming wars by enemy custodians. These measures not only served the interests of I.G. but enabled its foreign empire to carry out the greatly intensified efforts of the Nazi government to strengthen Germany at the expense of other nations.

When war appeared to be a reasonable certainty just before the capitulation of Chamberlain at Munich in September 1938, the indictment continued, "a special procedure was worked out by the officials of the German government after consultation with I.G. authorizing the cloaking of German foreign assets through the transfer to neutral trustees as a protection against wartime seizure."[1]

To illustrate the device of a neutral front to conceal I.G.'s ownership from enemy custodians, the indictment singled out the case of the General Aniline and Film Company, I.G.'s most valuable American property. I.G. used its Swiss holding company, I.G. Chemie, as a cloak for its prime American asset. The camouflage of General Aniline was a consummate example of I.G.'s corporate deception and by all odds its most successful one. In this case I.G. weaved a corporate tangle with such craft that not only were the Nuremberg prosecutors and judges unable to follow the threads but for years thereafter a series of U.S. officials were unable to unravel it. Before the General Aniline case had run its course through the United States government bureaucracy and the courts, it left a trail of corruption and scandal; no place seemed too high to remain untainted.

The extraordinary success of I.G.'s operation camouflage was, in effect, a tribute to the genius of a single individual, Hermann Schmitz, hand-picked by Carl Bosch in 1935 to be his successor as head of I.G. Farben. From the time I.G. was formed until it disappeared as a separate entity, Schmitz was in charge of its foreign empire and the principal architect of the program for camouflaging the company's vast overseas holdings. He was driven by a predisposition to distrust outsiders, a penchant for secrecy, and a talent for dissimulation. He rarely sought and never won popularity. Most of his peers regarded Schmitz with distaste coupled with fear. But none ever questioned his skill at corporate legerdemain or his curious practice of keeping the most complicated transactions and involved financial details in his head without committing them to paper. There were times when Schmitz did not confide in his intimate associates about such matters.

In accord with his suspicious and secretive personality, Schmitz exercised tight personal supervision over I.G.'s international empire. His control was established through a small circle of close family members, long-time associates, and personal friends whom he placed in strategic positions within I.G. and throughout its foreign outposts. This cadre of tried and faithful loyalists played a crucial role in the execution of Schmitz's master plan for the protection of the company's overseas holdings.

However, there was more to Schmitz than the two-dimensional portrait of cunning and deviousness drawn by the Nuremberg prosecution. The fact that Bosch chose him as his successor is an accolade not easily dismissed. Moreover, Schmitz was an intimate of many of the great and powerful of his time, who respected him for his broad knowledge of foreign affairs and his ability to cope with the most complex economic problems. Schmitz's advice and support was eagerly sought by the powerful of his day. Chancellor Bruening offered him a position in his cabinet as economic minister. When Schmitz refused, Bruening persuaded him to serve as an unofficial adviser and took him along to meetings around the world with heads of state, including President Herbert Hoover at the White House. When the world-respected *Frankfurter Zeitung,* the great German liberal newspaper, was in financial difficulty, Schmitz probably saved it with a sizeable investment. Later, during the Nazi period, as the excesses against the Jews mounted, Schmitz personally found places for high Jewish I.G. officials and lesser staff members in I.G.'s foreign offices. Some of these émigrés have insisted that Schmitz's long and repeated support for Hitler's internal repression and foreign expansion was a matter of necessity and opportunism rather than commitment. One instance in the summer of 1938 may be revealing on this score. An I.G. lawyer informed Schmitz that according to the newly enacted Reich citizenship laws, I.G. was legally a Jewish company. Like the Southern miscegenation laws of the United States whereby a single drop of Negro blood was sufficient to declare a person a Negro, under the new Nazi law a single Jewish director was enough to classify a corporation as Jewish. Schmitz replied to his shaking subordinate, "Have you anything against working in a Jewish company?"[2] The astounded lawyer retold this story in an affidavit prepared for Schmitz's defense at Nuremberg.

Obviously Schmitz was a complex personality. Despite his lifelong pursuit of success, he died a relative pauper in 1960 at the age of seventy-nine. To this day no one has been able to explain what happened to his fortune. Few who knew him can believe it does not exist.

Hermann Schmitz was born of impoverished working class parents in Essen, Germany, in 1881. Although he was blessed with unusual intelligence, Schmitz was from too poor a family to attend any but a commercial school. Yet it did not take Schmitz very long to make the most of his opportunities. In 1906 he went to work as a clerk in the Metallgesellschaft firm in Frankfurt, the largest nonferrous metal company in the world; there his talents surfaced quickly.

Schmitz's ability with figures and his general creativity, coupled with driving ambition and hard work, soon caught the eye of Wilhelm Merton, the patriarchal head and principal owner of the firm. Thereafter, his rise within the organization was rapid. Before he was thirty, Schmitz was in charge of all Metallgesellschaft's foreign operations, which covered every country that mined, manufactured, or bought and sold nonferrous metals. The American Metal Company, a highly profitable and important Merton outpost in the United States, was of special interest to Schmitz. He made frequent trips across the Atlantic to check on the progress of this American asset. And since he was a skilled observer, Schmitz became Merton's expert on the nature and habits of American politics and industry.

Under Schmitz's direction, Metallgesellschaft's foreign business boomed, and he came to superintend an ever increasing flow of foreign currencies into the headquarters at Frankfurt. The growing size of the German government's tax levy on these profits became a concern for the elder Merton. He decided to find some way to evade a major portion of this burden, a not unique desire for businessmen generally. Schmitz was assigned the problem, and he promptly proved his worth. He suggested the creation of a separate holding company in Switzerland as a repository for a substantial portion of the firm's foreign funds. The Swiss enforcement of its financial secrecy laws would keep these funds out of the reach of the German tax authorities. Merton was convinced. The result was the formation of a Merton-owned holding company incorporated in Zurich under the German name Schweizerische Gesellschaft fuer Metallwerte and the French, Société Suisse pour Valeurs de Métaux ("Swiss Company for Precious Metals"). This was Schmitz's first venture into corporate camouflage. Although its initial purpose was to conceal Metallgesellschaft's holdings from the German government, later the Schmitz mechanism of a neutral cloak would conceal its holdings from enemy governments. This period also marked the beginning of Schmitz's love affair with Switzerland, a land of sound currency and useful financial secrecy laws.

When World War I broke out, Schmitz was commissioned as a first lieutenant in the Wehrmacht. The war had hardly begun when he was severely wounded. After recovering, he was assigned to Rathenau's War Raw Materials Office, where he first met Carl Bosch and actively helped him get the German government's support for a nitrate plant at Leuna. When Wilhelm Merton died in 1916, his sons Richard and Alfred inherited both the leadership of Metallgesellschaft and Hermann Schmitz.

Although the United States had not yet entered the war, Merton, probably on the advice of Schmitz, decided to conceal the German control of the American Metal Company. The forty-nine percent recorded ownership thereupon was placed in the names of a few trusted members of the American Metal Company management, all of them American citizens. Beneficial ownership, however, remained with the Mertons.

When the United States entered the war in 1917, Congress passed the Trading with the Enemy Act, which required disclosure of enemy-held assets in the United States. Carl M. Loeb, President of the American Metal Company, reported to the U.S. Alien Property Custodian that the Mertons were the true owners of the stock held in the names of American dummies.[3] The Custodian thereupon seized the cloaked American Metal Company stock. Merton, however, did not surrender easily. Despite the state of war between the United States and Germany he began to search for ways to sell the vested shares to the American management and recoup as much of the value of the seized property as possible. When the U.S. War Trade Board—to the amazement of all concerned—gave permission for two officers of the American Metal Company to visit Switzerland and negotiate the purchase of these controlling shares with Richard Merton, the project appeared on the verge of success. An agreement was actually reached to pay the Mertons $7 million for the vested shares.[4]

When the chief investigator of the Alien Property Custodian Office, Francis P. Garvan (who later became its head), learned of the War Trade Board's action, he entered a strong objection to American citizens' negotiating with the enemy about seized property. He forced the War Trade Board to rescind its permission, and the deal collapsed.

At that time serving as a member of the War Trade Board was a young Army major whose poor eyesight had kept him from combat service.[5] He was John Foster Dulles, the nephew of Robert Lansing, the Secretary of State. Within two years Richard Merton would become Dulles's client, and a lot more commotion was in store.

In 1919 at the Versailles Peace Conference, the two Metallgesellschaft men, Richard Merton and Schmitz, were present as representatives of the German Ministry of Economics, Merton as a high-ranking Commissioner,

Schmitz as an expert. Carl Bosch was present as an expert representing the chemical industry.

Aside from their personal compatability, the three men were bound by a common interest, to reacquire their company's properties seized by the American Alien Property Custodian during the war. Merton and Schmitz were most concerned about the vested shares of the American Metal Company; Bosch's interest centered on the scores of valuable BASF patents vested by the American Alien Property Custodian, including those covering the Haber-Bosch process, as well as the assets of the Kuttroff & Pickhardt Company, BASF's American selling agent. At Versailles, the three men used their official positions to advance their cause. Bosch and Merton managed to secure places on the committees involving their particular interests; Merton even entered an official inquiry about the status of the seized American Metal Company shares. It was the kind of activity that infuriated the German delegation's commissioner in chief, Walter Simons. He complained bitterly of the difficulty of collaborating with the "fifty or more experts who have been saddled upon us. For each of them, apparently, the welfare of Germany depended upon safeguarding of his particular interest, and it was treason to expect sacrifices from him."[6]

Bosch, Merton, and Schmitz's efforts at Versailles to include in the peace treaty a provision for the return of the confiscated properties, however, did not succeed. Nevertheless, the time they spent together at Versailles resulted in an alliance of the two German industrial giants, BASF and Metallgesellschaft. Bosch and Merton joined each other's organizations as directors and at Bosch's request, Merton released Schmitz to become BASF's top financial officer and chief of its international setup. Schmitz, however, preserved his close personal and business ties with Merton, retaining his directorship in the Metallgesellschaft system and continuing as an adviser to Merton on financial and international affairs.

In November 1919 Merton learned that the Alien Property Custodian had sold the confiscated American

Metal shares to a Wall Street syndicate at public auction for $5 million, the largest amount ever received up to that time for a vested property.[7] In a frantic effort to protect his interests, Merton sought out and retained John Foster Dulles, now a partner in the Wall Street law firm of Sullivan and Cromwell.[8] Dulles, like Merton, had been an official at Versailles.

In December 1920, a month after Warren Harding was elected president, Dulles received a letter from Richard Merton stating that the auction of the American Metal stock by the Alien Property Custodian in November 1919 had not been legal because the shares were owned by a Swiss neutral, not a German enemy.[9] He contended that six days before the auction, the Swiss holding company Société Suisse pour Valeurs de Métaux had purchased the shares from Metallgesellschaft. The rationale behind Merton's action was that Société Suisse was a national of neutral Switzerland, and the United States had no legal right to look behind the corporate veil for Merton's enemy interest because of the Swiss secrecy laws. Thus the vehicle which Schmitz organized to hide Metallgesellschaft's profits from German tax authorities was now to be used as a camouflage to conceal the enemy interests in the American Metal Company.

It did not appear very realistic of Merton to expect the United States to recognize the validity of the relatively transparent scheme he had cooked up. Yet Merton was neither a fool nor an unsophisticate in business and politics. Ways to convince the United States, which he did not care to reveal to Dulles, may have already been churning around in his mind.

In the early spring of 1921, Dulles discussed Merton's claim with officials of the U.S. Department of Justice without revealing the name of his client or the companies involved, and presenting the facts as "hypothetical." The response was not encouraging, and after the meeting Dulles reported to Merton that the U.S. government would not even consider the claim under the facts outlined in his letter. In the opinion of the Department of Justice, Société Suisse's purchase of the

American Metal stock in November 1919 was two and a half years too late; the only claims of this nature that the Alien Property Custodian could consider would be those involving assets acquired by neutrals *before* the United States severed diplomatic relations with Germany in March 1917—certainly not assets acquired after the declaration of war in April.

Dulles's negative message soon brought Merton to the United States to discover the lay of the land for himself. He arrived not long after Harding appointed Thomas Miller as the new Alien Property Custodian. Very quickly, Merton, the wartime "investigator of bribery in the occupied areas," assessed the changed political climate. What he saw convinced him to ignore Dulles and retain a better connected political intermediary, John King, Republican committeeman from Connecticut. King was not a lawyer, but it was commonly known that he wielded great influence with the Harding administration and especially with Harding's new attorney general, Harry M. Daugherty. Throughout the Justice Department King was treated as a member of the attorney general's official family although he had no official position. Merton learned from King that the new Alien Property Custodian had little regard for Dulles. Miller's distaste for the New York lawyer apparently had begun when both men were at the Versailles conference.

After a number of false starts while Merton was learning the facts of political life in the new administration, he finally struck a deal with King. He paid him a nonreturnable fee of $50,000 in cash and agreed in addition to pay five percent of the amount recovered, provided the claim was approved within two and a half months after filing or two and one-half percent if approved within three and a half months. King promptly put things in motion by splitting the $50,000 cash payment with Jesse Smith, Daugherty's "bag man." The first bribe involving the Harding administration had now been paid.

These formalities completed, Merton was briefed by an Alien Property Custodian official on how to prepare the claim. He needed properly sworn documents "proving" that Société Suisse had received beneficial title to the seized American Metal shares before April 1917 by means of an oral contract from Metallgesellschaft and Metallbank, its banking affiliate. Merton was cautioned that the claim and the supporting documents had to be sworn to before an official authorized by law to administer oaths; an ordinary notary was not enough.

Merton returned to Europe, where he gathered the supporting documents and statements required for the Société Suisse claim. The oaths were administered by Felix Iselin, a Société Suisse employee who did not have the legal authority to do so. Merton was aware that this made the oaths a nullity.

Merton filed the claim on September 20, 1921. Within three days it was approved for payment. By that time the amount involved totaled almost $7 million, some $1.5 million in interest and dividends in addition to the $5.5 million from the auction. Under the terms of Merton's agreement with King, he was now obligated to pay the latter almost $350,000.[10]

A week later, on September 30, Merton, King, Smith, and Miller celebrated at a plush champagne dinner at the Ritz Carlton Hotel in New York. King, politically an ardent prohibitionist, supplied the champagne. Merton, who paid for the rest of the feast, presented each of the guests with a $200 gold cigarette case. To cap the affair, Miller ceremoniously handed Merton $6.5 million in U.S. Treasury checks and $514,000 worth of Liberty Bonds.[11] Merton deposited $123,000 with Eduard Greutert, a Merton banking partner. Next he fulfilled his contract with King, presenting the intermediary with Liberty Bonds in the face amount of $391,000. (Because the market for Liberty Bonds was below par at the time, King demanded enough bonds to yield the $350,000 agreed upon.)

Merton then returned to Germany, richer by more than $6.5 million and confident that he had mastered the elements of traditional American politics. He also appreciated the wisdom of Hermann Schmitz. Switzerland was indeed a useful country.

Very soon after the champagne party at the Ritz Carlton Hotel was over, the hangover began. The *St. Louis Post-Dispatch* and the *New York World* of the Pulitzer chain, suspicious about the speed with which the Merton claim had been approved, assigned a number of reporters to investigate Miller's conduct in the American Metal case. Before long, the suspicions about corruption in the Harding administration became a raging issue in the press and in the Congress. On August 22, 1923, as the disclosures were reaching their peak, President Harding died. The new president, Calvin Coolidge, appointed Harlan F. Stone to replace Attorney General Daugherty, whose involvement appeared greater with each disclosure. Under the pressure of the mounting scandal, Stone appointed a special prosecutor, Hiram C. Todd, to head a criminal investigation of Miller's conduct of the American Metal case. On October 30, 1925, a grand jury indicted Miller, Richard and Alfred Merton, Metallgesellschaft and its subsidiary, Metallbank, Société Suisse and its president; and the president of the prestigious Swiss Bank. John T. King was listed as a co-conspirator but not indicted; Jesse Smith had earlier committed suicide under very suspicious circumstances.

The indictment set forth the details of the multi-million dollar payment to Richard Merton and his bribery of Miller through King and Smith. It charged that the Mertons filed false papers with the alien property custodian to support the Société Suisse claim. It further charged that the papers supporting a "verbal transfer" were sworn to before an individual (Felix Iselin) who was not authorized to administer oaths and that the defendants knew the oaths were illegal.

Special prosecutor Hiram Todd, in explaining why King was not indicted, disclosed that he had waived immunity in appearing before the grand jury. The implication was clear: King had struck a bargain with Todd and would be a key witness for the prosecution. Todd further disclosed that Miller had refused an invitation to appear before the grand jury.

The failure of Todd to indict Harry Daugherty, the

attorney general who had resigned under fire, raised serious questions in the press and in the Senate. Suspicions were voiced that Todd was engaged in a cover-up to protect Daugherty and probably others even higher up. Evidence mounted that Todd was a Daugherty crony and had been something less than diligent in presenting all the facts to the grand jury. As a matter of fact, Daugherty had appointed Todd a U.S. Attorney for the Northern District of New York early in the Harding administration. The stories of Todd's failure to investigate Daugherty with vigor finally took their toll. The special prosecutor resigned, and Emory Buckner, the U.S. Attorney for the Southern District of New York, took over. Buckner soon suspected that Todd's investigation was in fact a cover-up. He assigned an assistant, Kenneth Simpson, to investigate. When Simpson reported his findings, Buckner knew his suspicions were correct. He assigned ten men to dig further into the case.

They discovered very quickly that of the $391,000 worth of Liberty Bonds handed over to King by Merton, only $50,000 worth had been traced by Todd. These had been sold through intermediaries for the account of Miller. Buckner turned his attention to the remaining bonds.

Buckner now had reason to believe that former Attorney General Daugherty had received part of the bonds and had deposited them in the Midland National Bank of Washington Court House, Ohio, of which Daugherty's brother Mal was president. Mal had appeared before Todd's grand jury for only twenty minutes and he had been required to produce no records. Harry Daugherty had never been called to testify at all.

Buckner remedied this oversight by summoning both Mal and Harry Daugherty before a new grand jury. Mal was asked for the records, which Buckner was convinced would show what happened to the bonds. Mal said Harry had destroyed them after Mal's appearance before the previous grand jury. Harry Daugherty was asked about the records, and his reply has become an American classic:

> "Having been personal attorney for Warren G. Harding before he was Senator from Ohio and while he was Senator, and thereafter until his death,
>
> "—And for Mrs. Harding for a period of several years, and before her husband was elected President and after his death,
>
> "—And having been attorney for the Midland National Bank of Washington Court House, Ohio, and for my brother, M. S. Daugherty,
>
> "—And having been Attorney-General of the United States during the time that President Harding served as President,
>
> "—And also for a time after President Harding's death under President Coolidge,
>
> "—And with all of those named, as attorney, personal friend and Attorney-General, my relations were of the most confidential character as well as professional,
>
> "—I refuse to testify and answer questions put to me, because:
>
> "The answer I might give or make and the testimony I might give might tend to incriminate me."[12]

The accumulation of new evidence against Daugherty, together with his refusal to testify, led Buckner to revise his conception of the case. With Richard Merton out of reach in Germany and with little chance of the United States government's ever recovering the $7 million, Buckner began to consider the possibility of trading Merton for Harry Daugherty as a defendant in return for his testimony. As bait he was even willing to permit Merton to keep the $7 million.

Buckner dispatched Kenneth Simpson to Germany to discuss this deal with the Mertons. At the time, Buckner wrote his former professor at Harvard, Felix Frankfurter. "I have hopes of getting something, though

I confess I cannot see why they should talk, since they can easily remain out of this country the rest of their lives."[13]

Nevertheless, Buckner's slight hope was rewarded. Richard Merton appeared before the grand jury in New York, and the testimony he gave satisfied Buckner. On May 7, 1926, the grand jury returned with a new indictment that named both Harry Daugherty and John T. King, along with Miller, as defendants. Significantly omitted were Richard and Alfred Merton and all the other German and Swiss defendants indicted earlier. Buckner had kept his bargain with the Mertons.

Miller's lawyer, Robert S. Johnstone, attacked this new development:

> There is one peculiar difference between the old and the new indictments—neither Merton nor any of his alien associates is included as a defendant in the new indictment. Why not? Why are the persons who got the six million odd dollars left out? Why are those who according to the prosecution's theory swindled the Government out of this money not indicted? What deal was made with Merton and why?[14]

King could not be reached for comment. He was now in deeper trouble with the law than the other defendants. Buckner had indicted him for perjury in his testimony to the grand jury. He had also been indicted for violating the Internal Revenue Act: he had not reported his share of the Merton Liberty Bonds on his 1921 tax return.

Five days after his indictment King was diagnosed as critically ill with double pneumonia. A day later he was dead. There was no autopsy.

The trial of Daugherty and Miller began on September 7, 1926. For the first time in the history of the United States, a U.S. attorney general was being tried for bribery. The courtroom was jammed; many lawyers as well as the general public came to witness the contest that was about to take place between two giants

221

of the legal profession, Max Steuer for Daugherty and Emory Buckner for the people.

In his opening statement, Buckner made it obvious that the most important witness for the prosecution would be Richard Merton. It was the prosecution's intention, Buckner said, to lead Merton through the train of events from the moment King was "retained" until the "bribe" was passed at the champagne party at the Ritz Carlton. Buckner had set for himself a delicate task. The *New York Times* speculated,

> considerable interest has been manifested as· to how fully Mr. Merton will fulfill the expectations of the Government prosecutor. . . . His role is regarded as somewhat difficult because he will be asked to blacken his own success in the Société Suisse–American Metal "deal."[15]

During Buckner's direct examination, Merton proved urbane, literate, and extremely loquacious. He did not hide his own eminence, referring several times to his position as a delegate at the Versailles conference as well as his standing in Germany's financial and industrial community. Throughout the questioning of Merton, Buckner hammered home the point that King was not a lawyer and had nothing to sell but his influence and his close relationship to the attorney general; that Merton had pulled together his claim after instruction and "coaching" from the Department of Justice; and that large amounts of money had been passed clandestinely to government officials.

In recounting the facts that led to the approval of his claim and how much the settlement cost him, Merton was not an enthusiastic witness. But he answered questions to the reasonable satisfaction of prosecutor Buckner. However, Miller's lawyer, Colonel William S. Rand, grasped the opportunity during the cross-examination of Merton to question the German witness about the validity of the claim. When Rand put the specific query to him, "Did the claim reflect utter good faith?" Merton answered with emphasis, "Yes!"[16] The answer took Buckner by surprise, and he showed obvious distress.

The next day, still under cross-examination by Rand, Merton answered categorically that it was *his* idea to make the deal with King and pay him a retainer. What is more, he disclaimed knowledge that any part of the $391,000 worth of Liberty Bonds and the $50,000 delivered to King as a "fee" was passed to Miller and Daugherty.

Buckner could not let this testimony stand unchallenged. He claimed that Merton's answers on cross-examination took him by surprise. He submitted a memorandum of law to Judge Mack arguing that Rand had made Merton his own witness and therefore Buckner should have the right to subject him to cross-examination. Judge Mack granted Buckner's motion.

With permission to cross-examine his own witness, "Mr. Buckner fairly shot through the newly opened door."[17] He drew from Merton the damaging admission that in requesting John Foster Dulles to present the hypothetical case to the Department of Justice, he had not informed the lawyer of any March 1917 "oral" transfer. Instead, Dulles had been told that the Société Suisse had secured rights to the American Metal stock from Metallgesellschaft and Metallbank on November 20, 1919.

Merton did not regard Dulles as much of a lawyer. This became clear when Merton went on to testify that Dulles had suggested that Metallgesellschaft declare bankruptcy so that Société Suisse would have a better chance to collect from the Custodian. He characterized the advice as asking "a man to cut off his nose to spite his face." To Merton it made no sense for the giant Metallgesellschaft to declare bankruptcy to collect a mere $7 million claim. The exchange between Merton and Buckner about the Dulles advice about the bankruptcy of Metallgesellschaft was not missed by Steuer.

A few days later, Buckner called Dulles as a prosecution witness. Dulles startled everyone in the courtroom when he announced he was appearing for the prosecution under protest and pursuant to a subpoena: "However, as Mr. Merton has waived the question of professional privilege concerning my relations with him while he was my client, I suppose I must answer."[18]

Buckner then took Dulles through the substance of the hypothetical case presented to the Department of Justice. Dulles had not been informed of an "oral transfer" or in fact of any transfer before 1919 and he made no such representations to Justice. Dulles's testimony was crucial in showing that a transfer in March 1917 never really took place; that this was a later concoction by Merton, upon the advice of officials in the alien property custodian's office. Dulles also angrily denied that he advised Merton to place Metallgesellschaft in bankruptcy.

When Steuer cross-examined Dulles, part of his strategic plan of defense began to unfold. The fraudulence of the Merton claim was to be charged to the advice of lawyer Dulles and not to the venality of Miller and Daugherty. For ninety minutes Steuer subjected Dulles to a withering cross-examination. Steuer, with obvious contempt for Dulles's answers, sought to unnerve the witness: "You are evidently trying to avoid responsibility in this case. I don't understand your anxiety. Everyone knows you are involved only in your professional capacity."

"I am not worried," responded a shaken Dulles.

The *New York Evening Post* reported that at the end of the ninety minutes "Mr. Steuer sat down with the air of a man who had accomplished his purpose."[19]

On October 7, the time for summations arrived. The surprises were not yet over. In the course of presenting his defense of Daugherty to the jury, Steuer brought everyone in the courtroom to attention by the intensity of his attack on John Foster Dulles.

"Do you recall the evidence Merton gave about his first attempt to collect the claim through Dulles before he turned it over to John T. King?" Steuer asked the jury.

Now I don't want to besmirch any lawyer, but you take it from me, if John Foster Dulles wasn't Lansing's nephew and that gave him the privilege of going to the Peace Conference carrying a bag [to collect the bribe] and if he lived in Rivington Street [in the Jewish ghetto of New York] and if his client went on the stand as Merton did and testified, as Dulles advised him, to go into bankruptcy to collect the $7,000,000 claim, Rivington Street would be turned upside down and the Grievance Committee would not rest until that lawyer had been disbarred.

John Foster Dulles, said Max Steuer, was a "scoundrel who should be disbarred."[20] Not very often has a federal court in New York heard such an unbridled attack on so prominent and distinguished a lawyer.

When the time came for Buckner to sum up, he felt an obligation to defend Dulles. He did so by showing that Dulles was the first witness to establish the fact that there was no oral transfer or transfer of any kind prior to 1919. Then, taking up Steuer's intemperate attack, he read from the transcript of Merton's testimony to prove that Dulles had not provided his client with unethical and improper advice: "The synthetic defense," Buckner charged, "comes from a lack of witnesses. Wouldn't it be better to talk a little about the bribe than to offer Dulles as a sacrifice?"[21]

On the night of October 8 at 9:43 P.M. the jury retired to deliberate. Sixty-five hours later it was hopelessly deadlocked. According to newspaper reports, the final vote on Daugherty was seven votes for conviction, five for acquittal; on Miller it was ten for conviction, two for acquittal. Up to that time no jury had deliberated so long in the Southern District of New York without coming to a verdict.

Immediately after the trial was over Judge Mack told Steuer that his assault on Dulles was not justified, showed him portions of the transcript, and suggested that he take appropriate action to rectify matters. Steuer apologized to Dulles by letter on October 14, three days after the jury was dismissed.

My attention has been called by Judge Julian W. Mack today to the fact that comments concerning you that I made upon the evidence given by Mr.

Merton in the trial of United States vs. Daugherty and Miller were unwarranted by the record. I have never read a word of the testimony that was given during the trial and relied entirely upon my recollection thereof, and believed implicitly that which I was stating was borne out by the testimony as given. I had not prepared a summation for this case, nor have I ever for any other. I was led by my false impression of the testimony to make statements concerning you which, of course, I would not have made but for my false belief. I cannot tell you how much I regret those utterances. No one could regret them more. I completely apologize, therefore, and make absolute withdrawal thereof.

I shall be glad if this communication obtains publicity so as to counteract any effect resulting from the publicity given my original statement concerning you.[22]

The Department of Justice, undeterred by the hung jury, decided to try Daugherty and Miller again. On February 9, 1927, testimony began at the second trial. Several changes were noticeable. District Judge John C. Knox now presided; Steuer had been replaced as counsel for Daugherty by his partner Harold Corbin; and the well-known Chicago criminal lawyer Aaron Sapiro had replaced Colonel Rand as attorney for Miller.

Buckner prosecuted the case with the same young associates as in the first trial, including Carl Newton, George Leisure, and John Harlan. (The first two later formed the prestigious law firm of Donovan, Leisure, Newton, and Lombard; John Harlan went on to become a Supreme Court Justice.)

The second trial was a shorter, more efficient version of the first. To the surprise of many observers, Merton, despite his rough handling by Buckner, appeared again as the chief prosecution witness. This time the defense did not cross-examine him. Dulles, too, received gentler handling from the defense. The role of King as a non-lawyer and his close relationship to Attorney General Daugherty was again hammered home by Buckner. As in the first trial, the defendants did not take the stand in their own defense. And again Buckner pleaded with the jury to convict Daugherty as well as Miller: "Don't let the big one get away."

But once again the "big one" got away. By the vote of one juror, Daugherty avoided conviction. Buckner succeeded against the "little one"; Miller was convicted and Judge Knox sentenced him to eighteen months in prison plus a $5000 fine. Then Judge Knox dismissed the indictment against Daugherty. He announced that he had done so at the request of U.S. Attorney Buckner. Felix Frankfurter, however, in a letter to Senator Burton K. Wheeler a few days after the verdict, took issue with Judge Knox's comment that the dismissal was Buckner's idea: "That isn't true. The motion was made by him against his wishes and upon the insistence of the court. . . . Judge Knox told Buckner that if he did not move to nol prosse the indictment, he, the Judge, of his own motion 'would take the bull by the horns and nol prosse the indictment.' "[23] Later Judge Knox was to state that "guilty or not, the evidence presented against Daugherty *was* not conclusive" and that he would have voted like the lone juror for acquittal.[24] Buckner and his staff, however, did little to conceal their feeling that the juror in question had been fixed. (Years after the hung jury, Westbrook Pegler, a well-known columnist, ran into Daugherty in Florida. After the usual amenities, he asked Daugherty whether or not he had bribed that lone juror. Daugherty answered, "Take your pick, Peg, take your pick.")

Richard Merton returned to Germany. Although humiliated by his experience as a prosecution witness in the two trials, he received what he had bargained for.

The U.S. government did not press a claim to recover the $7 million until Merton himself, unable to let well enough alone, forced the issue. On March 10, 1928, an amendment to the Trading with the Enemy Act was passed, requiring the return to German interests of eighty percent of seized enemy property and, in addition, payment of accrued interest for the period of seizure. Société Suisse thereupon put in a claim for interest covering the period from 1919, when the American Metal Company stock was sold, to 1921, when Miller turned over the funds to Merton. Because of the fraud established in the conviction of Custodian Miller, the government rejected the application. Société Suisse thereupon filed suit against the attorney general as acting alien property custodian to recover the interest it claimed was due it. The government grasped the opportunity to file a counterclaim seeking restitution for the amount fraudulently paid Merton plus interest, totaling roughly $15 million.

For the next eight years the claim and counterclaim journeyed back and forth in the federal courts. Finally, on July 25, 1938, the litigation reached its end when the United States circuit court for the District of Columbia denied Merton's claim and awarded the government its entire counterclaim of $15 million.[25] The United States, however, could find only about $60,000 worth of assets upon which to levy.[26] Long before, Merton had stripped Société Suisse: now it was a hollow shell. The government therefore proceeded against the Swiss Bank Corporation as a party to the original conspiracy to defraud the United States. Ultimately the United States claim was compromised, through the intervention of the Swiss minister, for $3,030,769. By this time World War II was under way, Switzerland was a friendly neutral, and Merton was a refugee from Hitler living in England and writing attacks on the Nazi regime.

At about the same time that Merton was making his first contact with the Harding administration in the spring of 1921, a case much closer to Schmitz in his new role as head of BASF's international operations began to unfold. It involved the Alien Property Custodian's seizure of the assets of Kuttroff & Pickhardt Company, the American selling agency of BASF. Included in the assets confiscated was almost half a million dollars in Liberty Bonds. Because of his instinct for behind-the-scenes manipulation, the extent of Schmitz's involvement in this incident must remain a matter of conjecture.

Nevertheless his position within BASF, his history, and his personality argue persuasively that there was little about Kuttroff & Pickhardt's activities that Schmitz did not know or that was not reported to him. Relations with the Alien Property Custodian were clearly within his responsibility and his competence.

After Harding assumed office, Adolf Kuttroff and Carl Pickhardt filed a claim with the president for the return of the seized assets as provided by the Trading with the Enemy Act. They insisted that theirs was a wholly American-owned firm and therefore the property had been confiscated wrongfully. As a matter of record the stock ownership of the BASF agency was listed in the names of American citizens, all employees of Kuttroff & Pickhardt. They included Adolf Kuttroff, Carl Pickhardt, and Ernest S. and Ernest K. Halbach (father and son), all longtime *Vertrauensmaenner*, or trusted agents of BASF. In keeping with their past history, these American shareholders of record, however, were nothing more than fronts for BASF. Each of them had signed a secret option agreement requiring them to return the shares to BASF upon request. Not only ultimate control but also actual control remained in BASF's hands. Hiring, firing, salary increases, leasing of space, and even stationery purchases required BASF's permission.[27]

When the former alien property custodian, Francis P. Garvan, who had investigated and seized the assets of Kuttroff & Pickhardt, heard of the application, he personally mounted an attack on it. In every forum available, including newspapers and congressional hearings, he repeatedly charged that "Adolf Kuttroff and Carl Pickhardt never owned a dollar's worth of the company here. They never have been and never will be anything but clerks of the German I.G."[28]

President Harding paid no attention to Garvan. Instead, on November 21, 1921, he wrote a remarkable letter to his own Office of the Alien Property Custodian directing swift return of seized property of Kuttroff & Pickhardt.

I have had my attention brought to the claim of Messrs. Adolf Kuttroff and Carl Pickhardt, for $440,500 Liberty Bonds seized by the Alien Property Custodian on March 19, 1919.

Quite apart from any official information or any representations by counsel, I happen to know of of the thorough Americanism of these claimants and I think we are doing them a very great injustice by longer retaining their property in the hands of the Custodian. Inasmuch as Colonel Miller is absent from the City, I am writing to request you to proceed with the arrangements for the restoration of these bonds to their lawful owners. I do not mention the sum above as indicative of the exact detail. I am only writing to say that I would like to have this property restored to its proper and loyal American owners at the earliest possible day.[29]

The instructions to the Alien Property Custodian were unambiguous and direct. Yet Custodian Miller chose to ignore the president's order. Instead, upon Miller's recommendations, Attorney General Daugherty delivered to President Harding an "opinion of disallowance." There the matter rested until Harding died on August 2, 1923, when the "opinion of disallowance" inexplicably was found among his private papers in his personal desk instead of the official files of the White House.

It would be a euphemism to say that the entire transaction emitted a strange odor. Why did Miller and Daugherty refuse Harding's request? Certainly these two officials of dubious virtue would hardly disobey a presidential order as a matter of principle. Only two months before, Daugherty's "bag man," Jesse Smith, and Miller attended the celebration at the Ritz Carlton Hotel where Merton received the $7 million in return for a $350,000 bribe. Equally curious was the failure of Kuttroff and Pickhardt to press their claims during Harding's lifetime in spite of the president's personal representation "I happen to know of the thorough Americanism of these claimants."

Political scientists and historians may have been unaware of Harding's letter, but not Kuttroff and Pickhardt. After Harding's death, they renewed their claims with the new president, Calvin Coolidge, presenting Harding's letter as evidence that the matter had already been decided in their favor. Coolidge then sought from the Department of Justice an explanation for the "opinion of disallowance" in face of the Harding letter. The Justice Department, now under Attorney General Harlan F. Stone, referred the question to Alien Property Custodian Miller, who was under pressure but had not yet resigned.

Miller replied,

> In connection with this matter, I might state that the Kuttroff and Pickhardt claim was before President Harding from some time in November 1921 until the time of his death. As a matter of fact, the opinion of disallowance forwarded by your Department to President Harding in November or December 1921 was in President Harding's personal desk and was found there after he died. A number of times between December 1921 and up to the time I last saw President Harding, he discussed this matter with me several times. It is submitted that this letter has no force and effect, when, for over a period of nineteen months after he wrote his letter of November 21, 1921, this matter was pending before the President, and the fact that he did not act in accordance with his expressions to Mr. Meekins would seem to indicate that he had changed the opinion so expressed in his letter.[30]

Upon the advice of the Justice Department, Coolidge denied the claim and Kuttroff and Pickhardt took the matter to court. There Harding's letter proved decisive and the judge ordered the Alien Property Custodian to return the seized assets.

The Merton and Kuttroff & Pickhardt episodes would not have been wasted on Schmitz. They provided him

231

with invaluable insight into some of the darker aspects of the conduct of government and business in the United States. As future events would prove, he learned well, very well indeed.

It was not until the spring of 1929 that Schmitz decided to use the foreign holding company device on behalf of I.G. The immediate pressure to move at this time was the agreement between I.G. and Standard Oil concerning the sale of the world hydrogenation rights for $35 million in Standard Oil stock. Schmitz had no intention of I.G.'s paying the German taxes on this huge windfall. Instead, he fell back on the same sort of device he had created for Wilhelm Merton in organizing Société Suisse. Now, to keep the Standard Oil payment out of the reach of the German tax authorities, he planned to set up two foreign holding companies—one in Switzerland and one in the United States. The scheme so intrigued Schmitz that he decided to use it to evade taxes on a number of other of I.G.'s profitable foreign properties as well. The most substantial of these were the General Aniline Works (composed basically of the prewar Bayer dyestuff plants) and the Agfa Ansco Company, a photographic concern second in size in the United States only to Eastman Kodak. In Schmitz's calculations, the earnings of these I.G. assets in the United States represented a German tax liability worth evading.

The concealment of I.G. Farben's foreign assets, however, was not Schmitz's only aim in creating the holding companies. By 1929 the cost of Bosch's ambitious program for converting coal into gasoline was getting out of hand. To keep the project moving forward, Schmitz planned to use the holding companies to raise capital in the booming Swiss and American money markets.

At an I.G. Farben special stockholders meeting on February 20, 1929, Schmitz announced the creation of a new Swiss holding company, Internationale Gesellschaft fuer Chemische Unternehmungen (known as I.G. Chemie). At the same time, he informed the I.G. Farben shareholders that this corporation was going to raise $19 million through a stock issue to be sold to Swiss investors. Schmitz proposed that I.G. back the project by guaranteeing the purchasers the same dividends as those received on I.G. Farben shares. In exchange, I.G. would retain control through an old and trusted device, an option to buy the assets of I.G. Chemie at any time at market value.

As an inducement to vote for the dividend guarantee proposal, I.G. Farben stockholders would have the right to purchase I.G. Chemie shares at half price. Attracted by the chance to buy the Swiss company's stock at a bargain price, the I.G. Farben stockholders overwhelmingly approved Schmitz's plan.

To insure his personal influence in the Swiss holding company, Schmitz made himself president of I.G. Chemie and filled the board with established friends and trusted associates, including Eduard Greutert and Felix Iselin—both alumni of the Merton empire. Schmitz obviously regarded experience with the Mertons as valuable preparation for I.G. Farben's new enterprise. Moreover, he had had a hand in their training and they were personally loyal to him. Greutert and Iselin's involvement in the alien property custodian scandals in the United States was clearly no impediment. For what he had in mind such experience was perhaps helpful.

When the I.G. Chemie stock was offered to the public, the dividend guarantee by I.G. Farben worked its magic. The entire issue was sold almost the moment it was offered to the investing public. Once I.G. Chemie was successfully launched, the next step in Schmitz's scheme was the creation of its U.S. counterpart, the American I.G. Chemical Company.

On April 26, 1929, an advertisement appeared in the financial sections of the leading American newspapers announcing a $30 million issue of American I.G. Chemical Company five and a half percent convertible debentures. I.G. Farben's backing was set forth in bold type: *Principal and Interest and Premium, if any, upon redemption unconditionally guaranteed by endorsement on each Debenture by I.G. FARBENINDUSTRIE AK-*

TIENGESELLSCHAFT (I.G. Dyes) Frankfurt on the Main, Germany."[31]

To inspire investor confidence, the board of directors of American I.G. included four impressive figures from American industry and finance: Walter Teagle, president of Standard Oil (New Jersey); Edsel Ford, president of the Ford Motor Company; Charles E. Mitchell, chairman of the National City Bank; and Paul M. Warburg, a member of the financially powerful Warburg banking family. I.G. Farben was represented by Carl Bosch and Hermann Schmitz, who were listed, respectively, as chairman and president of the new company.

The sale of the debentures was an immediate success. Before the morning of the offering was over, the entire issue was sold.[32]

In offering the $30 million worth of debentures to the American public, Schmitz had no intention of surrendering an iota of control. The securities sold to the public could be converted only into nonvoting A shares. It had been arranged with the primary underwriter, the National City Company of New York, that three million B shares, containing all the voting rights, were to be retained by I.G. Farben "or some company or individuals affiliated with it."[33] Not a single voting share would be in the possession of the Americans who purchased the debentures. As soon as he could, Schmitz designated Greutert to hold the B shares.

Greutert then parceled out this voting stock to a small group of non-German corporations including Standard Oil (New Jersey), I.G. Chemie, Chemo Maatschappij voor Chemische Ondernemingen (a Dutch company known as Chemo), Greutert himself, and a number of American banks acting as temporary fronts for Greutert. A small number of shares were also held by such I.G. notables as Bosch and Schmitz. In time other non-German fronts were included among the B shareholders such as the Dutch company N.V. Maatschappij voor Industrie en Handelsbelangen (known as Voorindu), and the Swiss concern Osman Werke.

Within Standard Oil the entire venture was viewed with nervousness if not suspicion. When objections were raised about the propriety of the company's acting as a front for I.G. Farben, Teagle assumed the ownership personally. He was still in a state of euphoria over having purchased the hydrogenation rights from Bosch. He had no strong objection to performing such a small favor for I.G. Farben, which after all now owned two percent of the giant Standard Oil Company and next to the Rockefeller family was the largest single stockholder. Later, in 1933, the shares in Teagle's name as well as those held by Bosch, Schmitz, Greutert, I.G. Chemie, and some others were transferred to Mithras A.G., an obscure company in Zurich, with suspiciously close ties to Greutert. It was a company with no other assets operated by a single lawyer and his secretary from a tiny office. Mithras was obviously an I.G. dummy controlled by Greutert. Although he now was no longer a stockholder of record, Teagle continued to serve as a director of American I.G.

When Schmitz organized his scheme for camouflaging the ownership of American I.G. through a series of non-German fronts, he could not have anticipated the problems that he would face from such disparate systems as Hitler's Third Reich and Roosevelt's New Deal. These twin dangers for Schmitz arrived in 1933.

The trouble with the Nazis began almost immediately. Soon after Hitler assumed power, the Nazis enacted a law with the ominous title of Treason against the Nation, which specified the death penalty for anyone violating foreign exchange regulations or concealing foreign currency.[34] Rather than risk the consequences of such a frightening law, I.G. reported to the German government for the first time that it had sold the world rights to hydrogenation (except for Germany) to Standard Oil for $35 million worth of stock.[35] As a result, the tax authorities in the Ministry of Finance began an in-depth investigation to determine the extent of I.G.'s concealed foreign holdings. Especially targeted for inquiry were I.G. Chemie and American I.G. since the control of I.G. Farben, I.G. Chemie, and American I.G. "all seem[ed] to meet in the person of Hermann Schmitz," who at the time was the chief executive officer of all three concerns. But when the tax officials demanded the records of Greutert & Company and I.G. Chemie, the Swiss bank secrecy laws stymied the investigation. Schmitz, who was not without influence among Nazi officials, apparently convinced them, after protracted and uncomfortable negotiations, that to inquire too deeply into the ownership and control of I.G. Chemie, American I.G., and Greutert & Company would endanger I.G.'s foreign "strong points" to the detriment of German interests. As a result, a compromise was reached in which I.G. paid $5 million in taxes on the Standard Oil stock and the investigation stopped.[36] But from then on I.G. was careful to pay taxes on its foreign earnings and on its camouflaged as well as admitted assets.

In the United States a parallel problem developed for I.G. Farben. The 1934 Securities and Exchange Act required American I.G. to file a sworn application for the registration of its securities. In the course of completing the Securities and Exchange Commission form, American I.G. was confronted with the question of whether it had a corporate parent. Failure to identify I.G. Farben as the ultimate power behind American I.G.'s policies and operations was to flirt with the penalties for perjury and making false statements. Nevertheless, the officials of American I.G. "bit the bullet" and during the years 1934–1936 repeatedly perjured themselves by answering "None."

It was a dangerous game. In 1936 an attempt was made to reduce the legal hazard for the American I.G. officials in the signing of future S.E.C. registration statements. D. A. Schmitz, the brother of Hermann Schmitz and a naturalized United States citizen since 1909, became president of American I.G., and Hermann Schmitz took over the less active role of chairman of the board from Carl Bosch. As one German I.G. official noted, D. A. Schmitz as president would now have the duty of testifying on behalf of the company and yet as a newcomer he would be in a perfect position to plead ignorance to any potentially embarrassing questions.

Within a year the merit of this move became apparent. In 1937 the S.E.C., obviously dissatisfied with American I.G.'s response to the question on corporate parents, demanded that the company state specifically whether I.G. Farbenindustrie of Germany was its corporate parent. If not, did American I.G. have any other corporate parent? Did I.G. Farben or any other corporation or individual have the power to elect the directors or dictate the policies of the firm through stock ownership, contract or agreement, or any other means? It must have been a very nervous group of American I.G. executives who made the decision to reply "No" to all these questions.

Sensing that this answer was less than the truth, the S.E.C. staff undertook an investigation in depth. They "requested" D. A. Schmitz, as president of A.I.G., and Walter Duisberg, as first vice-president and treasurer, to attend an S.E.C. conference in Washington to discuss the subject more fully. The government investigators were not unmindful that D. A. Schmitz, although a naturalized U.S. citizen, was the brother of Hermann Schmitz, the head of I.G. Farben, and that Walter Duisberg, a U.S. citizen since 1933, was the son of Carl Duisberg, the founder of I.G. Farben.

At the meeting, the S.E.C. officials inquired about the large American I.G. stockholders of record. They noted that although Chemo and Voorindu of Holland and Mithras of Switzerland were record owners of large controlling blocks of American I.G. stock, investigation revealed that they were totally unknown and their names could not be found in any of the trade manuals or usual sources that normally listed companies with such important assets. Were they acting for I.G. Farben? Searching questions were also asked about the sale to I.G. Chemie and Greutert & Company. To all the inquiries, Schmitz and Duisberg exhibited a general ignorance. They claimed that they just did not know who owned American I.G.

Distrustful of the answers, in fact suspecting they were false, the S.E.C. directed written inquiries to I.G. Farben, Greutert, and I.G. Chemie. I.G. was unequivocal in its response: "We beg to say that we have no direct or indirect participation in the American I.G. Chemical Corporation nor in the other corporations [Greutert and I.G. Chemie] mentioned in your letter."[37] This was clearly a false statement. The Greutert firm was more careful. It refused to provide any information, pleading the strict provisions of the Swiss bank secrecy law. I.G. Chemie refused to answer as "a matter of principle."

The S.E.C., totally dissatisfied, continued to press its inquiry. On February 4, 1938, D. A. Schmitz, Walter Duisberg, and Walter Teagle appeared as witnesses at an S.E.C. hearing on investment trusts. Their testimony revealed an extraordinary lack of knowledge on the part of these men about the ownership and control of the company of which they were top officials and directors. Schmitz admitted upon questioning by David Schenker, S.E.C. counsel, that he had no idea who the beneficial stockholders of the company were. Duisberg testified that he did not know either. Duisberg even went so far as to deny that he was related to anyone in I.G. Farben despite the fact that his brother Carl served on I.G.'s supervisory board and his brother Curt worked in the pharmacy department at Leverkusen. He never even mentioned his father. However, it was Teagle, former president and now chairman of the largest oil company in the world, who commanded the most interest. Though a director of American I.G. since the company's founding, he testified that he had never known who were the principal owners. The S.E.C. counsel pressed the matter:

MR. SCHENKER: "And you do not know, at the present time who controls that corporation, is that not so?"

MR. TEAGLE: "That is correct; yes."

MR. SCHENKER: "Have you ever made any attempt, Mr. Teagle, to ascertain who were really the beneficial owners of the Class A and Class B stock?"

MR. TEAGLE: "No, sir."

238

COMMISSIONER HEALY: "When you say you do not know who controls it, Mr. Teagle, it is apparent it is controlled by European interests, is it not?"

MR. TEAGLE: "Well, I think that would be a safe assumption.

COMMISSIONER HEALY: "That is about the only assumption you can draw from the list of stockholders."

MR. TEAGLE: "That is correct, certainly."

MR. SCHENKER: "But precisely who these foreign interests are, if we predicate our conclusion on that assumption, you have never known and still do not know?"

MR. TEAGLE: "That is correct."

A bit later Teagle was asked about Edsel Ford, president of Ford and a fellow director of American I.G.

MR. SCHENKER: "Is he still on the Board of Directors?"

MR. TEAGLE: "I believe so; yes."

MR. SCHENKER: "Do you think he knows of the control of that company?"

MR. TEAGLE: "No; I do not think he knows any more about it than I do."[38]

When Teagle's extraordinary ignorance was headlined in the newspapers the next day, there was consternation at Standard Oil. An interoffice memo from a Standard executive assessed Teagle's predicament.

Mr. Teagle as a director was placed in a most embarrassing position at the hearing and also in press releases because he did not know the beneficial ownership of any of the large blocks of American I.G. shares. To the public, at any rate, it seems impossible that a man in his position would not know something as to who owns the company. . . . It seems to us also that the best thing Mr. Teagle can do is to resign from the American I.G., for while the present inquiry, I believe, is closed, we have certainly not heard the last of it.[39]

Frank Howard was determined to do something about the matter and he knew, even if Teagle seemed not to, exactly with whom to discuss it. In a letter to a Standard representative in Europe, he wrote, "I am afraid that one of us, or both of us, will have to have some pretty straight talk with . . . Schmitz about the American I.G. Chemical business."[40]

Howard's talk with Hermann Schmitz took place in Berlin a few weeks later, on March 11, 1938, the day Germany invaded Austria. After this meeting, Howard wrote to Teagle about Schmitz's attitude toward the S.E.C. inquiry.

> He knows what happened in Washington, and despite everything he still believes that his course has been the best course that could be taken and he wishes to continue it. He has pointed out to me, however, reasons why he believes there will be no recurrence of any of the past troubles in connection with the American I.G. company. Unfortunately, these are matters which I can only talk about when I see you—this at Dr. Schmitz' specific request.[41]

It is not known what Schmitz told Howard about resolving the American I.G. problem that could not be put down in writing. However, it is known that about three weeks later Hermann Schmitz was in Basel at a high level meeting of I.G. Chemie and I.G. Farben officials to discuss the S.E.C. probe. The solution was the de-Farbenization of I.G. Chemie so that it could be reported as American I.G.'s corporate parent. It was agreed that "any strong influence of I.G. Farben . . . has to be considered undesirable from the American point of view"[42] and would be extremely dangerous in case of "international entanglements"—a euphemism for war.

As long as I.G. Farben maintained its option on the I.G. Chemie stock, its control of I.G. Chemie and therefore American I.G. was undeniable. In the event of war, American I.G. would be highly vulnerable. Any solution, of course, would have to be approved by the

German government because of the strict foreign exchange regulations established by the Nazis. Kurt Krueger, Max Ilgner's deputy, was assigned to start working out a plan.[43]

Krueger soon found that securing permission to dissolve the I.G. Farben option on I.G. Chemie stock was a difficult matter. The Ministry of Economics official in charge of such matters, Gustav Schlotterer, posed no objections and in fact was favorably disposed to I.G.'s request. But the all-powerful foreign organization of the Nazi party, the Auslandsorganisation (A.O.), was another matter. It maintained a liaison man in the Ministry of Economics who had to be informed about major transactions involving the operation of German firms abroad. This proved a major obstacle to I.G.'s hopes. The A.O. had always opposed the cloaking of German foreign interests. It contended that cloaking was a pretext employed by big business, particularly I.G., to deprive German companies abroad of their German character.[44] Such actions smacked of "internationalism," a very nasty word in the Nazi lexicon and a reminder of I.G.'s early troubles with the Nazis. Moreover, cloaking was a device inspired by defeatism. A victorious Germany had no need to cloak; this tactic was useful only in the event of defeat. As far as the Nazi A.O. was concerned, foreign subsidiaries and affiliates, instead of concealing their German ties, should flaunt them. That I.G. was now preparing to conceal the German control of its overseas operations only made the A.O. more suspicious of I.G.'s international Jewish flavor. Added to this, important members of the Ministry of Economics long suspected that I.G. was hiding foreign exchange in its overseas holdings.

The outbreak of war on September 1, 1939, emphasized the fact that time was running short if I.G. Farben's foreign assets were to be successfully cloaked. A week later the problem was seriously complicated. Eduard Greutert, I.G.'s chief *Vertrauensmann* in Switzerland, suddenly died. I.G. officials were so preoccupied with the camouflage problem that they could hardly talk of anything else at his funeral.

In American I.G. some superficial cloaking steps were taken immediately. American I.G. changed its corporate name to General Aniline and Film Corporation (G.A.F.), eliminating the incriminating I.G. initials. The change, a public relation spokesman frankly explained, resulted from "a belief that German names caused business prejudice in this country."[45] Hermann Schmitz and Carl Bosch resigned from the board. The Germanic complexion of the executive committee, however, remained: D. A. Schmitz, Rudolf Hutz, and Wilhelm H. vom Rath were all I.G. related figures.

But the de-Farbenization of G.A.F. could not proceed on any legally effective level until the damning I.G. Farben option on I.G. Chemie stock was removed. As long as this formal tie remained, I.G. Chemie could not be designated as American I.G.'s Swiss parent. Instead, I.G. Chemie's Dutch dummy subsidiaries, Chemo and Voorindu, would remain the stockholders of record.

Just before Hitler unloosed his assault on the west in the spring of 1940, several "American friends" of I.G. Farben, including D. A. Schmitz and Hugh Williamson, went to Basel to confer with officials of I.G. Farben and I.G. Chemie about "the best and most successful measures to be taken to avoid the danger [of seizure of G.A.F. by the U.S. government] in the event of war with the U.S."[46] It was agreed that if anything constructive were to be accomplished, the I.G. Farben option on I.G. Chemie stock would have to be eliminated.

While these conferences were going on, the problem was suddenly made more complicated and a solution more urgent. Germany invaded Holland on May 10, and all Dutch assets in the United States were blocked by the U.S. Treasury Department. This included the stock of G.A.F. because the major stockholders of record, Chemo and Voorindu, were Dutch companies. It was a dangerous consequence that Hermann Schmitz had failed to contemplate when setting up his elaborate scheme of camouflaging American I.G. From now on all financial transactions would have to be approved by the Treasury Department. To free General Aniline from the grip of the U.S. government, it became imperative to establish that G.A.F.'s corporate parent was not the Dutch dummy fronts but rather I.G. Chemie itself. But as long as the telltale dividend guarantee option was in effect, I.G. Chemie could not claim it had no connection with I.G. Farben.

Within days, Krueger was back in Schlotterer's office urgently requesting approval of an application for the "revamping of our relations with . . . I.G. Chemie." He pleaded for permission to release I.G. Chemie from all links that might be interpreted as "being under German influence." For this approach to be ostensibly effective, the I.G. option on I.G. Chemie stock would be canceled and Hermann Schmitz would resign as chairman of I.G. Chemie. Krueger explained that I.G. had not embarked on this drastic course without long deliberation: "Our American friends are handicapped in their work for us by the existing links and believe that we must help them in the defense of our interests by carrying out the measures described above which they recommended to us." In this connection he pointed out that "the difficulty of the present situation is that the American company [G.A.F.] is considered excessively dependent on Switzerland, with the inference that the Swiss company [I.G. Chemie] is too strongly obligated toward the I.G., so the American company can be regarded as being under German influence."[47]

The problem was immediate and real. I.G.'s "American friends" were under increasing pressure from the Securities and Exchange Commission for disclosure of the parentage of G.A.F. The commission had set a deadline of May 30, 1940, for a definitive answer. It was now obvious, especially with the turn in world events, that no further delays would be tolerated. G.A.F. was no longer in a position to plead ignorance about control of the company. Yet, it dared not claim I.G. Chemie as its parent until the I.G. Farben tie was severed. In the meantime G.A.F. was blocked as a Dutch asset of Chemo and Voorindu. Krueger wrote to the Ministry of Economics:

The matter is particularly urgent because the final expiration date of the statement [to the S.E.C.] of the parentage of the American company which has been renewed several times, is May 30, 1940. Mr. D. A. Schmitz, President of the American company, who is staying in Basel at the moment and who has to embark for America at Genoa on May 18 at the latest, is prepared to take immediately in the U.S. all steps required on account of the measures described above . . . provided . . . the permits required from the authorities concerned have been promised to us in principle.[48]

In private discussions with Schlotterer, Krueger gave assurances that "the ties between I.G. Farben and I.G. Chemie would not be completely severed but would continue to exist in other forms." The German government, Krueger said, need have no fears; I.G. would continue to exert its influence in General Aniline and Film. In fact, it "had taken all necessary measures to insure that end."[49] I.G. could not have been more specific in pointing out the consequences of the failure to approve its application to dissolve the option: "Do you want us to lose G.A.F. through its being seized because of claims that we did not make a separation after all?"[50] This time I.G.'s arguments and assurances were apparently enough for Schlotterer. He approved the application.

The I.G. Chemie annual stockholders meeting was held at the end of June. The "revamping" measures approved by the German Ministry of Economics were overwhelmingly approved by the stockholders. Open "legal" ties between I.G. Chemie and I.G. Farben were formally severed.[51] To add credence that the decision taken at the stockholders meeting turned "I.G. Chemie . . . into a Swiss company," Hermann Schmitz resigned as its president and was replaced by a Swiss citizen, Felix Iselin. To those with a sense of history, Iselin was an odd choice. He was, it will be recalled, the Société Suisse employee who administered the

244

illegal oaths for the benefit of Merton in the American Metal Company case.

Moreover, the resignation of Hermann Schmitz did not eliminate the entire aroma of I.G. Farben influence. Still remaining on the I.G. Chemie board with suspiciously close ties to I.G. Farben were August Germann, Eduard Greutert's brother-in-law; Albert Gadow, Hermann Schmitz's brother-in-law; and Hans Sturzenegger, Greutert's protégé and successor. Sturzenegger set up Sturzenegger & Company to take over the interests of Greutert & Company.

Once the I.G. Chemie option was terminated, G.A.F. finally answered the S.E.C.'s question about its parentage. It identified I.G. Chemie as the owner of 91.05 percent of its controlling stock. With regard to the control of I.G. Chemie, G.A.F. reported that "we have also been advised by I.G. Chemie that it has no parent, that the majority of its voting power is owned by nationals of Switzerland, and that no one has an option under which I.G. Chemie would be required to sell any of its holdings of stock of the registrant."[52] The S.E.C. was still not satisfied, however. In a report to Congress on its investigation of G.A.F. it stated: During the course of the study, all attempts to ascertain the beneficial owners of the controlling shares have been unsuccessful."[53]

Of no less importance, the Department of Justice and the Treasury Department let it be known publicly that they regarded General Aniline and Film as a Nazi front. In view of the Nazi excesses reported daily in the American press, this identification became an increasingly intolerable burden to carry for the American-born directors. Hugh Williamson, one of the American directors (and also secretary of the company), was beside himself looking for a way to change G.A.F.'s public image. With the support of the law firm Breed, Abbott & Morgan, the general counsel to G.A.F. from which he originally came to the company, Williamson decided that the only solution to that problem, as well as to his own vulnerability to prosecution by the United States government, was to find a purchaser

245

with unassailable American bona fides. Williamson and the other American directors were not unaware that securing the approval of I.G. Chemie for this action might not be a simple matter. And what role would I.G. Farben play in such a decision?

As it turned out, I.G. Chemie, the newly identified parent of G.A.F., however, had other ideas and these did not include selling G.A.F. At the recommendation of the Swiss minister to the United States, Charles Bruggemann, it had earlier retained as its authorized representative Werner Gabler, a young, naturalized American citizen of Swiss birth, who had New Deal connections. The fact that Gabler was a Jew and his mentor, Bruggemann, was a brother-in-law of Vice-President Henry Wallace added to Gabler's credentials. His first and probably most brilliant move was to retain John J. Wilson as U.S. legal counsel for I.G. Chemie.

Gabler's next mission was to convince the interested government agencies, principally Justice and Treasury, that I.G. Chemie was an independent Swiss concern unconnected to I.G. Farben. In the course of this activity, Gabler proposed a plan to the Treasury Department whereby I.G. Chemie's controlling shares of G.A.F would be placed in a voting trust with two equal trustees, one appointed by I.G. Chemie and the other by the U.S. government.[54] The Treasury rejected the proposal almost as soon as it was made. Too much evidence already pointed to Gabler's principal as a creature of I.G. Farben.

The British took an active part in pressuring the United States to do something about General Aniline and Film. Hugh Dalton, the British minister of economic warfare, on May 1, 1940, issued a detailed public statement urging the United States to freeze Axis owned properties.[55] He warned that German interests, in anticipation of such an action, had already placed their assets in the names of neutral dummies. Dalton recommended that a system be instituted by which the neutral veil concealing Axis ownership would be torn aside. The most important German property concealed by a Swiss front, charged Dalton, was the General Aniline and Film Company, and he urged that something be done about this concern. Not long after Dalton's plea, on June 14 President Roosevelt ordered that the assets of continental European nationals in the United States be frozen. Roosevelt assigned the secretary of the treasury, Henry Morgenthau, Jr., the task of implementing the freezing order. The order required that by July 14, 1940, all property in the United States in which any foreign national had a direct or indirect interest must be reported. After the issuance of this order, there began what the *New York Times* described as "the greatest bit of detective-like ferreting this government has ever undertaken, since it is well known here that the Axis governments had long tried to conceal their American assets in anticipation of a move of this kind directed at them."[56]

By specifying *every* continental European country, Roosevelt caught the Swiss in his net. Switzerland's ownership of $1.5 billion worth of assets in the United States was too suspicious a concentration to be ignored. General Aniline had already been blocked at the time of the invasion of Holland. Now, with Roosevelt's action, the establishment of a de-Farbenized I.G. Chemie as the parent of G.A.F. would not result in the "unblocking" of General Aniline.

At the same time, the General Dyestuff Corporation was also blocked. This concern was composed of the I.G. Farben sales companies that had been seized by the alien property custodian in World War I. They all found their way back to I.G. Farben during the twenties and were merged to form the General Dyestuff Corporation. To exercise ultimate control of General Dyestuff, I.G. Farben resorted to the traditional option device, relying on such I.G. *Vertrauensmaenner* as Adolf Kuttroff and, most significantly, Ernest K. Halbach, on whom I.G. had relied in more than seven transactions involving "control by option." In August 1939, just before Germany's attack on Poland, I.G. sold the controlling interest in General Dyestuff to Halbach. Because the Treasury Department had strong

247

suspicions and reservations about Halbach's history, General Dyestuff was also blocked after Roosevelt's order. Henceforth the company's activities were subject to Treasury licenses.

All of these adverse developments prodded Williamson, the leader of the so-called American majority of the G.A.F. board, to push his plan to free G.A.F. from its present ugly difficulties even more vigorously. He approached a number of companies, including Standard Oil (New Jersey), the Ford Motor Company, and International Telephone & Telegraph. Standard and Ford, having been burned during the S.E.C. inquiry of American I.G., manifested a short-lived interest. But I.T.T.'s interest was genuine.

Colonel Sosthenes Behn, the president of I.T.T., went directly to what he regarded as the ultimate power in the matter, the German government. Obviously, he regarded I.G. Farben as the true owner of G.A.F. and therefore German government permission was necessary before any deal could be made. Behn actually reached a tentative agreement with the German government, and he dispatched Frank Page, a vice-president of I.T.T., to inform the U.S. State Department. According to a State Department memorandum,

> Colonel Behn reports that the German government has offered to exchange the ownership of the American [sic] Aniline and Film Company for the ownership of the German company owned by the I.T.&T, which manufactures telephone wire and other equipment. Mr. Page said that the value of each of the two companies was approximately the same, and the exchange would be of advantage to the I.T.&T. in that they would have their money transferred into an American asset.[57]

An International Telephone & Telegraph representative then entered into negotiations with I.G. Chemie officials in Switzerland, and Behn was led to think the matter was near settlement. In early July he scheduled a meeting in Basel. He apparently believed this would be one of the final steps in closing the deal. So did Williamson and most of the other General Aniline and Film board members. D. A. Schmitz, the president of G.A.F., however, indicated more skepticism than enthusiasm.

On July 3 the reasons for Schmitz's attitude took on greater meaning for Williamson. The G.A.F. representative in Basel had just reported that I.G. Chemie had lost interest in making a deal with I.T.T. Williamson called Hans Sturzenegger, who had inherited Greutert's position as the principal stockholder of record of I.G. Chemie, to check on what had caused the breakdown in negotiations.

The conversation had hardly begun when Sturzenegger confirmed Williamson's fears that the I.T.T. deal was off. It was based, said Sturzenegger, "on erroneous assumptions." He then dropped what must have seemed like a bombshell to Williamson. I.G. Chemie, he revealed, was now negotiating with Ernest Halbach. Sensing Williamson's dismay, Sturzenegger said that he had been reliably informed that Halbach was acceptable as a purchaser to the United States government. With that, Williamson exploded: "Ach du liebe Zeit. That is ridiculous. Halbach is blocked right now, you know."[58]

When Sturzenegger asked why Halbach was unacceptable to the U.S. government, Williamson almost screamed, "His background, Hans, on the record, all in writing, is even worse than our own." Halbach's signature on some seven option agreements as an I.G. trustee agent was enough to doom him. But Sturzenegger pursued the issue of Halbach's bona fides. Williamson explained: "It's just like selling to D.A. Schmitz. . . . It's just inconceivable." At the end of the conversation, Williamson charged that in addition to everything else, Halbach was not in a financial position to buy G.A.F.: "He hasn't anything like the money with which to do it . . . as a physical banking act, he cannot do it."[59]

Convinced that I.G. Chemie was about to sell to Halbach, Williamson in desperation called Sturzenegger again that day. He acknowledged that under ordinary circumstances, I.G. Chemie in selling to Halbach "couldn't ask for a better trustee—that's just switching pennies from one pocket to another" and that Halbach was "our own hired man."[60] The trouble was that the Treasury Department would take the same view.

Williamson's efforts proved futile. I.G. Chemie was determined to sell to Halbach. On July 14 the General Dyestuff Corporation (G.D.C.), now owned by Halbach, received a cable in code giving it an option to buy the controlling stock of G.A.F. in the possession of the U.S. Treasury Department. The price was $5,812,500. Upon receipt of the option agreement, G.D.C. filed an application with Treasury, requesting approval to purchase the G.A.F. shares.[61]

Williamson continued his objections to Halbach, arguing that the entire project was pointless and would only result in the loss of valuable time because the U.S. government would never approve the sale. It would be much more productive to work at selling G.A.F. to a company with unquestioned American credentials. General Aniline's general counsel, Breed, Abbott & Morgan, even prepared an opinion setting forth the reasons why the United States government would never approve Halbach as a purchaser of General Aniline and Film. I.G. Chemie was unmoved. It continued its all-out support for the sale to Halbach. Ignoring both Williamson's warning that precious time was being wasted and the Breed, Abbott & Morgan opinion on the unacceptability of Halbach, it waited for the Treasury's approval of Halbach's G.D.C. application. A bitter split was now developing among the G.A.F. directors. Felix Iselin demanded that the sale to Halbach go forward. D. A. Schmitz abandoned his seemingly noncommittal stand and sided openly with Iselin. So did Ernst Schwarz, formerly a high official of I.G. in Germany but now a Jewish refugee in the United States. Schwarz was loyal to Hermann Schmitz, who had found a place for him in G.A.F. Strongly opposing this trio was the majority of board members—the American-born directors, Hugh Williamson, William Breed, and Walter Bennett, and the German-born American citizens, Wilhelm vom Rath, Hans Aikelin, and Rudolf Hutz.

By September, the struggle on the G.A.F. board had grown so intense that the majority demanded the resignation of D. A. Schmitz as president. Breed wrote him a letter on September 14 pointing out that his past, especially the fact that he was the brother of Hermann Schmitz, made him unsuitable for the position and suggesting he resign immediately. When Schmitz refused, the board took summary action and dismissed him as president, although he continued to remain as a director. Upon learning of this action, Felix Iselin struck back and sent a cable from Basel peremptorily demanding the resignations of all the American directors. The cable was ignored.

Barely a week later, as Williamson predicted, on October 2 the Treasury rejected Halbach's application to buy control of G.A.F. It gave no reason for the denial. The reason was obvious.

With the Halbach problem out of the way, the majority directors of G.A.F. turned their attack against I.G. Chemie. On October 31 they elected John Mack to succeed the deposed D. A. Schmitz as president. The political benefits the new appointee brought to the post were clear. He was a friend and neighbor of President Roosevelt's. In fact, Mack made the principal nominating speech for Roosevelt at the 1932 Democratic convention. As for improving relations with the S.E.C. and the Justice and Treasury departments it was considered a politically wise selection.

On November 30 the majority directors pressed their attack by demanding the resignations of the minority directors—D. A. Schmitz, Ernst Schwarz, and Felix Iselin. All refused. On December 5 the majority faction continued the policy of acquiring politically important figures to help their cause. They elected William C. Bullitt to the board. Like Mack, Bullitt was an intimate friend of Roosevelt's. He had influenced Roosevelt to recognize the Soviet Union and had been named ambassador to the U.S.S.R. Later, when war seemed inevitable in Europe, Bullitt had been appointed to the critical post of ambassador to France. The majority directors, in a public statement, described Bullitt's election to the

251

board as "another step to place control . . . unmistakably in the hands of American interests."[62]

On December 7 the Japanese attacked the United States at Pearl Harbor. On December 10, Germany declared war on the United States.

Within days Attorney General Francis Biddle moved to strike at I.G. Chemie's control of General Aniline. He drafted an amendment to the Trading with the Enemy Act empowering the president to vest the property of *any* foreigner not just of enemy nations.

Before a hastily convened executive session of the Senate Judiciary Committee, Biddle explained, "Under the Trading with the Enemy Act . . . there is no power whereby the United States can take title to and operate certain businesses of aliens, or even alien enemies—for instance where a majority of the stock is owned by a Swiss company and we might have no way of preventing that Swiss company from acting for the Nazi government."[63] He left no doubt that he was referring to G.A.F. and its ownership by I.G. Chemie.

The day before, December 18, only a week after Biddle presented the proposed legislation, it was passed by the Congress and signed into law by President Roosevelt. Now Swiss-owned assets were subject to vesting. G.A.F. was seized by the alien property custodian on April 24, 1942, and G.D.C. two months later.

With the seizure, all attempts by the board to Americanize G.A.F. came to an end. The Custodian, Leo Crowley, replaced all the past directors with his own appointees, who took over active operation of the company for the rest of the war.

When the Nazi government received newspaper reports that the United States might be planning to liquidate the confiscated enemy properties, including G.A.F., it proposed to retaliate by liquidating United States assets in the Reich. The idea of retaliation was opposed by the Reichsbank and the Foreign Office. By such an act they warned, "we would thereby furnish the Americans with a frank admission of what we have been so far trying to conceal by cloaking—i.e., that these actually exert German interests in the companies involved, and on a considerable scope."[64] It was a damning admission, which surfaced among the captured German documents immediately after the end of the war.

11

The Strange Case
of
General Aniline and Film

As the war approached its last year, the problem of what action should be taken by I.G. Chemie with regard to the seized General Aniline and Film shares became a serious question. I.G. Chemie's lawyer, John J. Wilson, counseled delay. He wisely reasoned that the chances for success increased as the passage of time dimmed the passions of war. Within a very short period the wisdom of Wilson's advice was affirmed.

Standard Oil (New Jersey) felt it could not afford the luxury of waiting for a change of climate. It had good reason to believe that Crowley, under pressure from the Justice Department's Antitrust Division, was about to issue licences under the vested Jasco and Standard-I.G. Company's patents. It decided "to take the bull by the horns." On July 13, 1944, Standard and its affiliates, Standard Oil Development Co., Standard Catalytic Co., and Jasco, filed a complaint under section 9 (a) of the Trading with the Enemy Act against the Alien Property Custodian in U.S. district court for the Southern District of New York. The companies charged that the patents and stock of the Standard-I.G. Company and Jasco had been wrongfully seized and demanded their return. After all the preliminaries were out of the way, the trial began on May 21, 1945, two weeks after Germany surrendered unconditionally. There were some voices within Standard who urged delay until the emotional climate became more favorable. It was hardly the time to be defending relations with an "enemy" company. But those who argued that time would work against Standard prevailed.

Representing Standard was John W. Davis of the Davis, Polk firm. Davis, an eminent member of the American bar, had been the Democratic nominee for president of the United States in 1924. Heading the trial team that represented the Alien Property Custodian was Philip Amram, a trial lawyer from Philadelphia who had been drafted for the task by Attorney General Biddle.

Judge Charles E. Wyzanski, Jr., of the U.S. district court in Boston, had been specially designated by Chief Justice Harlan Stone to preside over the case. It would have been difficult to improve on the quality of either the defense and prosecution teams or the judge.

The chief contention of Standard's lawyers during the trial was that at the time the Jasco and Standard-I.G. shares and patents were vested on March 25, 1942, Standard was their rightful and legal owner— that all vestiges of I.G.'s interest in the properties had disappeared in September 1939 with the Hague agreement.

The government's defense of the seizure was that the transfer of the stock and patents to Standard as provided by the Hague agreement was a camouflage to conceal the enemy ownership by I.G.

In the course of preparing for the trial, Amram received word from the War Department that August von Knieriem, chief legal counsel of I.G., had been captured by General Patton's Third Army. Amram sensed that the approaching defeat of Hitler might make Knieriem a cooperative witness. He caught the first available military plane for Paris, where Knieriem was brought for the interrogation. The I.G. lawyer not only agreed to appear as a U.S. government witness but also promised to provide documents in support of Amram's case. These would include papers involving the Hague agreement as well as correspondence about the transaction between I.G. and the German High Command. All this material was intact because when the bombing of Frankfurt had begun, Knieriem had moved all his files to a farm outside of Heidelberg, which as a protected university city had not been bombed by Allied air forces. Amram arranged for Knieriem to bring these papers to New York for the trial.

When the trial was in its second week, Amram received word that Knieriem had arrived at Ellis Island with his documents. Amram went to meet him and Knieriem said he was ready to testify. He asked Amram to do something for him first, however—buy him a new white shirt and tie so he would not have to face his old Standard associates in a shabby prisoner of war uniform. Amram gladly complied.

Amram was now ready to unveil his mystery witness. He called Knieriem to the witness stand. Wearing the new shirt and tie, Knieriem entered the courtroom under military guard. He clicked his heels and bowed to the judge and the attorneys on both sides. "The faces of the Standard Oil executives were something that I will never forget,"[1] Amram later recalled.

Judge Wyzanski asked Knieriem if he would like a translator, but the German lawyer proudly declined. Then in clipped and impeccable English, with only a trace of an accent, he proceeded to identify the documents he had brought from Germany. Amram was now ready to deal Standard a devastating blow. He offered in evidence Knieriem's own copy of the Hague agreement, with the latter's handwritten notes in the margin, some in English and some in German.[2] Beside the preamble stating that under the original 1930 agreement Jasco was the owner of certain patent rights including the Buna process, Knieriem had written *"Nachkrieg Camouflage"* ("Postwar camouflage")! Amram then introduced correspondence that Knieriem had supplied between I.G. and the High Command. In one document I.G. explained, "By this transfer . . . the patents in German possession will be removed from enemy seizure . . . we consider it right to transfer the patents to an American holder who is on friendly terms with us and who will cooperate with us on a friendly basis in the future."[3]

After strong objections by the Standard lawyers, Judge Wyzanski finally admitted Knieriem's documents. In Amram's view, this evidence "exposed the falsity of the Hague Memorandum . . . and showed conclusively that the whole scheme was a transparent device to conceal the property from the Alien Property Custodian in the event of United States participation in World War II"[4]

Five months later, on November 7, 1945, Judge Wyzanski rendered his verdict. He held that all transfers of assets from I.G. to Standard after the Hague agreement were a sham designed to create the false appearance of Standard ownership of property interests that both parties continued to regard as owned by I.G. "The court is satisfied," Wyzanski wrote,

> that the overriding real agreement of the Jersey group [Standard] and I.G. was that . . . these transfers both of legal title and equitable interests were to be null and void at the pleasure of I.G., and the parties intended that after the close of World War II, the Jersey group and I.G. would make whatever deal then deemed to be appropriate.[5]

Judge Wyzanski concluded,

> In short, the Hague Agreement and the subsequent transactions in reality, though not always in form, left I.G. with unaltered legal and equitable rights. . . . And so the United States government and the Alien Property Custodian were entitled to seize those rights on March 25, 1942, as properties of an enemy.[6]

The Jasco stock and patents, including the Buna patents, were therefore to be retained by the custodian. But the government did not win a complete victory. Wyzanski found that the transactions between I.G. and

257

Standard that took place *before* the Hague conference had been in good faith and had not contemplated later substantial readjustments. The securities and patents involved must be returned to Standard since they were not to be construed as the property of an enemy.

On September 22, 1947, the circuit court upheld the decision and findings of Judge Wyzanski.[7] Judge Charles Clark, who wrote the opinion, sharpened the findings of the lower court. For example, in connection with the initial transfer of title of I.G.'s Jasco stock to Walter Duisberg, Clark wrote that "the inference is inescapable that Duisberg was just another dummy used to hide the real ownership of I.G. property."[8] In a footnote in the opinion, Judge Clark volunteered a startling observation—that Standard Oil could have been considered an enemy national in view of its relationship with I.G. Farben after the United States and Germany had become active enemies: "Though the defendent does not make the argument, it would seem possible to contend that, under this extensive definition, plaintiffs became enemy nationals after the outbreak of the war, since their concealment of I.G. assets continued thereafter."[9]

Clark's decision became final on April 19, 1948, when the U.S. Supreme Court denied all writs of certiorari. This date marked the end of the disastrous I.G.-Standard marriage. As a result of the lawsuit, the Alien Property Custodian turned over to Standard Oil the prewar interests of I.G. in the Standard-I.G. Company but retained I.G.'s half interest in Jasco, along with almost all of the patents that presumably had been transferred to Jasco by I.G. after the beginning of the war, including the Buna patents.

However, Standard's fears, expressed back in 1939, that I.G.'s interests would "fall into unfriendly hands" were not realized. In April 1953, the Alien Property Custodian offered the Jasco stock at auction to the highest bidder. After receiving six sealed bids, he announced that the Standard Oil Development Company was the high bidder at $1.2 million.

The decision in the Standard Oil case was hardly a

source of comfort for I.G. Chemie or its American lawyer, John J. Wilson. Even more disquieting was the directive issued by the reparations conference held in Paris in December 1945 that each Allied member look to confiscated German assets in their respective countries as reparations for war damages. Neutral nations likewise were required to liquidate known German assets found within their borders and transfer proceeds to the Inter-Allied Reparations Agency, which was to divide the assets among claimants in accordance with a fixed quota—the United States and Great Britain were each to receive twenty-eight percent with the remaining forty-four percent to be divided among the other Allies. Of frightening significance to I.G. Chemie was the fact that German assets cloaked in neutral countries were included: "The German enemy assets to be charged against reparation shares shall include assets which are, in reality, German assets despite the fact that the nominal owner of such assets is not a German enemy."[10] No one doubted that I.G. Chemie and its alleged offspring, General Aniline Film, were prime targets of this resolution. While the reparations conference was under way, a special meeting of I.G. Chemie stockholders was held in Basel to take protective measures against the decision of the Paris conference. The climate of German defeat pervaded the atmosphere of the meeting, whose purpose was to obliterate, as far as possible, any taint of I.G. Farben. The famous I.G. initials were dropped as the corporation formally changed its name to Internationale Industrie und Handelsbeteiligungen A.G. From now on I.G. Chemie would be known as Interhandel. The bylaws were amended to eliminate the use of bearer shares, one of the traditional mechanisms used by I.G. Farben to exercise hidden control. Finally Albert Gadow, managing director since 1935 and brother-in-law of Hermann Schmitz, resigned. Gadow was succeeded by Walter Germann, a Swiss citizen, and a nephew of the late Eduard Greutert.

While I.G. was involved in these attempts at de-Farbenization and de-Germanization, the Swiss Compensation Office undertook an investigation into the degree of German ownership of Interhandel. The agency examined every scrap of paper in Interhandel's files that might be relevant to determining the ownership of Interhandel. It made an equally complete examination of the records of Sturzenegger, the successor to Greutert.

When the inquiry was completed, the Swiss Compensation Office concluded that I.G. Chemie (Interhandel) was not controlled or owned by I.G. Farben and was indeed a genuine Swiss company owned and operated by Swiss interests. In Allied circles the decision met with disbelief, and it was entirely unacceptable to the United States government. Fortified by thousands of captured I.G. Farben documents, the United States stood its ground that Interhandel was a German controlled concern. There was a growing impression among U.S. officials concerned with the matter that the Swiss government was more and more dominated in this matter by internal pressures than by the need for a legally valid adjudication.

The tough United States position brought some results. In May 1946, at a conference in Washington, D.C., Switzerland entered into an agreement with the United States, France, and England to deal with the problem of Nazi involvement in camouflaged assets and looted gold in Switzerland. According to the terms of the agreement, the Swiss Compensation Office, in collaboration with a commission composed of representatives of the four parties to the Washington Accord, was to examine all questions of disputed ownership and liquidate all property determined to be German owned. In the event of a disagreement between the Swiss Compensation Office and the Joint Commission, the dispute was to be submitted to the Swiss Authority of Review.

Almost immediately Interhandel became the subject of a major disagreement. The Swiss Compensation Office continued to hold that Interhandel was truly a Swiss company and not a camouflaged holding of I.G. The Joint Commission vigorously disputed this finding and appealed to the Swiss Authority of Review, which supported the Swiss Compensation Office. After the prescribed period of thirty days, the Swiss government declared the Swiss Authority of Review decision final, removed the freeze on Interhandel's assets in Switzerland, and presented the United States government with a demand that the General Aniline and Film stock be released to Interhandel. Two could play this game, however, and the United States refused. The Americans replied that the Washington Accord dealt only with assets located in Switzerland and did not affect assets in the United States: non-enemies such as Swiss nationals seeking the release of property vested in the United States were to rely on the legal remedies provided for in the Trading with the Enemy Act. For practical purposes United States law would govern the disposition of the General Aniline property. By July 1948, this proposition was strengthened by an amendment to the Trading with the Enemy Act providing that no enemy assets were to be returned to their former owners. Instead, they were to be deposited in a special fund for the payment of war claims.

This addition to the Trading with the Enemy Act seemed to settle the question of whether Congress would pass legislation, as it had in 1928 after World War I, returning seized assets to their former owners. With that option apparently gone, John J. Wilson, now confronted by the running of the statute of limitations, finally filed a section 9 suit on behalf of Interhandel for the recovery of the G.A.F.[11] shares that had been seized by the Alien Property Custodian. Since the Office of the Alien Property Custodian had been transferred some two years earlier to the Department of Justice, the suit named Attorney General Tom C. Clark as the defendant. It is a matter of historical interest that the suit was filed not in Interhandel's German name, under which it did business in German-speaking Basel, but in the rarely used French name, Société Internationale pour Participations Industrielles et Commerciales S.A.

The Interhandel complaint charged that the G.A.F. stock had been wrongfully seized by the alien property custodian because Interhandel had never been either an enemy or an ally of an enemy of the United

States and because Interhandel was the real and beneficial owner of the vested shares. Significantly, Interhandel did not dispute the U.S. claim that I.G. Farben controlled and dominated I.G. Chemie before June 1940. It contended, however, that after that date, changes had occurred that cut all ties to I.G. Farben. What Interhandel was alluding to were the de-Farbenization measures undertaken in 1940, just before G.A.F. informed the Securities and Exchange Commission that I.G. Chemie was its corporate parent. These included the cancelation of the dividend option agreement, the rsignation of Hermann Schmitz from I.G. Chemie, and I.G. Chemie's purchase of a large portion of its own stock held by German shareholders.

In its reply, the United States charged that all these changes were nothing more than further attempts at camouflage. It charged that Interhandel, from its incorporation in 1921 until Germany's surrender in 1945, had participated in a conspiracy with I.G. Farben, Eduard Greutert, and the latter's successor, Hans Sturzenegger, "to conceal, camouflage and cloak the ownership, control and domination by I.G. Farben of properties and interests in many countries of the world, including the United States."[12] Moreover, the government charged, the real and beneficial owner of the G.A.F. shares was I.G. Farben.

Thus began a legal contest that was to journey up and down the judicial ladder of the federal courts until it reached a surprise conclusion some fifteen years later. During those fifteen stormy years, there were innumerable efforts to reach a settlement. Frequently these attempts were complicated by the intrusion of political influence and the appearance of volunteer intermediaries and others of dubious credentials. Nevertheless, several times a settlement appeared to be a real possibility. In 1950, for example, Interhandel offered to accept $14 million to compromise its G.A.F. claim.

The assistant attorney general in charge of alien property recommended U.S. government acceptance. However, Attorney General Tom Clark rejected the $14 million figure and countered with an offer of $12 million. The Justice staff, which argued that principle rather than money should be the determining factor, heatedly objected to any settlement. Only a legal adjudication in court would satisfy them. Now in possession of captured Nazi and I.G. documents, they could prove in a court of law that G.A.F. and Interhandel were camouflaged I.G. Farben properties.

However, in the middle of the negotiations, two Jewish refugees, Interhandel stockholders, entered the scene of action. On May 11, 1950, Eric G. Kaufman and Aenni C. Kaufman, who owned eighty-six shares of Interhandel stock, filed a motion in district court on behalf of all non-enemy stockholders to intervene in the pending case. In their petition, the Kaufmans alleged that Interhandel was presently dominated and controlled by officers, agents, and stockholders who had engaged in a conspiracy with German nationals and with the German government to operate Interhandel's business in the interest of Germany during the war. In fact, they contended that the present Interhandel suit was controlled by the very stockholders whose background and conduct had caused the U.S. Alien Property Custodian to seize the G.A.F. assets in the first place. The Kaufmans charged that the management, fearing permanent confiscation of its enemy-tainted interests, was about to settle the claim for a great deal less than the true value of the non-enemy holdings. Finally, the Kaufmans alleged that this "enemy" group in control of Interhandel could not be expected to protect the interests of non-enemy shareholders. Their intention to divide the proceeds of such a settlement equally among enemy and non-enemy stockholders would deprive the non-enemy stockholders of their rightful interest in the assets. Moreover, it would result in a substantial benefit to a former enemy.[13]

Both the Interhandel management and the United States government opposed the Kaufman intervention, each insisting that the interest of all stockholders be treated alike. The Interhandel management objected to the opprobrium implicit in dividing the stockholders into enemy and non-enemy classifications, which car-

263

ried the even more odious connotation of Nazi and anti-Nazi. The United States, for its part, simply preferred a settlement of all the claims at once so that the G.A.F. stock could be sold in one package.

The Kaufmans' petition to intervene was denied by the district court two weeks after it was filed,[14] and the denial was affirmed by the U.S. court of appeals.[15] However, the Kaufmans persisted and in October 1951 the Supreme Court granted them a writ of certiorari.[16]

In the last week of 1951 the Interhandel shares rose sensationally on the Zurich stock exchange on rumors of a settlement with the U.S. government. These rumors were soon given substance.[17]

On January 2, 1952, the Supreme Court heard the argument on the Kaufmans' right to intervene[18]—the first time the Supreme Court had ever considered the complicated question of safeguarding the rights of minority stockholders in a company alleged to be enemy controlled. During the course of the proceeding, the Department of Justice lawyer was asked how high a sum had been named in the compromise settlement discussions between Interhandel and the United States. The Justice lawyer replied that no figure had yet been reached.[19] It was the first public intimation that the settlement was being negotiated seriously.

Shortly thereafter the Interhandel management increased its demand in the settlement negotiations from $14 to $35 million, the total estimated net worth of G.A.F. at the time of the vesting. The Department of Justice officials, who had not been willing to pay $14 million a few months earlier, were certainly not interested in the new figure. The $35 million demand wrecked the negotiations and for practical purposes ended the possibility of settlement at that time.[20]

On April 7, 1952, the Supreme Court ruled in favor of the Kaufman petition to intervene[21] on behalf of the minority stockholders of Interhandel, almost burying any chance for a United States–Interhandel settlement. Continued litigation seemed the only solution in sight.

Early the next year Interhandel received an even more serious legal setback. The district court for the

District of Columbia, where Interhandel had sued for recovery of the G.A.F. assets, dismissed the Interhandel suit because of Interhandel's failure to produce the Sturzenegger & Company documents that the court had ordered to be submitted as evidence.[22] The American court would not accept the Swiss secrecy laws as a defense. Interhandel's attorney, John J. Wilson, appealed the decision and for the next five years he battled the Justice Department through the courts on the procedural question of whether the case could be tried without the Sturzenegger papers.

In the meantime, another route was opened for Interhandel to recover G.A.F. In 1954 Senator Everett M. Dirksen introduced a bill in the United States Senate providing for the return of vested enemy property to its former owners.[23] The Department of Justice, under Attorney General Herbert Brownell, vigorously opposed the Dirksen bill. [24] But now John Foster Dulles, Eisenhower's secretary of state, made his presence known. To the surprise of the Justice Department and America's wartime allies, he testified in support of the Dirksen bill before the Senate committee.[25] Dulles acknowledged that the bill contravened the 1945 reparation agreement to which the United States was a signatory, but he maintained that the agreement was a purely executive one that could not limit the power of Congress to deal with alien property as it saw fit. Dulles did not appear concerned that the word of the State Department was at stake.

The Dulles testimony sent shock waves through the Allied capitals. If the United States repudiated its obligations on reparations, Germany, it was feared, would demand similar concessions from the other Allied countries. The Dutch were particularly disturbed. They had acquired as reparation more than $100 million worth of German assets in Holland—actually a fraction of the value of what had been destroyed by the Germans. One high Dutch official, in a *New York Times* interview, said, "We believe in honoring agreements"[26] and then added ruefully that in the future the Netherlands would have to be very careful in concluding agreements with the United States.

Dulles's support notwithstanding, the opposition of the Department of Justice prevailed and the legislation was killed.

In June 1958, the Interhandel suit was legally reinstated when the U.S. Supreme Court decided in favor of Interhandel and reversed the lower courts.[27] It held that Interhandel, even without the submission of the Swiss documents, was entitled to a hearing on the merits of the case. Another long journey through the courts was in prospect.

A few days after the Supreme Court decision reinstating the suit, a dramatic change took place in Interhandel. On June 25, at the Interhandel annual meeting, in a further attempt at de-Farbenization, Felix Iselin resigned, along with three other members of the board.[28] They were replaced by four prominent members of the Swiss banking community with impeccable reputations and no links to I.G. Farben. The new directors were the president of the Swiss Bankers Association and the general managers of the three most important Swiss deposit banks—Swiss Bank, Crédit Suisse, and Union Bank. Union Bank, the smallest of the three, was reported in the press to have made large-scale purchases of Interhandel stock during the preceding few months.[29] These purchases had an especial meaning. They were composed of the bulk of the shares owned by Hans Sturzenegger, which eliminated the last remaining important link to I.G. Farben. Sturzenegger, in fact, had resigned from the board earlier when the Swiss banks yielded to "pressure from conservative Swiss circles that insisted on the eradication of all vestiges of doubt about the real ownership of Interhandel."[30] But until Sturzenegger sold his remaining stock, I.G. Farben influence in Interhandel was suspected.

The Union Bank thus became the controlling force in Interhandel. At the next stockholders meeting in June 1959, Union's representative on the Interhandel board, Alfred Schaefer, was elected general manager and vice-chairman. He was now the dominant figure in the affairs of the company.

In the fall of 1959 Schaefer was approached by Robert A. Schmitz—son of D.A. and nephew of Hermann—with a written plan for settling the G.A.F. matter. Robert Schmitz had spent most of his adult years in the pursuit of a solution to the G.A.F. problem. His announced purpose was to clear the name of his father and to make some money. At the end of World War II, immediately after his discharge from the U.S. Navy, Schmitz had gone to Switzerland with his father to confer with Sturzenegger as to the best way to try to recover the vested G.A.F. stock from the U.S. Alien Property Custodian. The Schmitzes recommended that the only hope for Interhandel to recoup the value of General Aniline was to sell the company to an American purchaser acceptable to the United States government. Sturzenegger agreed that the proposal was worth pursuing. The Schmitzes thereupon began the search for a buyer.

After D.A. Schmitz died, Robert continued the project with the passion of a crusader. In the years that followed, Robert Schmitz became associated with a number of American companies interested in acquiring G.A.F. Among these were Remington Rand, Shields and Company, W. R. Grace and Company, Food Machinery, and Chemical Corporation. Remington Rand even succeeded in securing an option in 1947 from Interhandel to buy the G.A.F. stock for $25 million when and if Interhandel regained the stock from the United States government.

In the early 1950s, when Robert Schmitz was employed by W. R. Grace, he came to know Charles E. Wilson, who had retired as president of General Electric and had become chairman of the executive committee of W. R. Grace to help that company in its plans for diversification. Schmitz convinced Wilson that General Aniline would be a perfect acquisition. Although Schmitz left W. R. Grace in 1957 after a disagreement wtih Peter Grace, he maintained his friendship with Wilson, who recommended him to a number of companies also interested in acquiring G.A.F.

In late 1958 Schmitz was in Basel on behalf of one of these concerns and went to see his old friend Sturzenegger. He knew that the Swiss banks had moved into Interhandel that summer and Sturzenegger was no longer on the board. But he also knew that Sturzenegger still owned the largest block of Interhandel stock at that time and retained a strong voice in Interhandel affairs.

Sturzenegger told Schmitz that the new banking group in Interhandel had decided to abandon the effort to interest an American company in buying G.A.F. and instead to concentrate on recovering G.A.F. for Interhandel itself. In that case, Schmitz said, he had a suggestion. Interhandel had failed in its efforts so far because it had never been able "to command the interest of those who counted in the highest echelons of the American government."[31] He counseled a new approach. Interhandel should convey full and irrevocable powers of negotiation and final settlement to an outstanding American who "would be above politics and yet would have entree to every door of the admistration."[32] Schmitz's recommendation was Charles E. Wilson. Schmitz pointed out that Wilson had served two Democratic administrations in positions of the most vital importance to the country's safety (high official of the War Production Board in World War II and defense mobilizer during the police action in Korea.) Wilson's Republican connections were even more impressive: he was a close friend of both Vice-President Nixon and President Eisenhower.

Sturzenegger thought enough of Schmitz's advice to begin discussions with Wilson. However, when Sturzenegger sold the bulk of his stock and bowed out of the Interhandel picture completely, the negotiations with Wilson collapsed.

Schmitz had to start over again. In the fall of 1959, he was back in Basel to present his plan to Schaefer, the new power in Interhandel. Schaefer expressed immediate interest and authorized Schmitz to continue his efforts to persuade Wilson to accept the trusteeship. In late April 1960, Wilson and Schaefer met in Paris. The conference was kept secret since Schaefer was afraid that the highly volatile G.A.F. stock would plummet if Wilson refused the trusteeship. Not even John J. Wilson, who was in charge of the litigation, knew about either the meeting or the Schmitz plan to obtain the services of Charles E. Wilson as a trustee. Shortly after the meeting Charles Wilson accepted the trusteeship.

Charles Wilson was given what appeared to be an irrevocable power of attorney wth absolute discretion and control. However, Wilson and Schaefer entered into private side agreements modifying the basic understanding and rendering the trusteeship somewhat less than irrevocable and absolute. It was orally agreed that Wilson's power of attorney could be terminated at the simple request of Interhandel. It was also agreed in writing that Wilson would come to no settlement of the G.A.F. matter without first submitting the plan to Interhandel for approval. Wilson refused any compensation, asking only that his expenses be covered. His attorney, Charles Spofford, a senior partner in the prominent Davis, Polk law firm, however, was to receive compensation for legal services.

When Wilson's acceptance of the trusteeship was made public on June 6, 1960, the value of Interhandel shares jumped more than $50 million on the stock exchange.[33]

The first goal Wilson set for himself was to convince Attorney General William Rogers of the legitimacy of Interhandel's cause. But the attorney general repeatedly refused to see Wilson after he assumed the Interhandel trusteeship. He was referred instead to Dallas Townsend, the assistant attorney general in charge of alien property. On his several visits Wilson received less than a hearty welcome from Townsend and his staff, who expressed the strongest reservations about the independence of Interhandel from German control.

Wilson and Schmitz, anticipating the election of Richard Nixon in November, were making plans to present their views to the new president, who they thought would be more receptive. When John Kennedy was elected, Wilson switched plans and made arrangements through Kennedy's prospective secretary of the treasury, Douglas Dillon, to see representatives of the new president before he assumed office. Such a meeting took place in late 1960 in Palm Beach at the home of Joseph P. Kennedy, the father of the president-elect. The meeting ended on an inconclusive note.

Schaefer began to entertain doubts about Wilson's influence with the new administration. Disappointed, he wrote Robert Schmitz on November 14, "It probably will be doubtful whether Mr. Charles Wilson will find the same friendly ear at the future highest instance of the administration as has been the case up till now."[34]

In early 1961, when Kennedy took office, William H. Orrick was appointed assistant attorney general in charge of alien property. Charles Spofford, Wilson's attorney, promptly paid him a visit to discuss the G.A.F. case and the nature of Wilson's trusteeship. Orrick asked Spofford for a written account of these matters and the latter agreed to supply one.

Spofford, while in Zurich to put the finishing touches on the memorandum for Orrick, was informed by Schaefer that he was concerned about the lack of progress and had decided to go to Washington to see for himself what was going on.

Schaefer arrived in the United States in May 1961. Spofford arranged for him to see a few senators and a number of government officials, none of higher rank than Orrick. Schaefer was appalled by the antagonistic reception he received from the government officials charged with resolution of the case. His meeting with Orrick was especially stormy. The assistant attorney general became so enraged by Schaefer's attack on the U.S. government's handling of the Interhandel case that he ordered Schaefer to leave his office immediately. According to Orrick's testimony: "I recall him pacing up and down in my office making uncomplimentary remarks about the United States government, which irritated me very much, and I recall asking him to leave my office."[35]

A month after Schaefer's fruitless visit to the United States, a friend and lawyer, a Dr. Gutstein, made a suggestion to him. One of his clients was personally familiar with the new Democratic president. Why not ask this client to use his influence to arrange a meeting between Schaefer and the new attorney general, Robert F. Kennedy? Schaefer readily agreed.

Promptly after the meeting with Gutstein and his "influential client," Schaefer wrote Spofford, cryptically informing him that something important was afoot.

> I am pleased to tell you that we have been able to make a new contact with one of the highest authorities through the intermediary of a third party. I would ask you to treat this news very confidentially and hope I can report to you on further developments within a few days. My message will, however, probably again be private and personal.[36]

Schafer gave no indication as to the identity of the "third party" through whom contact with "one of the highest authorities" was to be made.

A month later, on August 24, he wrote both John Wilson and Spofford asking them to suspend activities with the Department of Justice. He deliberately did not specify why he gave this order but said only that he was planning to be in Washington himself in connection with "a new proposal of ours." At that time, he would discuss the matter with them.[37] It was obvious Schaefer had taken matters into his own hands.

Spofford was in France on vacation, but Schaefer's letter was forwarded to him. Shortly thereafter, Spofford received a phone call from Orrick. Orrick asked whether Spofford was aware that a new figure had come to the Justice Department on behalf of Interhandel. Spofford admitted he was not. Orrick then dropped the bombshell: *Prince Radziwill,* he reported, *was representing Interhandel!*[38] Spofford was jolted by

271

the news. Radziwill was not even a lawyer. But he was the brother-in-law of President Kennedy.

The disturbing call sent Spofford to see Schaefer in Zurich. He demanded to know whether or not Orrick's information was correct. Schaefer confirmed that Radziwill had indeed been retained. Spofford expressed his reservations about the president's brother-in-law in the bluntest terms. He believed that all approaches should be "on a professional basis between the lawyers and not through stray intermediaries."[39] However, he recognized that Radziwill's special relationship to President Kennedy was a powerful element. Therefore, despite his misgivings, he reluctantly agreed that this new and extraordinary development probably had to be pursued.

Schaefer then told Spofford about Interhandel's new proposal: the Department of Justice would return G.A.F. to Interhandel, which would sell it and with the proceeds establish a European development bank to supply credit to underdeveloped countries.[40] It was Prince Radziwill's assignment to feel out the attorney general's reaction to such a plan. The essence of the proposal was to benefit the poor of the world first and Interhandel second, if such a notion could be believed by the attorney general or anybody else.

Upon Spofford's return to the United States a few days later, he told Charles Wilson about these developments. Wilson and his counsel agreed that they should wait for the results of the "initiatives" that Schaefer had taken "through other channels." They were clearly referring to Prince Radziwill's efforts.[41]

On September 13, Charles Wilson received a cable from the Union Bank asking that he arrange an early conference between Schaefer and Robert Kennedy.

Spofford immediately went to Washington and met with Orrick, who informed him that the attorney general did not even want to discuss the project of the European development bank. In Kennedy's view it did not represent an appropriate solution to the G.A.F. problem.[42]

Spofford cabled the discouraging news to Switzerland: "Advised that Attorney General does not believe conference useful at this time and cannot fix future date."[43] Schaefer wrote in reply, "I heard from *my friend in London* that the Justice Department felt they could not entertain our proposal." He had therefore asked *"the party in question* to contact Washington in order to solicit an appointment there for the next or following week, if possible."[44] In the extensive correspondence between Schaefer and Spofford, never once did either of the men write the name Radziwill. Instead, such vague terms as "intermediary," "friend in London," "party in question," and "third party" were used.

In little over a week after Schaefer asked "the intermediary" to arrange an appointment, Orrick called Spofford with the information that Robert Kennedy would meet with Schaefer on October 30 or 31 "as a courtesy to the intermediary."[45] Spofford reported this conversation to Schaefer. He wrote that he assumed that the primary purpose of the meeting would be to discuss the European development bank, a proposal that Spofford now thought should be pursued: "I believe that despite what Orrick has told me of the Attorney General's view of that plan you should, in view of the sponsorship you have given it and the advice you have gotten from this intermediary . . . present the plan."[46] Schaefer replied that the purpose of his visit was to find out why his proposal was rejected and to learn on what basis the Department of Justice would be interested in an arrangement.[47] Schaefer made it a point not to include Spofford, John Wilson, Charles Wilson, or Radziwill in the meeting with Attorney General Kennedy. According to Schaefer, he was told by "our mutual friend" that the attorney general would only see the Swiss banker alone—"no intermediary, no counselor, no advisor, because this must be a talk from man to man."[48]

The meeting was set up by a letter from Prince Radziwill to Robert Kennedy requesting an appointment for Alfred Schaefer. It was the prince's first formal appearance in the case. According to the Justice lawyer who

273

was present when the letter arrived, it looked like a royal wedding invitation, enclosed in two richly appointed envelopes and embossed with the Radziwill crest.

When the men met, according to Schaefer, Kennedy said " he had heard so much about interferences, intermediaries, and all sorts of people trying to make transactions that he was glad that something could be talked about directly between him and myself."[49] Kennedy immediately dismissed the idea of a European development bank. But he did not dismiss the idea of a settlement. He told Schaefer that a settlement would take a great deal of courage on his part because of the unanimous opposition of his staff. But if the General Aniline and Film matter was to be settled, it would have to be on at least a fifty-fifty basis. He gave his tentative approval, and the two men agreed that the details could be worked out by Interhandel and the Justice Staff.[50]

A few days after the conference with Robert Kennedy, Schaefer met with Charles Wilson and Spofford in New York. It was a stormy meeting. Wilson complained that the injection of Prince Radziwill underminded his authority. Spofford agreed, complaining that the Radziwill action seemed "highly unusual, if not improper."[51] Even if Schaefer used Prince Radziwill only as a Washington leg man, or to open doors, "this was obviously very tricky politically, and unprofessional as far as we were concerned, and I thought if it got to the press or got to the floor of Congress, why there would be an uproar."[52]

The next week, after Schaefer returned to Zurich, he called Orrick to say that the Interhandel board had agreed to Kennedy's offer. There followed an exchange of cables between the Department of Justice and Schaefer. In mid-December, Orrick was in Zurich and called Schaefer to discuss the settlement further.[53] In January Attorney General Kennedy and Schaefer talked about the terms of settlement by transatlantic telephone. Schaefer shortly thereafter received a cable from Kennedy confirming and clarifying their conversation:

Assume proposal mentioned in our telephone conversation contemplates United States will receive first eleven percent of proceeds of sale as compensation for shares to which Interhandel makes no claim and remainder will be divided fifty-fifty between Interhandel and United States. If this assumption is correct, we shall again be willing to discuss this and other aspects of the proposed agreement with you. Robert F. Kennedy.[54]

The cordial relations developing between the Kennedy administration and Interhandel convinced Schaefer that Wilson's position had become politically and practically untenable and the time had arrived to relieve him of the trusteeship. He wrote to Wilson on February 12, 1962, in effect revoking the latter's authority. In setting forth the reasons for this decision, Schaefer pointedly reminded Wilson that the meeting with the attorney general had been arranged "through the intermediary of a mutual friend." The meetings and subsequent "repeated telephone conversations" indicated "that our negotiations are approaching a medium line and we are therefore hopeful to reach an agreement by continuing along this road, which, as you know, was opened for us direct." So that there would be no doubts "as to Interhandel's right to conduct . . . direct negotiations with Washington," Schaefer asked Wilson "to consider the trusteeship you so kindly agreed to accept two years ago as being no longer valid."[55]

Six weeks later Wilson replied that he had decided to surrender his power of attorney as soon as the necessary formalities could be completed. The Radziwill matter still rankled.

For my part, I am frank to say that you have dealt with me in a less open manner than a satisfactory relationship requires, and that your methods of proceeding are not what I understood they would be when I accepted the power of attorney. I am referring particularly to the extraordinary steps you took to reach the Attorney General without my knowledge....[56]

In April, Orrick and Schaefer met in Munich and reached a general understanding. According to the Munich agreement the settlement terms were more or less those outlined in the Kennedy cable, the details to be negotiated later by both parties' lawyers.

Schaefer's high hopes for a prompt disposal of the conflict were, however, premature. It was almost a year before a settlement was reached. Nevertheless, for Schaefer the climate had changed considerably, and it now seemed a long time since Orrick threw him out of his office.

In mid-1962, Orrick left the Department of Justice to become a deputy undersecretary of state, and Deputy Attorney General Nicholas Katzenbach took over responsibility for the G.A.F. negotiations. Katzenbach's first move was to find a relatively unassailable vehicle by which a fair price could be established. Apparently he recognized the dangers implicit in any settlement of the case. He decided that a competitive sale at a public auction would blunt at least some of the anticipated criticism. To permit such a sale, however, required an amendment to the Trading with the Enemy Act. In fact, an amendment was then pending in Congress, introduced by Senator Kenneth Keating of New York,[57] against whom Robert Kennedy intended to run in the 1964 senatorial election in New York. For over a decade the Department of Justice had been trying to get this amendment passed by Congress but the Interhandel interests had always succeeded in blocking it.

Although the Justice-Interhandel deal was not yet firm in all details, Katzenbach asked John Wilson, as an act of good faith, to drop opposition to Keating's amendment. Let the legislation pass, Katzenbach suggested to Wilson, because otherwise Keating's opposition to a settlement would be formidable. With the reluctant acceptance of Katzenbach's assurance that the gentlemen's agreement reached in Munich would be adhered to in drafting the final settlement, Wilson dropped

Interhandel's opposition to congressional action and the bill that permitted the sale of G.A.F. without court action passed the Congress. President Kennedy signed the bill into law on October 22, 1962.[58] With that stroke of the pen, the sole remaining company in active operation under the supervision of the office of alien property was now ready for disposal by the United States government. The *New York Times* commented, "The General Aniline provision is expected to open still another chapter in the long and tangled legal history of that corporation."[59]

The *New York Times* was right. There was still another chapter. It had been John Wilson's understanding that before the government and Interhandel shared the net proceeds of the proposed sale of G.A.F., $24 million in tax and other claims would be deducted "off the top." Katzenbach now insisted that such a formula was not acceptable; instead, Interhandel would have to bear the entire burden of the $24 million.[60] This turn of events led Wilson to remark, "It was my worst Christmas." Upon reflection, however, Interhandel decided to accept Katzenbach's new condition. Its share of the proceeds was still expected to be substantial. Attorney General Kennedy was informed of Interhandel's acquiescence.

Attorney General Robert Kennedy called a press conference on March 4 to announce the settlement of the Interhandel suit. Apparently anticipating criticism, he said, "Our fundamental aim throughout has been for the government to step out of its unnatural role as the owner of a private corporation and to end the extensive litigation in this case." Kennedy argued that if the government were to go ahead and sell G.A.F. without first settling the suit—as the law now allowed—it would be faced with from one to three years of litigation over its right to do so.[61]

Deputy Attorney General Katzenbach also felt compelled to explain the reasons for the settlement to the press. If there had been a sale without a prior settlement, Interhandel would have fought the constitutionality of the 1962 sales amendment in the courts; if it lost in the U.S. courts, Interhandel would have carried the case to the International Court of Justice at The Hague.[62]

The uneasiness betrayed by Kennedy and Katzenbach was warranted. The Department of Justice announcement of the G.A.F. settlement brought the anticipated storm of criticism. President Kennedy was questioned about it at his next press conference two days later.

Mr. President, for twenty years the Justice Department has assured Congress that it had evidence showing that the Interhandel was a cover for the German firm of I.G. Farben, and therefore the seizure of General Aniline & Film in this country during World War II was justified. Now, in the past few days, there has been an agreement between Justice and Interhandel on the division of the proceeds from the sale of Aniline. Has the Justice Department discovered that its facts are wrong . . . or is this the result of pressure from the Swiss government?[63]

President Kennedy replied,

No, I would say that the agreement is an equitable agreement. It could have gone on ten years more in the courts, and it has been now fifteen or twenty years and lawyers have enjoyed it, but I don't think that there is anything else. I don't think we would get a better arrangement if we continued the litigation for another ten years. We feel that the arrangement which has been worked out will return the assets to those who have a claim to them, and I think the division of resources is fair.[64]

The explanations of President Kennedy, Attorney General Kennedy, and Deputy Attorney General Katzenbach did little to stem the criticism in the Congress, particularly from several members of the House Interstate and Foreign Commerce Subcommittee dealing with enemy assets and war claims. Representative John Dingell, second-ranking member of the Democratic majority of the subcommittee, fairly exploded: "I don't think Interhandel has a nickel coming."[65] As a lawyer, he said, he was aware of the general rule that a bad settlement is often better than a good lawsuit, but in this case "Interhandel has behaved shamefully and shamelessly. I don't think there is any question that Interhandel is a cloak or a front."[66] Representative Willard S. Curtin, a Republican member of the same subcommittee, pointed out that if G.A.F. were truly a Swiss asset, then it should have been returned to Interhandel. On the other hand, "if it were a completely German asset, as we have always thought, then I think it was not a good settlement."[67] Another Republican member of the subcommittee, Hastings Keith, joined in the criticism. The three congressmen expressed their disappointment that the attorney general had not seen fit to inform their subcommittee of the settlement.[68]

Undeterred by opposition in the Congress, in the press, and among the working staff of the Department of Justice, the government and Interhandel proceeded to work out the details for approval by the court. On December 20, 1963, a stipulation of settlement was signed by the Department of Justice and Interhandel that provided for the sale of G.A.F. to the public and the division of the proceeds between the government and Interhandel in the agreed proportions.[69] The proposed compromise of the litigation was presented to the U.S. district court. In April 1964 the court approved the settlement and authorized the sale.[70]

During the next year, while the Department of Justice was preparing for the public auction of General Aniline and Film, criticism of the settlement continued in the press. In May 1964 revelations about the G.A.F. case appeared in the syndicated column of Drew Pearson.[71] He pointed out that a long succession of attorneys general, both Democratic and Republican—Clark, McGranery, McGrath, Brownell, and Rogers—had refused to settle with Interhandel: "But last year Attorney General Robert F. Kennedy strangely took a contrary position . . . despite the unanimous opposition of the Justice Department staff. The big mystery, therefore, has been: Why the change?"[72]

Pearson answered this question by suggesting two clues. The first had to do with the interest in General Aniline shown by Joseph P. Kennedy, father of the president and of the attorney general. Ever since the Justice officials who approved the settlement learned of the postelection visit of Charles Wilson to the Joseph Kennedy home in Palm Beach, they feared the active intrusion of America's preeminent father. In their view, the size of the financial stakes involved was far too great for Joseph Kennedy to leave the matter alone. This fear crystallized very early when Robert Kennedy appointed William Payton Marin vice-chairman of the board of G.A.F. Marin, Joseph Kennedy's principal counsel, was acknowledged to be one of his closest advisers. Very swiftly Marin became the dominant figure on the General Aniline board. The hand of the elder Kennedy was also seen in the appointment to the board of his public relations man, Harold E. Clancy, a former editor of the *Boston Traveler*. Pearson concluded his column with the second clue—a potential blockbuster that he indicated was leaked from the Department of Justice: "Finally," wrote Pearson, "a memo turned up in Justice Department files signed by Dr. Alfred Schaefer of Interhandel. The memo read, 'We want to keep dealing through Radziwill.'"

This was the only known time in his pursuit of G.A.F. that Schaefer took the risk of naming Radziwill*

---

* So sensitive about the name Radziwill were the various parties to the settlement negotiations that even four years later, when the matter had become academic, it still remained a fact to be suppressed. In 1968, in a deposition in a suit about a finder's fee, Spofford found it difficult to mention the name. During his deposition, he was asked about the time Orrick had informed him that a new representative was appearing on behalf of Interhandel at the Department of Justice. John J. Wilson, the attorney for Interhandel, on cross-examination, asked Spofford, "Who was he?"

SPOFFORD: "I am hesitating, Mr. Wilson, because it's a well-known name and I don't want—this is not to become public in any sense, is it?"
WILSON: "Yes, it is."
SPOFFORD: "Well, I am under oath and I am testifying, trying to be helpful in this case. I will give you the name of the individual. It's Prince Radziwill, the brother-in-law of Bob Kennedy."

on paper.[73] Surprisingly, this revelation was not followed up by any newspaper or by political opponents of the Kennedys such as Senator Keating. However, it created a commotion within the Department of Justice, where there was an intensive investigation to determine the source of the leak. In any event, Pearson's mention of Radziwill's role was the first public identification of the "royal intermediary" by name.

However, pointed questions about the settlement were being asked that could not be ignored—especially in view of Robert F. Kennedy's plans to run for the Senate from New York. In July an official of the Jewish War Veterans asked the Justice Department if any of the proceeds from the sale of G.A.F. would find their way to former Nazis. Deputy Attorney General Katzenbach's reply appeared in the July–August issue of the *Jewish Veteran*.

> According to all the information available now, no money in the property sale [of G.A.F.] would revert to any former Nazis. The bulk of the proceeds of the sale will go to the Government and will be used to compensate Americans who suffered injury or loss in World War II. The remainder of the proceeds go to Interhandel, a holding company now controlled by Swiss interests.[74]

Katzenbach said it would be "very difficult" to prove that Interhandel was a blind for German interests.

On March 9, 1965, the General Aniline and Film stock was sold by sealed bid at the largest competitive auction in Wall Street history. Representatives of the two contending syndicates—one headed by Kuhn Loeb, Lehman Brothers, Glore Forgan & Company, and Merrill Lynch, Pierce, Fenner and Smith, the other by Blyth & Company and the First Boston Corporation—awaited the results as the bids were opened in the office of Attorney General Katzenbach in the presence of Senator Robert F. Kennedy and other notables. The Blyth & Company syndicate with a bid of $329,141,-

926.49—almost a third of a billion dollars—was the winner![75]

The Blyth syndicate had no trouble selling the General Aniline and Film stock to the public. On the first day of trading, all of the 11,166,438 shares were sold for a total of $341 million. The stock opened at $30.60, traded as high as $36, and closed at $32, still five points over the issue price. Payment to Interhandel netted about $122 million—an impressive amount, especially in view of the fact that in 1950 Interhandel had been willing to settle for $14 million.

Nevertheless, the General Aniline and Film story was not quite over. In January 1967, Robert Schmitz filed suit against Interhandel in United States district court for the District of Columbia. In his complaint, after outlining his extensive efforts on behalf of Interhandel to settle its claim against the United States government, he demanded a judgment of $11,250,000, plus interest. From the complaint, as well as from public statements made by Schmitz, it was obvious that he felt the payment of $124 million to Interhandel by the U.S. goverment ultimately was the result of his initiatives and perseverance. These were worth at least as much as Prince Radziwill's influence. Such was the basis of Schmitz's not insignificant claim.

With the cost of litigation threatening to "bankrupt" him, Schmitz accepted a relatively nominal settlement from Interhandel. It was nothing, he said, compared to what was paid Radziwill for a simple introduction to Robert Kennedy.

The strange case of General Aniline will not rest. After the payment of $124 million to Interhandel some eyebrows were raised when Alfred Schaefer was elected to the board of BASF. A few years later, on December 13, 1974, the now American-owned GAF, together with BASF, Bayer, Du Pont, and five other companies, was indicted for a conspiracy to fix the price of dyestuffs in the United States. With the exception of one smaller concern all the defendants, including GAF and BASF, pleaded guilty and were punished with heavy fines.

And on April Fools' Day 1978 it was revealed[76]

that GAF sold to BASF its dyestuff plant at Rensselaer, New York, originally built by Carl Duisberg and seized as enemy property by the Alien Property Custodian in both World Wars I and II. Apparently the parties expect no interference by the U.S. government under the Trading with the Enemy Act.[77] Once again, the wartime confiscation and peacetime recapture of I.G. Farben property has completed its cycle. Herman Schmitz can now rest content in his grave—mission accomplished.

"Those who do not remember the
past are condemned to repeat it."
George Santayana

Notes

ABBREVIATIONS USED IN NOTES

Published Nuremberg War Crimes Trials Records:

NCA: *Nazi Conspiracy and Aggression* (United States Government Printing Office, 1946).

TMWC: *Trial of the Major War Criminals Before the International Military Tribunal* (Nuremberg, Germany, 1947–49).

TWC: *Trials of War Criminals Before the Nuremberg Military Tribunals, Under Control Council No. 10* (U.S. Government Printing Office, 1953).

Documents in National Archives Collection, World War II Crimes Records (some of which have been included as exhibits in above publications, some of which are available only at the Archives):

NI: "Nuremberg, Industrialists"
PS: "Paris, Storey [Col. Robert Storey]"
NO: "Nuremberg, Organizations"
NG: "Nuremberg, Government."

INTRODUCTION

1. U.S. Group Control Council, Finance Division, Germany, *Report on Investigation of I.G. Farbenindustrie,* September 12, 1945. Classification canceled by authority of the Joint Chiefs of Staff; microfilmed by the Library of Congress.

1. WORLD WAR I

1. Rathenau, Walther, "Germany's Provisions for Raw Materials," in *Economic and Social History of the World War*, ed. James Shotwell, Carnegie Endowment for International Peace, Yale University, 1924, pp. 78–79.
2. *Ibid.*, p. 80.
3. Holdermann, Karl, *Im Banne der Chemie: Carl Bosch, Leben und Werk*, 1954, p. 136.
4. *Ibid.*
5. Kessler, Harry, *Walther Rathenau: His Life and Work* (Harcourt, Brace & Co., New York, 1930), p. 175.
6. Holdermann, p. 137.
7. Haber, Fritz, "Chemistry in War," in *Journal of Chemical Education*, November, 1945, p. 528.
8. Churchill, Winston, *The World Crisis*, vol. I, p. 474.
9. Bauer, Max, *Der Grosse Krieg im Feld und Heimat*, Tuebingen, 1921, p. 67.
10. *Ibid.*
11. Bundesarchiv, Koblenz, Bauer's Papers, Letter from Carl Duisberg to Major Max Bauer, March 3, 1915.
12. Bauer, p. 68.
13. Goran, Morris, *The Story of Fritz Haber*, Univ. of Oklahoma Press, Oklahoma, 1967, p. 68.
14. Lefebure, Victor, *The Riddle of the Rhine*, W. Collins Sons & Co., Ltd., London, 1921, p. 27.
15. Goran, p. 68.
16. *Ibid.*, p. 69.
17. *Ibid.*, p. 72.
18. Lefebure, p. 85.
19. *Ibid.*, p. 144.
20. *Ibid.*, p. 144.
21. Bundesarchiv, Koblenz, Bauer's Papers, Letter from Carl Duisberg to Major Max Bauer, July 24, 1915.
22. Hearings before a Subcommittee of the Committee on Military Affairs, U.S. Senate, 79th Congress, 1st Session (1945), *Elimination of German Resources of War*, part X, p. 1167.
23. Feldman, Gerald D., *Army, Industry, and Labor in Germany, 1914–1918*, Princeton University Press, Princeton, N.J., 1966, p. 152.
24. Bundesarchiv, Koblenz, Bauer's Papers, Letter from Carl Duisberg to Lt.-Col. Max Bauer, September 10, 1916.
25. Feldman, p. 164.

26. Feldman, p. 167, footnote 26.
27. Halsey, Francis Whiting, *The Literary Digest History of the World War,* vol. I, p. 372, Funk & Wagnalls Company, New York and London, 1919.
28. *Ibid.,* p. 371.
29. *Ibid.,* pp. 371–372.
30. Passelecq, Ferdnand, *Unemployment in Belgium during the German Occupation and Its General Causes,* Hodder & Stoughton, London, New York, Toronto, 1917.
31. Feldman, p. 359.
32. *Ibid.,* p. 391.
33. *Ibid.,* p. 521.
34. *Ibid.,* p. 398.
35. *Ibid.,* p. 398.
36. *Ibid.,* p. 399.
37. *New York Times,* July 10, 1916, p. 1, col. 5; *New York Times,* August 15, 1916, p. 1, col. 2.
38. Manchester, William, *The Arms of Krupp, 1587–1968,* Little, Brown, Boston, 1968, p. 310.
39. Holdermann, pp. 155–156.
40. *New York Times,* December 24, 1918, p. 3, col. 5.
41. Norris, Lt. Col. James F., "The Manufacture of War Gases in Germany," in *Journal of Industrial and Engineering Chemistry,* September, 1919, pp. 817–819.
42. McConnell, Lt. Robert E., "The Production of Nitrogenous Compounds Synthetically in the U.S. and Germany," in *Journal of Industrial and Engineering Chemistry,* September, 1919, p. 839.
43. Lefebure, *The Riddle of the Rhine.*
44. Geschaeftsstelle fuer die Friedensverhandlungen, Berlin, 1919, Drucksache, No. 28.
45. *Ibid.,* Drucksache, No. 27.
46. Holdermann, p. 166.
47. U.S. Department of State, *The Treaty of Versailles and After: Annotations of the Text,* Greenwood Press, New York, 1944, Articles 227–230.
48. *Ibid.,* Article 306.
49. *Ibid.,* Annex VI.
50. *Ibid.,* Articles 168–172.
51. *Ibid.,* Articles 42–44.
52. Luckau, Alma, *The German Delegation at the Paris Peace Conference,* Columbia University Press, New York, 1941, p. 305.
53. Holdermann, pp. 167–168.
54. Letter from Compagnie Française des Matières Colorantes

S. A. to Joseph Borkin, April 14, 1970, re biography of Joseph F. Frossard.

55. Holdermann, p. 168.
56. *Ibid.*
57. *Ibid.,* pp. 168–170.
58. Luckau, p. 190.
59. *New York Times,* November 15, 1919, p. 11, col. 1.
60. Goran, p. 83.
61. *New York Times,* January 27, 1920, p. 14, col. 5.
62. *Ibid.*
63. *Ibid.,* January 28, 1920, p. 10, col. 6.
64. Luckau, p. 372.
65. *New York Times,* October 31, 1921, p. 14, col. 2.
66. *New York Times,* September 25, 1921, Sec. II, p. 9, col. 2.
67. NI-6768, p. 16, affidavit of Carl Krauch.
68. National Archives Collection, World War II Crimes Records, Krauch Document Book I, pp. 9–10.
69. NI-6768, p. 16, affidavit of Carl Krauch.

2. POSTWAR GERMANY AND BOSCH'S DREAM

1. Hearings before Special Committee Investigating the Munitions Industry, U.S. Senate, 73d Congress, part XXXIX, p. 13438.
2. *Ibid.,* part XI, p. 2572.
3. *New York Times,* February 21, 1921, p. 15, col. 4.
4. Hearings, *op. cit.,* part XXXIX, p. 13445.
5. *New York Times,* February 21, 1921, p. 15, col. 4.
6. Hearings, *op. cit.,* part XXXIX, p. 13446.
7. Private Papers of Captain Herman E. Osann, pp. 1–2.
8. Holdermann, Karl, *Im Banne der Chemie: Carl Bosch, Leben und Werk,* 1954, p. 187.
9. *New York Times,* October 8, 1923, p. 3, col. 5.
10. *New York Times,* August 16, 1923, p. 3, col. 4; and *Frankfurter Zeitung,* August 12, 1923.
11. Hearings before a Subcommittee of the Committee on Military Affairs, U.S. Senate, 79th Cong., 1st Sess. (1945), pursuant to S. Res. 107 and 146, *Elimination of German Resources for War,* part X, p. 1391.
12. Holdermann, p. 188.
13. *Ibid.,* p. 192.
14. *Ibid.,* p. 201.
15. NI-5187, p. 5, affidavit of Fritz ter Meer.
16. *New York Times,* August 3, 1926, p. 5, col. 3.

17. *New York Times,* August 5, 1926, p. 7, col. 3.
18. Federal Oil Conservation Board Report, September 6, 1926, p. 5.
19. Gibb, George Sweet and Knowlton, Evelyn H., *The Resurgent Years, History of Standard Oil Company (N.J.), 1911–1927,* Harper Brothers, N.Y., 1956, p. 554.
20. Howard, Frank A., *Buna Rubber,* D. Van Nostrand Co., Inc., New York, 1947, p. 10.
21. Holdermann, p. 225.
22. Howard, p. 13.
23. Berge, Wendell, *Cartels: Challenge to a Free World,* Public Affairs Press, Washington, D.C., 1944, p. 210.
24. *New York Times,* May 23, 1945, p. 21, col. 5.
25. Howard, p. 15.
26. Holdermann, p. 228.
27. Federal Oil Conservation Board Report, p. 6.
28. Howard, pp. 20–21.
29. Hearings before the Committee on Patents, U.S. Senate, 77th Cong., 2nd Session (1942), *Patents,* Part VI, pp. 3433–3436.
30. *New York Times,* August 9, 1927, p. 12, col. 1.
31. Holdermann, pp. 254–256.
32. Howard, pp. 21–27.
33. Hearings before a Special Committee Investigating the National Defense Program, U.S. Senate, 77th Cong., 2nd Session (1942), *Investigation on the National Defense Program,* Part II, p. 4312.
34. *Ibid.,* p. 4561.
35. NI-5186, p. 7, affidavit of Ter Meer.

3. I.G. PREPARES HITLER FOR WAR

1. National Archives Collection, World War II Crimes Records, Krauch Document Book I, p. 19; Holdermann, Karl, *Im Banne der Chemie: Carl Bosch, Leben und Werk,* 1954, p. 155.
2. NI-8637, p. 15, affidavit of Dr. Heinrich Buetefisch.
3. NI-6767, p. 4, affidavit of Carl Krauch; Carl Bosch, "Erdoel und Synthetisches Benzin," *Petroleum,* XXIX (1933), p. 7.
4. NI-6765, affidavit of Friedrich Jaehne.
5. *New York Times,* November 13, 1931, p. 10, col. 2.
6. NI-8788, p. 1, affidavit of Heinrich Gattineau.
7. National Archives Collection, World War II Crimes Rec-

ords, Heinrich Gattineau's letter to Dr. Karl Haushofer, June 6, 1931.

8. NI-4833, pp. 1–2, affidavit of Heinrich Gattineau.
9. TWC, VII, p. 539, NI-14304 extracts.
10. NI-4833, p. 3, affidavit of Heinrich Gattineau.
11. NI-8637, p. 15, affidavit of Heinrich Buetefisch.
12. NCA, VI, pp. 796–798, Document 3901-PS, Petition to Hindenburg, November, 1932.
13. TWC, VII, p. 563, NI-406, extract from interrogation of Hjalmar Schacht.
14. TWC, VII, pp. 565–568, NI-391, items related to "National Trusteeship" account.
15. Holdermann, p. 272.
16. Goran, Morris, *The Story of Fritz Haber*, University of Oklahoma Press, 1967, p. 38.
17. Holdermann, p. 288.
18. Goran, p. 39.
19. NI-6787, p. 3, affidavit of Heinrich Hoerlein.
20. National Archives Collection, WI/IF 5.2507, *Geschichte der Deutschen Wehr und Ruestungswirtschaft, 1918/1943–44*, Document #1, 11/22/28, p. 494.
21. TWC, XII, p. 421, NG-4142.
22. TWC, VII, pp. 571–572, NI-4718.
23. TWC, VII, p. 573, NI-7123, von Bockelberg memo, 9/15/33; also National Archives, NI-6544, p. 14, affidavit of Max Ilgner.
24. NI-9784, p. 4, letter from Homer H. Ewing to Wendell R. Swint, July 17, 1933.
25. *Ibid.*, p. 9.
26. NI-881, Benzin Contract, December 14, 1933.
27. TWC, VII, pp. 752–753, NI-6930, correspondence between I.G. Farbenindustrie, Army Ordnance, and the Ministry of Economics.
28. NI-7241, p. 4, affidavit of Ernst Struss.
29. NI-5187, p. 10, affidavit of Fritz ter Meer.
30. NI-7241, p. 5, affidavit of Ernst Struss.
31. *London Times*, September 12, 1935, p. 12, col. 5.
32. TWC, VII, p. 782, NI-4713.
33. NI-7241, p. 4.
34. *New York Times*, February 16, 1936, p. 1, col. 3.
35. *New York Times*, March 13, 1936, p. 1, col. 8.
36. TMWC, IX, p. 448.
37. *New York Times*, April 28, 1936, p. 1, col. 3.
38. *New York Times*, May 3, 1936, p. 38, col. 1.
39. NI-9767, p. 2, affidavit of Erich Gritzbach.

40. TWC, VII, p. 1049, NI-4702.
41. NCA, III, p. 881, 1301-PS.
42. TWC, VII, p. 799, NI-5380.
43. NCA, III, p. 886, 1301-PS.
44. NI-7241, pp. 7–8, affidavit of Ernst Struss.
45. NI-8833, p. 3, affidavit of Johannes Eckell.
46. TWC, XII, p. 430, NI-4955.
47. Schacht, Hjalmar, *Confessions of "The Old Wizard,"* Houghton Mifflin Co., Boston, 1956, p. 337.
48. *Ibid.*
49. NCA, III, p. 892, 1301-PS.
50. *New York Times,* September 10, 1936, p. 1, col. 8.
51. TWC, XII, p. 446, 2071-PS.
52. *New York Times,* October 20, 1936, p. 1, col. 7.
53. TWC, XII, p. 447, NG-1221.
54. NI-9767, p. 2, affidavit of Erich Gritzbach.
55. NI-7241, pp. 9–10, affidavit of Ernst Struss.
56. NI-10,035, p. 38, Hagert affidavit.
57. NI-9945, p. 1, affidavit of Max Kuegler.
58. *Ibid.,* p. 2.
59. NI-9944, p. 1, affidavit of Max Kuegler.
60. NI-9945, p. 1, affidavit of Max Kuegler.
61. NI-7241, p. 10, affidavit of Ernst Struss.
62. NI-12,042, Chart of I.G. people and their membership in various organizations.
63. NI-7957, Chart of I.G. Supervisory Board membership.
64. NI-6768, p. 7, Krauch affidavit; TWC, VII, p. 1001, Krauch testimony.
65. NI-10,386, p. 1, affidavit of Paul Koerner.
66. NI-6768, p. 7, affidavit of Carl Krauch.
67. *Ibid.,* p. 8; NI-10,386, p. 2, affidavit of Paul Koerner.
68. NI-10,386, p. 2.
69. TWC, VII, pp. 890–893, NI-8800.
70. NI-10,386, p. 2.
71. TWC, VII, pp. 902–908, NI-8840.
72. TWC, VII, pp. 911–912, NI-8797.

4. THE MARRIAGE OF I.G. AND STANDARD OIL UNDER HITLER

1. TWC, VII, p. 1309, NI-10, 551, memorandum of June 6, 1944 from August von Knieriem to Schmitz, Ambros, Buetefisch, et al.
2. TWC, VII, p. 1204, August von Knieriem testimony.

3. TWC, VII, p. 1189.
4. Hearings before a Subcommittee of the Committee on Military Affairs, United States Senate, 78th Cong., 1st Session (1943), *Scientific and Technical Mobilization,* part VI, p. 939, letter from a Du Pont official to E. W. Webb, President of Ethyl Gasoline Corporation, dated December 15, 1934.
5. TWC, VII, p. 135.
6. TWC, VII, p. 1274.
7. TWC, VII, p. 1309, NI-10, 551.
8. TWC, VII, p. 1280, EC-223, circular of March 12, 1937, from V.W. re counterintelligence.
9. TWC, VII, p. 1275, NI-10, 437, report from the meeting at the Wehrmacht re secrecy, held July 14, 1937.
10. Hearings before the Committee on Patents, United States Senate, 77th Cong., 2d Session (1942), *Patents,* part VI, p. 2906, letter from F. A. Howard to R. P. Russell of Standard Oil Development Company, dated March 15, 1938.
11. TWC, VII, pp. 1281–1284, NI-10,455, file note of March 21, 1938, by ter Meer, concerning a meeting with General Loeb, Dr. Muelert, and Dr. Eckell on the status of the American rubber program.
12. Hearings before the Committee on Patents, United States Senate, 77th Cong., 2d Session (1942), *Patents,* part VI, p. 2907, letter from F. ter Meer to F. A. Howard, dated April 9, 1938.
13. *Ibid.,* p. 2912, letter from F. A. Howard to F. ter Meer, dated April 20, 1938.
14. *Ibid.,* p. 2910, letter from F. A. Howard to F. H. Bedford, Jr., dated April 14, 1938.
15. *Ibid.,* pp. 2912–2913, letter from F. A. Howard to F. H. Bedford, Jr., dated April 20, 1938.
16. *J. Robert Bonnar, et al.* v. *The United States, et al.* (Ct. Cl. 1971 No. 293–63), Defendant's Exhibit 286, letter from F. ter Meer to W. H. Duisberg, dated October 11, 1938.
17. Hearings before Committee on Patents, United States Senate, 77th Cong., 2d Session (1942), *Patents,* part VI, p. 2916, Executive Committee Memorandum, November 28, 1938.
18. *J. Robert Bonnar, et al.* v. *The United States, et al.* (Ct. Cl. 1971 No. 293–63), Plaintiff's Exhibit 155, Office of the Alien Property Custodian Report of Examiner re Walter Duisberg, p. 26, extracts of minutes of the Standard Oil Executive Committee meeting of August 30, 1939.
19. *Standard Oil Co. (New Jersey), et al.* v. *Tom C. Clark, At-*

torney General, as Successor to the Alien Property Custodian (2d Cir., Civ. Action No. 26-414), Joint Appendix to the Briefs, p. 993, Plaintiff's Exhibit 85, letter from W. C. Teagle to E. J. Sadler and F. H. Bedford, Jr., dated August 30, 1939.

20. *Ibid.*, pp. 1380–83, Defendant's Exhibit 392, letter from W. Schaefer to F. H. Bedford, Jr., dated September 8, 1937.

21. *Ibid.*

22. *Ibid.*, p. 994, Plaintiff's Exhibit 86, cable from Standard Oil Co. (N.J.) to I.G. Farbenindustrie, dated September 1, 1939.

23. Howard, Frank A., *Buna Rubber*, D. Van Nostrand Co., Inc., New York, 1947, p. 81.

24. *Standard Oil Co. (N.J.), et al.* v. *Clark*, Joint Appendix to the Briefs, p. 529, testimony of August von Knieriem.

25. *Ibid.*, pp. 1543–46, Defendant's Exhibit 572, letter from I.G. Farbenindustrie to the Economic Defense Headquarters, Oberkommando der Wehrmacht, dated September 16, 1939.

26. Howard, p. 82.

27. *New York Times*, April 1, 1942, p. 1, col. 2.

28. *Standard Oil Co. (N.J.)* v. *Clark*, Joint Appendix to the Briefs, p. 1560, Defendant's Exhibit 578, memorandum dated October 8, 1939, by Ringer "concerning a conference with Mr. Howard in The Hague on September 24 and 25, 1939."

29. *Ibid.*, p. 1292, Defendant's Exhibit 330, Cable from Standard Oil Development Co. to I.G. Farbenindustrie, dated September 15, 1939.

30. *Standard Oil Co. (N.J.)* v. *Clark*, Joint Appendix to the Briefs, p. 946, Plaintiff's Exhibit 67, memorandum re "readjustment of Jasco," bearing date of September 25, 1939 ("The Hague Memorandum").

31. *Ibid.*, p. 1560, Defendant's Exhibit 578, memorandum dated October 8, 1939, by Ringer "concerning a conference with Mr. Howard in The Hague on September 24 and 25, 1939."

32. *Ibid.*, p. 1563, Defendant's Exhibit 578, memorandum dated October 8, 1939, by Ringer "concerning a conference with Mr. Howard in The Hague on September 24 and 25, 1939."

33. *J. Robert Bonnar, et al.* v. *The United States*, No. 293–63 (Ct. Cl. 1971), Defendant's Exhibit 399, "Report on the Transfer of I.G. Patents to Third Parties."

34. *Standard Oil Co. (N.J.), et al.* v. *Clark* (2d Cir., 1947), Joint Appendix to the Briefs, p. 952, Plaintiff's Exhibit 70,

cable from I.G. Farbenindustrie to Standard Oil Development Co., dated October 16, 1939.

35. *Ibid.,* p. 1296, Defendant's Exhibit 333, cable from I.G. Farbenindustrie to Standard Oil Development Co., dated October 16, 1939.

36. *Ibid.,* p. 948, Plaintiff's Exhibit 68, letter from F. A. Howard to A. C. Minton, dated October 1, 1939.

37. *Ibid.,* pp. 1059–1061, Plaintiff's Exhibit 142, note re "New Arrangement Jasco," dated January 12, 1940, signed by Ringer.

38. *New York Times,* March 29, 1942, p. 1, col. 4.

39. *Ibid.*

40. *U.S.* v. *Standard Oil Co. (N.J.),* Department of Justice Criminal Case No. 682 and Civil Case No. 2091.

41. Department of Justice Press Release, March 25, 1942, re *U.S.* v. *Standard Oil Co. (N.J.).*

42. Standard Oil Company (N.J.) Press Release, March 25, 1942, re *U.S.* v. *Standard Oil Co. (N.J.).*

43. *Washington Daily News,* March 27, 1942, p. 5, col. 1.

44. Hearings before the Committee on Patents, United States Senate, 77th Cong., 2d Session (1942), part I, *Patents,* p. 11, Farish testimony.

45. *Ibid.*

46. *PM,* April 5, 1942, p. 10, col. 1.

47. Marson, Henrietta M.; Knowlton, Evelyn H., and Toptle, Charles S.; *New Horizons: History of Standard Oil Company (New Jersey)—1927–1950,* Harper & Row, New York, 1971, p. 443.

48. *Ibid.,* p. 449.

5. THE RAPE OF THE EUROPEAN
CHEMICAL INDUSTRY

1. TWC, VII, pp. 1404–1406, NI-4024.

2. TWC, VII, p. 1393, NI-9289.

3. TWC, VII, p. 1406, NI-4024.

4. TWC, VII, pp. 1399–1400, NI-3982; and pp. 1401–1403, NI-3981.

5. TWC, VII, pp. 1414–1415, NI-9289.

6. DuBois, Josiah, *The Devil's Chemists,* Beacon Press, Boston, 1952, p. 92.

7. Hilberg, Raul, *The Destruction of the European Jews,* Quadrangle Books, Chicago, 1961, p. 61; NI-10998, affidavit of Joham.

8. TWC, VII, p. 1408, NI-9289.
9. TWC, VII, p. 153.
10. TWC, VII, p. 42.
11. TWC, VII, p. 591, NI-2795.
12. TWC, VII, p. 43.
13. *Ibid.*, p. 43.
14. *Ibid.*, p. 43.
15. TWC, VIII, pp. 4–6, NI-9151, NI-9154, NI-9155.
16. TWC, VII, p. 181.
17. TWC, VIII, p. 7, NI-8457.
18. TWC, VIII, pp. 7–10, NI-2749.
19. TWC, VIII, p. 11, NI-1093.
20. TWC, VIII, p. 21, NI-8380.
21. TWC, VIII, p. 1143; and TWC, VIII, pp. 20–23, NI-8380.
21a. TWC, V, pp. 154–155, Greifelt testimony.
22. TWC, VIII, p. 1143.
23. Holdermann, Karl, *Im Banne der Chemie: Carl Bosch, Leben und Werk,* 1953, pp. 305–307.
24. NI-6525, p. 1, Krauch affidavit.
25. TWC, VII, p. 1452.
26. TWC, VII, p. 1439, NI-14897.
27. TWC, VII, p. 1461.
28. Hearings before a Subcommittee of the Committee on Military Affairs, U.S. Senate, 79th Congress, 1st Session (1945), pursuant to S. Res. 107 and 146, *Elimination of German Resources for War,* part X, p. 1387, Schnitzler affidavit.
29. *Ibid.,* p. 1387, Schnitzler affidavit.
30. TWC, VIII, 120.
31. TWC, VII, 1447.
32. TWC, VIII, 105–106, NI-6839.
33. TWC, VIII, p. 104, NI-6839.
34. TWC, VIII, p. 109, NI-795.
35. *Ibid.*
36. Hearings before a Subcommittee of the Committee on Military Affairs, U.S. Senate, 79th Congress, 1st Session (1945), pursuant to S. Res. 107 and 146, *Elimination of German Resources for War,* part X, pp. 1388–1389, Exhibit No. 37, Report of Dr. Kramer re conference with Mr. Frossard.
37. *Ibid.,* pp. 1388–1389, Exhibit No. 37, report of Dr. Kramer re conference with Mr. Frossard.
38. *Ibid.*
39. Shirer, William L., *The Rise and Fall of the Third Reich,* Simon and Schuster, New York, 1960, p. 815; see also

William Langer, *Our Vichy Gamble*, Alfred A. Knopf, New York, 1947, p. 97.

40. *Ibid.*, p. 817.
41. Hearings before a Subcommittee of the Committee on Military Affairs, U.S. Senate, 79th Congress, 1st Session (1945), pursuant to S. Res. 107 and 146, *Elimination of German Resources for War*, part X, pp. 1392–1393, Exhibit No. 39, interrogation of Schnitzler.
42. TWC, VIII, p. 113, NI-14224, file note by Kuegler re Paris conference.
43. TWC, VII, p. 47, Indictment, Count Two.
44. TWC, VIII, p. 110, NI-15228.
45. TWC, VIII, pp. 118–126, NI-6727, Wiesbaden meeting memorandum, November 21, 1940.
46. TWC, VIII, p. 113, NI-14224, Kuegler's file note re Paris conferences, November 28, 29, and 30, 1940.
47. TWC, VIII, p. 119, NI-6727.
48. TWC, VIII, pp. 120–121, NI-6727.
49. TWC, VIII, p. 121, NI-6727.
50. TWC, VIII, pp. 123–124, NI-6727.
51. TWC, VIII, p. 126, NI-6727.
52. TWC, VIII, p. 111, NI-790, Schnitzler's letter to Schmitz, November 21, 1941, re Wiesbaden conference.
53. TWC, VII, p. 47, Indictment, Count Two.
54. TWC, VIII, p. 114, NI-14224.
55. TWC, VIII, pp. 116–117, NI-14224.
56. TWC, VIII, p. 117, NI-14224.
57. Hearings before a Subcommittee of the Committee on Military Affairs, U.S. Senate, 79th Congress, 1st Session (1945), pursuant to S. Res. 107 and 146, *Elimination of German Resources for War*, part X, p. 1399, Exhibit No. 42.
58. *Ibid.*, p. 1398, Exhibit No. 42.
59. *Ibid.*, p. 1399, Exhibit No. 42.
60. *Ibid.*
61. *Ibid.*
62. *Ibid.*
63. *Ibid.*
64. TWC, VIII, p. 1149, Count Two.
65. TWC, VII, p. 47, Indictment, Count Two.
66. NI-4889, p. 12, affidavit of M. René Duchemin.
67. TWC, VIII, p. 1149, Count Two.
68. *Ibid.*, p. 1150.
69. TWC, VIII, p. 141, NI-6845.
70. TWC, VIII, pp. 130–131, NI-15220.

71. *Ibid.*, pp. 130–131.
72. Hearings before a Subcommittee of the Committee on Military Affairs, U.S. Senate, 79th Congress, 1st Session (1945), pursuant to S. Res. 107 and 146, *Elimination of German Resources for War,* part X, p. 1402, Exhibit No. 47.
73. *Ibid.*
74. *Ibid.*
75. *Ibid.*
76. *Ibid.*, part X, p. 1394, Exhibit No. 39.
77. *Ibid.*, part X, pp. 1394–1395, Exhibit No. 39.
78. TWC, VIII, p. 142, NI-6845, Francolor convention extracts, November 18, 1941.
79. TWC, VIII, p. 136, NI-15219.
80. *Ibid.*, p. 137.
81. *Ibid.*, p. 137.
82. TWC, VIII, p. 141, NI-6845, Francolor convention extracts, November 18, 1941.
83. TWC, VIII. p. 163, ter Meer testimony.
84. TWC, VIII, p. 145, NI-6845, Francolor convention extracts, November 18, 1941.
85. Hearings before a Subcommittee of the Committee on Military Affairs, U.S. Senate, 79th Congress, 1st Session (1945), pursuant to S. Res. 107 and 146, *Elimination of German Resources for War,* part X, p. 1393, Exhibit No. 39.
86. *Ibid.*, p. 1393, Exhibit No. 39.
87. TWC, VIII, p. 235, ter Meer Testimony.
88. *New York Times,* December 22, 1941, p. 31, col. 7.
89. *Ibid.*
90. TWC, VIII, p. 1150.
91. TWC, VII, p. 52.
92. *Ibid.*
93. *Ibid.*
94. *Ibid.*
95. *Ibid.*

6. SLAVE LABOR AND MASS MURDER

1. *New York Times,* August 27, 1943, p. 7, col. 2.
2. TWC, VI, p. x, Declaration on German Atrocities.
3. *Ibid.*
4. *New York Times,* March 24, 1944, p. 4, col. 2.
5. TMWC, vol. XXXVII, p. 433, Document 022-L, excerpt

from War Refugee Board Report, Washington, D.C., November 1944 (PE 1759).

6. *History of the War Refugee Board with Selected Documents, January 22, 1944–September 15, 1945.* Executive office of the President, War Refugee Board (3 volumes, mimeographed).

7. TWC, VIII, pp. 330–331, NI-11781, letter from Reich Ministry of Economics to Farben, dated November 8, 1940.

8. *Ibid.*, p. 331, letter from Reich Ministry of Economics to Farben, dated November 8, 1940.

9. TWC, VIII, pp. 336–338, NI-11784, Conference Report between Farben representatives and the Schlesien-Benzin Company, January 18, 1941.

10. TWC, VIII, pp. 349–351, NI-11113, file note on conference with ter Meer, Krauch, and Ambros, held February 6, 1941.

11. TWC, Prosecution's Final Brief, part IV, p. 54.

12. TWC, VIII, pp. 358–360, NI-11938, letter from Krauch to Ambros, dated February 25, 1941.

13. TWC, VIII, pp. 354–355, NI-1240, letter from Goering to Himmler, dated February 18, 1941.

14. *Ibid.*, p. 355, letter from Goering to Himmler, dated February 18, 1941.

15. TWC, VIII, pp. 356–357, NI-11086, letter from Krauch, signed by Wirth, to Ambros, dated March 4, 1941.

16. *Ibid.*, p. 357, letter from Krauch, signed by Wirth, to Ambros, dated March 4, 1941.

17. *Ibid.*

18. TWC, VIII, pp. 373–376, NI-15148, report on conference of Farben representatives with Auschwitz concentration camp officials, held March 27, 1941, p. 374.

19. *Ibid.*, p. 375.

20. *Ibid.*

21. *Ibid.*

22. *Ibid.*, pp. 374–375.

23. TWC, VIII, pp. 377–381, NI-11115, extracts from minutes of first construction conference on I.G. Auschwitz at Ludwigshafen held March 24, 1941.

24. TWC, VIII, pp. 374–375, NI-15148, report on conference of Farben representatives with Auschwitz concentration camp officials, held March 27, 1941.

25. *Ibid.*, p. 375.

26. NI-034, p. 4, affidavit of Rudolf Franz Ferdinand Hoess.

27. TWC, VIII, pp. 388–389, NI-11118, letter from Ambros to ter Meer and Struss, dated April 12, 1941, p. 389.

28. TWC, VIII, pp. 392–393, NI-14543, extracts from Farben-Auschwitz weekly report no. 11, for the period August 3–9, 1941.
29. *Ibid.*
30. TWC, VIII, pp. 404–405, NI-14556, extracts from Farben-Auschwitz weekly report no. 30, for the period December 15–21, 1941, p. 405.
31. *Ibid.*
32. TWC, VIII, pp. 406–409, NI-11130, extracts from report of fourteenth construction conference on Farben-Auschwitz, held December 16, 1941.
33. TWC, VIII, p. 410, extracts from Farben-Auschwitz weekly reports nos. 31 and 32, for the periods December 22–28, 1941, and December 29, 1941–January 4, 1942.
34. TWC, VIII, p. 425, NI-15256, extracts from Farben-Auschwitz weekly report no. 42, for the period March 9–15, 1942.
35. TWC, VII, p. 197.
36. DuBois, Josiah, *The Devil's Chemists,* Beacon Press, Boston, 1952, p. 229.
37. TMWC, I, p. 245.
38. Hilberg, Raul, *The Destruction of the European Jews,* Quadrangle Books, Chicago, 1961, p. 264.
39. Hilberg, Raul, p. 561; Judge Wladyslaw Bednarz (Lodz), "Extermination Camp at Chelmno," in *Central Commission for Investigation of German Crimes in Poland,* German Crimes in Poland, Warsaw, 1946, pp. 107–117.
40. Manvell, Roger, and Heinrich Fraenkel, *The Incomparable Crime,* Simon & Schuster, New York, 1960, p. 135.
41. TMWC, XI, p. 398, testimony by Rudolf Franz Ferdinand Hoess.
42. *Ibid.,* pp. 416–417, testimony by Rudolf Franz Ferdinand Hoess.
43. NI-034, affidavit by Rudolf Franz Ferdinand Hoess, p. 2.
44. TWC, Preliminary Brief, part III, p. 35, NI-9098, NI-9150, NI-12073, NI-6363; also NI-9540 (I.G. "Book of Participation").
45. *Ibid.,* p. 35, NI-12075.
46. Hilberg, Raul, p. 264; NG-2586-E.
47. *Ibid.,* p. 266; NG-2586-E.
48. *Ibid.,* p. 568; NI-9093.
49. *Ibid.,* p. 571; NI-9908.
50. NI-12110, memorandum from Dr. Heinrich to Mr. Amend, dated June 21, 1944.
51. Hilberg, Raul, p. 587; *Dokumenty i Materialy,* part I, pp.

115–117, letter from Sommer to Kommandant Auschwitz, dated January 27, 1943, and letter from Schwarz to WVHA D-11, dated February 20, 1943.

52. Hilberg, p. 587; *Dokumenty i Materialy,* part I, pp. 108–110, 117, letters from Schwarz to WVHA D-11, dated March 5 and 8, 1943, and to WVHA-D, dated March 15, 1943.

53. NI-7967, affidavit of Ervin Schulhof, taken June 21, 1947, p. 2.

54. TWC, VII, p. 199.

55. *Ibid.,* pp. 199–200.

56. TWC, Preliminary Brief, part III, p. 97, NI-4830, affidavit by Vitek about Auschwitz diet.

57. TWC, VIII, pp. 603–616, NI-11696, affidavit and testimony of Charles J. Coward, taken July 24, 1947, p. 604.

58. NI-11003 to NI-11017; NI-11019; NI-11027; NI-11029; NI-11031 to NI-11033; typical Auschwitz punishment reports by SS.

59. *Ibid.*

60. NI-7967, affidavit of Ervin Schulhof, taken June 21, 1947, p. 1.

61. NI-5847, affidavit by Berthold Epstein, taken March 3, 1947, p. 2.

62. TWC, VIII, pp. 532–535, NI-10040, letter from Krauch to Himmler, July 27, 1943.

63. TWC, VIII, pp. 558–559, NI-13512, file memorandum of Ritter and Duerrfeld, February 3, 1944, p. 558.

64. DuBois, p. 220; NI-7967, affidavit of Ervin Schulhof, taken June 21, 1947, p. 2.

65. TWC, Prosecution's Final Brief, part IV, p. 54.

7. I.G. LOSES THE WAR

1. NI-3767, U.S. Strategic Bombing Survey, September 30, 1945, p. 42.

2. Speer, Albert, *Inside the Third Reich,* Macmillan, New York, 1970, p. 346.

3. *Ibid.,* pp. 346–347.

4. *Ibid.,* p. 347.

5. TWC, VII, p. 1109.

6. Speer, p. 348.

7. *Ibid.*

8. *Ibid.,* p. 351.

9. NI-3767, pp. 41–42.

10. *Ibid.*, p. 42.
11. *Ibid.*
12. Letter from Harteck to J. Borkin, 1974; Irving, David, *The German Atomic Bomb*, Simon and Schuster, New York, 1967, p. 240.
13. *Petroleum Times,* December 13, 1943.
14. TWC, VII, p. 1318.
15. TWC, VII, p. 1319.
16. TWC, VII, Ambros testimony, p. 1045.
17. *Ibid.*, p. 1044.
18. *Ibid.*
19. *Ibid.*, pp. 1044–1045.
20. *Ibid.*, p. 1045.
21. *Ibid.*, p. 1044.
22. TWC, VII, p. 605, NI-4043, exchange of letters between Speer and Himmler.
23. *Ibid.*, p. 605.
24. TWC, VII, p. 605, NI-4043, exchange of letters between Speer and Himmler.
25. *Ibid.*, p. 605.
26. *Ibid.*, p. 606.
27. TWC, VII, p. 1045.
28. Speer, Albert, p. 414.

8. I.G. AT NUREMBERG

1. U.S. Department of State, Executive Agreement Series 472, Agreement by the Government of the United States of America, the Provisional Government of the French Republic, the Government of the United Kingdom of Great Britain and Northern Ireland, and the Government of the Union of Soviet Socialist Republics for the Prosecution and Punishment of the Major War Criminals of the European Axis, signed at London, August 8, 1945.
2. TMWC, I, pp. 27–68, Indictment, October 6, 1945, *U.S.A. et al.* v. *Hermann Goering et al.*
3. TMWC, I, pp. 118–133.
4. *Ibid.*, pp. 145–146.
5. TMWC, I, p. 147.
6. *Ibid.*, pp. 365–366.
7. *New York Times,* October 16, 1946, p. 1, col. 8.
8. TMWC, I, p. 365.
9. *Ibid.*, pp. 365–366.
10. Taylor, Telford, Final Report to the Secretary of the Army

on the Nuremberg War Crimes Trials under Control Council Law No. 10, August 15, 1949, Washington, pp. 269–270, Minutes of the Meeting of the Chief Prosecutors held April 5, 1946.

11. *Ibid.*, p. 285, note of January 22, 1947, from U.S. Government embassies in London, Moscow, and Paris, addressed to the British, French, and Soviet governments.

12. *Ibid.*, p. 285, note of January 22, 1947, from U.S. Government embassies in London, Moscow, and Paris, addressed to the British, French, and Soviet governments.

13. TWC, VII, p. 10–80, Indictment in *U.S.* v. *Carl Krauch, et al.*, filed May 3, 1947.

14. *Ibid.*, pp. 56–58.

15. Douglas, William O., *An Almanac of Liberty*, Doubleday, Garden City, N.Y., 1954, p. 96.

16. Mason, Alpheus T., *Harland Fiske Stone: Pillar of the Law*, Viking, New York, 1956, p. 716.

17. *New York Times*, October 6, 1946, p. 1, col. 4.

18. *Congressional Record*, November 28, 1947, p. 10938.

19. *Congressional Record*, July 9, 1947, p. 8564.

20. DuBois, Josiah E., Jr., *The Devil's Chemists*, Beacon Press, Boston, 1952, p. 69.

21. TWC, VII, p. 5.

22. *Ibid.*, pp. 99–101.

23. DuBois, p. 82.

24. *Ibid.*, p. 99.

25. National Archives Collection, World War II War Crimes Records, *U.S.* v. *Krauch et al.*, Prosecution Exhibit 2059, pp. 43–44.

26. *Ibid.*, Prosecution Exhibit 1871, transcript of trial, pp. 13566–13615.

27. NI-12373.

28. NI-4830.

29. NI-7967.

30. NI-12388, affidavit of Eric J. Doyle.

31. TWC, VIII, p. 621, testimony of Eric J. Doyle.

32. NI-11696, affidavit of Charles J. Coward.

33. DuBois, pp. 229–230.

34. National Archives Collection, World War II Crimes, Document Book XI, Schnitzler No. 214, pp. 64–66; affidavit of Richard von Szilvinyi.

35. *Ibid.*, Schnitzler No. 215, p. 68.

36. TWC, VII, pp. 628–629.

37. TWC, VII, p. 594, NI-13522.

38. *Ibid.*, p. 629.

39. *Ibid.*, pp. 414–415, Compulsion in Hitler's Third Reich and the Defense of "Window Dressing."
40. *Ibid.*, pp. 416–417, testimony of Defense Witness Field Marshal Erhard Milch.
41. *Ibid.*, pp. 417–421, testimony of Defense Witness Friedrich Flick, Head of the Flick Concern.
42. TWC, VIII, p. 921, closing statement for Defendant Krauch.
43. *Ibid.*, p. 914, closing statement for Defendant Krauch.
44. *Ibid.*, p. 1083, Opinion and Judgment of the U.S. Military Tribunal VI.
45. *New York Times,* July 29, 1948, p. 1, col. 8.
46. TWC, VIII, p. 1081.
47. *Ibid.*, p. 1081.
48. *Ibid.*, p. 1114.
49. *Ibid.*, pp. 1134–1136, Count Two.
50. *Ibid.*, pp. 1153–1167.
51. *Ibid.*, p. 1175.
52. *Ibid.*
53. *Ibid.*, p. 1179.
54. *Ibid.*, p. 1184.
55. *Ibid.*, p. 1185.
56. *Ibid.*
57. *Ibid.*, pp. 1186–1187.
58. *Ibid.*, p. 1187.
59. *Ibid.*
60. *Ibid.*, p. 1189.
61. *Ibid.*, p. 1190.
62. *Ibid.*, pp. 1191–1192.
63. *Ibid.*, pp. 1187–1196.
64. *Ibid.*, pp. 1206–1209, Formal Judgment and Sentences.
65. DuBois, p. 339.
66. TWC, VIII, p. 1211, Concurring Opinion on Counts One and Five of the Indictment.
67. *Ibid.*
68. *Ibid.*
69. *Ibid.*
70. *Ibid.*, p. 1212.
71. *Ibid.*, p. 1311, Dissenting Opinion on Count Three of the Indictment.
72. *Ibid.*, p. 1314.
73. *Ibid.*, p. 1319.
74. *Ibid.*, p. 1322.

9. I.G. WINS THE PEACE

1. U.S. Group Control Council, Finance Division, Germany, *Report on Investigation of I.G. Farbenindustrie,* September 12, 1945. Classification canceled by authority of the Joint Chiefs of Staff; microfilmed by the Library of Congress.
2. *New York Times,* October 21, 1945, p. 1, col. 6.
3. *Ibid.*
4. *Ibid.,* p. 12, col. 2.
5. Official Gazette of the Control Council for Germany, Allied Secretariat, Berlin, November 30, 1945, p. 34, Law #9.
6. *New York Times,* January 17, 1946, p. 14, col. 5.
7. *New York Times,* January 31, 1946, p. 7, col. 2.
8. Military Government Gazette, Germany, United States Area of Control, April 1, 1947, pp. 2–6.
9. *Ibid.,* p. 3.
10. *New York Times,* June 18, 1947, p. 5, col. 2.
11. *New York Times,* March 26, 1947, p. 11, col. 1.
12. Martin, James S., *All Honorable Men,* Little, Brown & Co., Boston, 1950, p. 232.
13. *New York Times,* December 20, 1949, p. 19, col. 1.
14. *New York Times,* December 27, 1951, p. 11, col. 2.
15. *Ibid.*
16. *New York Times,* March 19, 1953, p. 5, col. 2.
17. *New York Times,* March 29, 1953, Section III, p. 1, col. 3.
18. U.S. Department of State, *Treaties and Other International Acts Series 3425,* GPO (1954), "Termination of the Occupation Regime in the Federal Republic of Germany."
19. *Ibid.,* p. 1316, letter from Adenauer to the U.S. High Commissioner, October 23, 1954.
20. *New York Times,* January 15, 1955, p. 6, col. 4.
21. *New York Times,* May 30, 1955, p. 17, col. 8.
22. Farbenfabriken Bayer A.G., Annual Report for the Year 1955, p. 12.
23. Farbwerke Hoechst, Annual Report for the Year 1955, p. 8.
24. Farbenfabriken Bayer A.G., Annual Report for the Year 1956, p. 6.
25. *New York Times,* June 2, 1957, p. 21, col. 1.
26. Farbenfabriken Bayer A.G., Annual Report for the Year 1956, p. 12.
27. *New York Times,* April 13, 1956, Section IV, p. 4, col. 1.
28. *Fortune,* August 1977, p. 240.

10. CORPORATE CAMOUFLAGE

1. TWC, VII, p. 35.
2. National Archives Collection, World War II Crimes, Doc. Book 5, Schmitz, Doc. No. 76, Friedrich Liecher affidavit.
3. Alien Property Custodian Report of 1919, p. 100.
4. *New York Times*, September 21, 1926, p. 17, col. 2.
5. Hoopes, Townsend, *The Devil and John Foster Dulles*, Atlantic-Little Brown, Boston, 1973, p. 28.
6. Luckau, Alma, *The German Delegation at the Paris Peace Conference*, Columbia University Press, New York, 1941, p. 125.
7. *New York Times*, November 27, 1919, p. 22, col. 6.
8. *Société Suisse pour Valeurs de Métaux* v. *Cummings, Attorney General*, 99 F. 2d 387 at 390.
9. *New York Times*, September 9, 1926, p. 1, col. 1.
10. *Société Suisse* v. *Cummings*, p. 391.
11. *Ibid.*
12. *New York Times*, January 23, 1926, p. 32, col. 3.
13. Mayer, Martin, *Emory Buckner*, Harper and Row, New York, 1968, p. 212.
14. *New York Times*, May 18, 1926, p. 1, col. 3.
15. *New York Times*, September 10, 1926, p. 23, col. 6.
16. *Ibid.*
17. *New York Times*, September 15, 1926, p. 1, col. 4.
18. *New York World*, September 21, 1926, p. 1, col. 1.
19. *New York Evening Post*, September 21, 1926, p. 6, col. 2.
20. *New York World*, October 9, 1926, p. 6, col. 4.
21. *New York Sun*, October 8, 1926, p. 2, col. 1.
22. *New York Times*, October 15, 1926, p. 20, col. 2.
23. Mayer, Martin, p. 234.
24. Knox, John C. Clark, *A Judge Comes of Age*, p. 257.
25. *Société Suisse pour Valeurs de Métaux* v. *Cummings, Attorney General*, 97 F. 2d 387.
26. *New York Times*, September 10, 1940, p. 14, col. 1.
27. *J. Robert Bonnar et al.* v. *United States*, in the U.S. Court of Claims, No. 293-63, Defendant's Exhibit 381.
28. Hearings before Special Committee Investigating the Munitions Industry, U.S. Senate, 73rd Congress, part XI, p. 2397, *Alleged Dye Monopoly*, p. 252.
29. *Adolf Kuttroff* v. *Thomas W. Miller as Alien Property Custodian et al.*, in Equity No. E-30-251, District Court for the Southern District of New York, Complaint, November 7, 1924, p. 4.

30. *Ibid.*, Memorandum of Facts in Answer to Bill of Complaint filed November 18, 1924.
31. *New York Times,* April 26, 1929, Financial Section.
32. *New York Times,* April 27, 1929, p. 30, col. 2.
33. *J. Robert Bonnar et al.* v. *The United States,* in the U.S. Court of Claims, No. 293-63, Exhibit DSR 164.
34. *Gesetz gegen Verrat der Deutschen Volkswirtschaft,* June 12, 1933.
35. U.S. Department of Justice, Civil Division, *General Aniline and Film Liquidators Report,* p. 26f.
36. NI-7319, affidavit of August von Knieriem; and *J. Robert Bonnar et al.* v. *The United States,* in the U.S. Court of Claims, No. 293-63, Defendant's Exhibit 377, letter from Rospatt to Central Finance Administration, August 16, 1939.
37. *SEC Report on Investment Trusts and Investment Companies,* part IV, 1942, p. 146.
38. *Ibid.*, pp. 21538–9, Public Examination of American I.G. Chemical Corporation.
39. Hearings before a Special Committee Investigating the National Defense Program, United States Senate, 77th Cong., 1st Session (1941), *Investigation of the National Defense Program,* part II, p. 4897, memorandum re: American I.G., SEC Investigation of Investment Trusts, February 10, 1938.
40. *Ibid.*, p. 4896, letter from Frank Howard to H. von Reidemann, February 19, 1938.
41. *Ibid.*, p. 4903, letter from Frank Howard to Walter Teagle, March 11, 1938.
42. *J. Robert Bonnar et al.* v. *The United States,* in the U.S. Court of Claims, No. 293-63, Defendant's Exhibit 185, extract from conference, March 31, 1938.
43. *J. Robert Bonnar et al.* v. *The United States,* in the U.S. Court of Claims, No. 293-63, Commissioner Fletcher's Report, p. 58.
44. *Ibid.*, Defendant's Exhibit 163, statement dated October 3, 1947, made by Dr. Gustav Schlotterer to the U.S. Department of Justice, p. 15.
45. *New York Times,* October 31, 1939, p. 35, col. 2.
46. NI-5768, affidavit of Fritz ter Meer.
47. *Ibid.*
48. *Ibid.*
49. *J. Robert Bonnar et al.* v. *The United States,* in the U.S. Court of Claims, No. 293-63, testimony of Krueger, p. 1493.

50. *Ibid.*, testimony of Gustav Schlotterer, pp. 2114–2115.
51. *Ibid.*, Defendant's Exhibit 74.
52. General Aniline and Film Corporation, Interim Report to the SEC for the period April 1, 1939 to December 31, 1939.
53. SEC Annual Report to Congress, June, 1941.
54. *J. Robert Bonnar et al v. The United States*, in the U.S. Court of Claims, No. 293-63, DSR 437, p. 3.
55. *New York Times*, May 2, 1941, p. 1, col. 3.
56. *New York Times*, May 14, 1941, p. 9, col. 6.
57. *J. Robert Bonnar et al.* v. *United States*, in the U.S. Court of Claims, No. 293-63, DSR 437.
58. *Ibid.*, DSR 437.
59. *Ibid.*, DSR 437, pp. 4–5.
60. *Ibid.*, Defendant's Exhibit 141.
61. *Ibid.*, Report of the Commissioner to the Court, January 26, 1970, p. 80.
62. *New York Times*, December 6, 1941, p. 25, col. 4.
63. Hearings, Senate Judiciary Committee, U.S. Senate, 77th Cong., 1st Session, December 15, 1941.
64. *J. Robert Bonnar et al.* v. *United States*, in the U.S. Court of Claims, No. 293-63, Defendant's Exhibit 162.

11. THE STRANGE CASE OF
GENERAL ANILINE AND FILM

1. Letter to J. Borkin from Philip W. Amram, July 7, 1972.
2. *Standard Oil Co. (N.J.) et al.* v. *Clark*, Joint Appendix to the Briefs, pp. 547–549, testimony of August von Knieriem.
3. *Ibid.*, pp. 556–557.
4. *Ibid.*
5. *Standard Oil Co. (N.J.) et al.* v. *Clark*, 64 F. Supp. 656 at 665.
6. *Ibid.*, 671.
7. *Standard Oil Co. et al.* v. *Clark*, 163 F. 2d 917.
8. *Ibid.*, 163 F. 2d 917 at 927.
9. *Ibid.*, 163 F. 2d at 925.
10. Treaties and Other International Acts Series 1655, "Germany: Distribution of Reparation, Establishment of Inter-Allied Reparation Agency, Restitution of Monetary Gold," Department of State Publication 2966.
11. Société Internationale pour Participations Industrielles et Commerciales, S.A. v. McGranery, et al., 111 F. Supp. 435 (D.D.C. 1953).

12. *Ibid.*, at 437.
13. *Kaufman et al.* v. *Société Internationale pour Participations Industrielles et Commerciales, S.A. et al.*, 343 U.S. 156 at 157 (1952).
14. *Société Internationale pour Participations Industrielles et Commerciales, S.A. et al.* v. *McGrath et al.*, 90 F. Supp. 1011 (D.D.C. 1950).
15. *Kaufman et al.* v. *Société Internationale pour Participations Industrielles et Commerciales, S.A. et al.*, 188 F. 2d 1017 (D.C. Cir. 1951).
16. *Kaufman et al.* v. *Société Internationale pour Participations Industrielles et Commerciales, S.A. et al.*, 342 U.S. 847 (1951).
17. *New York Times*, January 14, 1952, p. 29, col. 7.
18. *Kaufman et al.* v. *Société Internationale pour Participations Industrielles et Commerciales, S.A. et al.*, 343 U.S. 156 (1952).
19. *New York Times*, January 14, 1950, p. 29, col. 7.
20. Department of Justice Report, June 25, 1962, "Price Settlement Efforts."
21. *Kaufman et al.* v. *Société Internationale pour Participations Industrielles et Commerciales, S.A. et al.*, 343 U.S. 156 (1952).
22. *Société Internationale pour Participations Industrielles et Commerciales, S.A.* v. *McGranery, et al.*, 111 F. Supp. 435 (D.D.C. 1953).
23. S. 3423, 83d Congress, 2d Session.
24. *New York Times*, August 15, 1954.
25. *New York Times*, August 10, 1954.
26. *New York Times*, August 3, 1954.
27. *Société Internationale pour Participations Industrielles et Commerciales, S.A., et al.* v. *Rogers* 357 U.S. 197 (1958).
28. *New York Times*, June 26, 1958.
29. *New York Times*, February 10, 1958, p. 34, col. 7.
30. *Ibid.*
31. *Schmitz* v. *Société Internationale et al.*, 249 F. Supp. 757 (D.D.C. 1966), affirmed without opinion in *Schmitz* v. *Société Internationale et al.*, No. 24, 600, February 15, 1972 (D.C. Cir.), Brief for Robert A. Schmitz, p. 10.
32. *Ibid.*, Brief for Robert A. Schmitz, p. 10.
33. *New York Times*, June 6, 1960, p. 44, col. 3.
34. *Schmitz* v. *Société Internationale et al.*, 249 F. Supp. 757 (D.D.C. 1966), affirmed without opinion in *Schmitz* v. *Société Internationale et al.*, No. 24, 600, February 15, 1972 (D.C. Cir.), Joint Appendix Exhibits, Plaintiff's Exhibit 80, p. 167, Alfred Schaefer's letter to Robert Schmitz on November 14, 1960.

35. *Ibid.*, Joint Appendix Volume I, p. 470, William Orrick's Testimony.

36. *Ibid.*, Joint Appendix Exhibits, Defendant's Exhibit 58, p. 489, Alfred Schaefer's letter to Charles Spofford on July 21, 1961.

37. *Ibid.*, Joint Appendix Exhibits, Plaintiff's Exhibit 143, p. 282, Alfred Schaefer's letter to Charles Wilson and Charles Spofford on August 24, 1961.

38. *Ibid.*, Deposition of Charles Spofford, taken February 27, 1968, p. 17.

39. *Ibid.*, Deposition of Charles Spofford, taken February 27, 1968, p. 22.

40. *Ibid.*, Testimony of Alfred Schaefer, February 2, 1970,, pp. 1114–1115.

41. *Ibid.*, Joint Appendix Exhibits, Defendant's Exhibit 62, p. 496, Spofford's letter to Schaefer on September 18, 1961.

42. *Ibid.*, Joint Appendix Exhibits, Defendant's Exhibit 62, p. 495, Spofford's letter to Schaefer on September 18, 1961.

43. *Ibid.*, Joint Appendix Exhibits, Defendant's Exhibit 62, p. 495, Spofford's letter to Schaefer on September 18, 1961.

44. *Ibid.*, Joint Appendix Exhibits, Plaintiff's Exhibit 198, p. 367, Schaefer's reply to Spofford on September 26, 1961.

45. *Ibid.*, Joint Appendix Exhibits, Plaintiff's Exhibit 198, p. 367, Schaefer's reply to Spofford on September 26, 1961.

46. *Ibid.*, Joint Appendix Exhibits, Defendant's Exhibit 63, p. 499, Spofford's letter to Schaefer, October 6, 1961.

47. *Ibid.*, Joint Appendix Exhibits, Plaintiff's Exhibit 197, p. 365, Schaefer's reply to Spofford, October 9, 1961.

48. *Ibid.*, Joint Appendix Volume II, p. 1124f, Schaefer's Testimony.

49. *Ibid.*, Joint Appendix Volume II, p. 1126, Schaefer's Testimony.

50. *Ibid.*, Joint Appendix Volume II, pp. 1126–1129, Schaefer's Testimony.

51. *Ibid.*, Deposition of Charles Spofford taken February 27, 1968, p. 21.

52. *Ibid.*, Joint Appendix Volume II, p. 1299, Deposition of Charles Spofford taken January 28, 1970.

53. *Schmitz* v. *Société Internationale et al.*, 249 F. Supp. 757 (D.D.C. 1966), affirmed without opinion in *Schmitz* v. *Société Internationale et al.*, No. 24, 600, February 15, 1972 (D.C. Cir.), Joint Appendix, Volume II, p. 501.

54. *Ibid.*, Joint Appendix Exhibits, Plaintiff's Exhibit 204, p. 373, Robert Kennedy's cable to Alfred Schaefer on January 18, 1962.

55. *Ibid.*, Joint Appendix Exhibits, Plaintiff's Exhibit 172, p. 313f, Alfred Schaefer's letter to Charles Wilson on February 12, 1962.

56. *Ibid.*, Joint Appendix Exhibits, Defendant's Exhibit 7, p. 406, Charles Wilson's reply to Alfred Schaefer on March 26, 1962.

57. H. R. 7283, bill passed by 87th Congress, 2d Session, on October 3, 1962, to amend the War Claims Act of 1948.

58. Public Law 87-846, 76 Stat. 1107, signed by President John Kennedy on October 22, 1962.

59. *New York Times,* October 23, 1962, p. 14, col. 4.

60. *Schmitz* v. *Société Internationale et al.,* 249 F. Supp. 757 (D.D.C. 1966), affirmed without opinion in *Schmitz* v. *Société Internationale et al.,* No. 24, 600, February 15, 1972 (D.C. Cir.), Brief for Société Internationale et al., p. 23.

61. *New York Times,* March 4, 1963, p. 1, col. 1, and p. 8, col. 4.

62. *New York Times,* March 4, 1963, p. 8, col. 4.

63. *New York Times,* March 7, 1963, p. 4, col. 5.

64. *New York Times,* March 7, 1963, p. 4, col. 5.

65. *New York Times,* March 8, 1963, p. 13, col. 1.

66. *New York Times,* March 8, 1963, p. 16, col. 6.

67. *New York Times,* March 8, 1963, p. 16, col. 6.

68. *New York Times,* March 8, 1963, p. 16, col. 6.

69. *Société Internationale pour Participations Industrielles et Commerciales, S.A.* v. *McGrath et al.,* 9F.R.D. (D.D.C. 1948), Stipulation of Settlement CA. 4360-48, signed December 20, 1963, by Attorney General Robert Kennedy and John J. Wilson.

70. *New York Times,* April 16, 1964, p. 51, col. 3.

71. *Société Internationale pour Participations Industrielles et Commerciales, S.A.* v. *McGrath et al.,* 9F.R.D. (D.D.C. 1948), order issued April 15, 1964, by Judge David A. Pine.

72. *Washington Post,* May 19, 1964, sec. B, p. 27 and *Washington Post,* May 25, 1964, sec. B, p. 11.

73. *Washington Post,* May 25, 1964, sec. B, p. 11.

74. *Washington Post,* May 25, 1964, sec. B, p. 11.

75. *New York Times,* August 23, 1964, p. 35, col. 1.

76. *New York Times,* April 1, 1978, p. 31, col. 1.

77. 50 U.S.C. App. 12: "Any person purchasing property from the Alien Property Custodian for an undisclosed principal, or for re-sale to a person not a citizen of the United States, or for the benefit of a person not a citizen of the United States, shall be guilty of a misdemeanor, and, upon conviction, shall be subject to a fine of not more than $10,000, or imprisonment for not more than ten years, or both, and the property shall be forfeited to the United States."

Index

311

313

317

320